S0-BYX-950

Frommer's®

P O R T A B L E

Maine Coast

2nd Edition

by Wayne Curtis

Macmillan • USA

ABOUT THE AUTHOR

Wayne Curtis is a travel writer who lives in Eastport, Maine. His stories have appeared in numerous magazines and newspapers, including the *New York Times, Yankee, House Beautiful,* and *Discovery Channel Online.* He's also the author of the Frommer's guide to Atlantic Canada, and *Maine: Off the Beaten Path* (Globe Pequot).

MACMILLAN TRAVEL USA

A Pearson Education Macmillan Company
1633 Broadway
New York, NY 10019

Find us online at **www.frommers.com**

ISBN 0-02-862761-X
ISSN 1093-0221

Editor: Margot Weiss
Production Editor: Michael Thomas
Design by Michele Laseau
Photo Editor: Richard Fox
Digital Cartography by John Decamillis and Ortelius Design
Page Creation by Carrie Allen, John Bitter, Jerry Cole, Natalie Evans, and Sean Monkhouse

SPECIAL SALES

Bulk purchases (10+ copies) of Frommer's and selected Macmillan travel guides are available to corporations, organizations, mail-order catalogs, institutions, and charities at special discounts, and can be customized to suit individual needs. For more information write to Special Sales, Macmillan General Reference, 1633 Broadway, New York, NY 10019.

Manufactured in the United States of America

Contents

List of Maps

AN INVITATION TO THE READER

In researching this book, we discovered many wonderful places—hotels, restaurants, shops, and more. We're sure you'll find others. Please tell us about them, so we can share the information with your fellow travelers in upcoming editions. If you were disappointed with a recommendation, we'd love to know that, too. Please write to:

Wayne Curtis
newengland@email.com
Frommer's Portable Maine Coast, 2nd Edition
Macmillan Travel
1633 Broadway
New York, NY 10019

AN ADDITIONAL NOTE

Please be advised that travel information is subject to change at any time—and this is especially true of prices. We therefore suggest that you write or call ahead for confirmation when making your travel plans. The authors, editors, and publisher cannot be held responsible for the experiences of readers while traveling. Your safety is important to us, however, so we encourage you to stay alert and be aware of your surroundings. Keep a close eye on cameras, purses, and wallets, all favorite targets of thieves and pickpockets.

WHAT THE SYMBOLS MEAN

✪ Frommer's Favorites

Our favorite places and experiences—outstanding for quality, value, or both.

The following abbreviations are used for credit cards:

AE	American Express	EU	EuroCard
CB	Carte Blanche	JCB	Japan Credit Bank
DC	Diners Club	MC	MasterCard
DISC	Discover	V	Visa
EN	enRoute		

FIND FROMMER'S ONLINE

Arthur Frommer's Budget Travel Online (**www.frommers.com**) offers more than 6,000 pages of up-to-the-minute travel information—including the latest bargains and candid, personal articles updated daily by Arthur Frommer himself. No other Web site offers such comprehensive and timely coverage of the world of travel.

Planning a Trip to the Maine Coast

*H*umorist Dave Barry once wryly suggested that Maine's state motto should be "Cold, but damp."

Cute, but true. There's spring, which tends to last a few blustery, rain-soaked days. There's November, in which Arctic winds alternate with gray sheets of rain. And then winter brings a character-building mix of blizzards and ice storms to the fabled coast. (The inland mountains are more or less blessed with uninterrupted snow.)

Ah, but then there's summer. Summer in Maine brings ospreys diving for fish off wooded points; gleaming cumulus clouds building over the steely blue, rounded peaks of the western mountains; and the haunting whoop of loons echoing off the dense forest walls bordering the lakes. It brings languorous days when the sun rises before most visitors and it seems like noontime at 8am. Maine summers bring a measure of gracious tranquillity, and a placid stay in the right spot can rejuvenate even the most jangled nerves.

The trick comes in finding that right spot. Those who arrive here without a clear plan may find themselves cursing their travel decision. Maine's Route 1 along the coast has its moments, but for the most part it's rather charmless—an amalgam of convenience stores, tourist boutiques, and restaurants catering to bus tours. Acadia National Park, for all its vaunted ocean vistas, also has world-class congestion along some of the byways in and around the park. In this it's no different than other national parks of its stature—whether Yosemite or Yellowstone. You need strategy to avoid the worst moments.

Fortunately, Maine's size works to the traveler's advantage. Maine is nearly as large as the other five New England states combined. Straighten out the state's convoluted coast and you'll discover you've got more than a continent's worth of exploring—some 4,500 miles of mainland shoreline. Add to that some 4,600 coastal islands, and you'll realize that with a little planning, you should easily be able to find your piece of Maine away from the bustle and crowds.

This chapter is designed to provide most of the nuts-and-bolts travel information you'll need before setting off to explore coastal Maine. Browse through the following sections before you hit the road to ensure you've touched all the bases.

1 Visitor Information & Money

VISITOR INFORMATION

It often seems that Maine's leading cash crop is the brochure. Shops, hotels, and restaurants often feature racks of colorful pamphlets touting local sights and accommodations. These mini-centers can be helpful in turning up unexpected places, but for a more comprehensive overview you should contact the **Maine Office of Tourism** (☎ 800/533-9595; www.visitmaine.com) or the **Maine Publicity Bureau** (☎ 800/782-6497 or 207/287-5711), either of which can provide information that offers a good overview of the state. For local and regional information, chambers of commerce addresses and phone numbers are provided for each region in the chapters that follow. If you're a highly organized traveler, you'll call in advance and ask for information to be mailed to you. If you're like the rest of us, you'll swing by when you reach town and hope the office is still open.

There's also a rapidly growing horde of information available on the web. A good place to begin an Internet search is at the official information site maintained by the state at **www.state.me.us**.

MONEY

Budget travelers accustomed to turning up basic motels for $25 or $30 in other parts of the country are in for a bit of a shock in Maine, at least during peak travel seasons. In midsummer there's virtually no such thing as a cheap motel along the Maine Coast. Motels where you might reasonably expect to pay $40 per night will command $90 on a Saturday in August. (To be fair, many of the innkeepers in these northern latitudes must make all their profit in what amounts to a 2- or 3-month season.)

What are the alternatives?

• Travel in the off-season. Inexpensive rooms are often available in April or May. If that's a little too bleak (trees often aren't in full leaf until late May), consider traveling between Memorial Day and July 4th, when you can often get room discounts and good deals on packages as innkeepers get ready for the crowds of high summer. The best off-season period to my mind is September. The weather is good, and many inns and hotels cut their prices for two or three weeks between the summer and foliage periods.

Maine

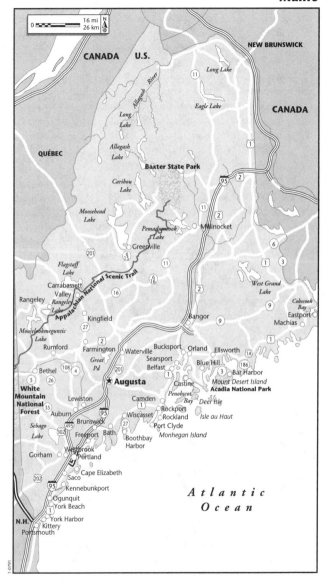

- **Commute from lower-priced areas.** If you're willing to drive a half-hour to an hour to reach prime destinations, you can often find cheaper lodging—including chain motels—in less glamorous settings inland.
- **Camp.** Maine's coast isn't so congested that campgrounds have been driven out to make room for condominiums. You should be able to find great camping at both public and private campgrounds, with prices ranging from $8 to $25 per night. Be aware that coastal campgrounds south of Portland tend to be fewer in number, a bit more crowded, and more expensive; northward, the opportunities expand and the prices tend to fall.

Traveler's checks are commonly accepted everywhere, although some shops may balk at cashing $100 checks for small purchases. Cash machines (ATMs) are easy to find in the more populated areas and regions that cater to tourists. But don't count on finding machines in the smaller villages in the more remote parts of the region. Stock up on greenbacks when you can. To locate the nearest machine in the **Plus** network, call ☎ **800/843-7587.** For the **Cirrus** network, call **800/424-7787.**

2 When to Go

THE SEASONS

The well-worn joke about Maine's climate is that it has just two seasons: winter and August. There's a kernel of truth to that, but it's mostly a canard to keep outsiders from moving here, repeated the same way Seattle "celebrates" its 11-month rain festival.

SUMMER

The peak summer season runs from July 4th to Labor Day. Vast crowds surge up the Maine Coast during and between the two holiday weekends, swelling traffic on the turnpike and Route 1, and causing countless motels and inns to hang "No Vacancy" signs. This should be no surprise: Summers are exquisite here. The forests are verdant and lush, the sky can be an almost lurid blue, and the cumulus clouds brilliantly white. Ocean breezes keep the temperatures down, sometimes producing atmospheric fogs that linger for days. (In Portland, it tops 90 degrees only 4 or 5 days a year on average.) Expect to pay premium prices at hotels and restaurants along the coast in mid season.

Maine's weather is largely determined by the prevailing winds. Southwest winds bring haze, heat, humidity, and often thunderstorms. The northwest winds bring cool weather and knife-sharp vistas. These systems tend to alternate during the summer, with the heat arriving stealthily and slowly, then getting exiled by stiff, cool winds rising from the north a few days later. (The change from hot to cool will sometimes occur in a matter of minutes.) Along the immediate coast it's often warmest in the late morning, since sea breezes typically kick up around lunchtime, pushing temperatures back down in the afternoons. Rain is rarely far away—some days it's an afternoon thunderstorm, sometimes it's a steady drizzle that brings a 4-day soaking. On average, about 1 day in 3 will bring some rain. Travelers should come prepared for it.

Also be aware that early summer brings out the blackflies and the mosquitoes in great multitude, a state of affairs that has spoiled many camping and hiking trips. While this is especially true in the inland areas, it applies along the coast and offshore islands as well. Outdoors enthusiasts are best off waiting until after July 4 for longer adventures if they want to avoid a fate as human pincushions.

AUTUMN

Don't be surprised to smell the tang of fall approaching as early as mid-August, a time when you'll also notice a few leaves turned fiery red in otherwise green-leafed maples at the edges of wetlands. Fall comes early to northern New England, puts its feet up on the couch, and stays for some time.

Happily, thanks to the low elevation and moderating influences of the ocean temperatures along the coast, the foliage season tends to run even longer along the coast. Inland mountains can be brown and brittle by mid-October, but coastal foliage is just hitting its stride by then, and the tart colors can linger into the first few days of November.

Keep in mind that fall gets the most intense short-term tourist traffic in New England. Maine's coast attracts fewer leaf peepers than Vermont or New Hampshire, but don't expect to be alone during early October. Hotels are often booked up, and reservations are strongly encouraged.

WINTER

Winters along Maine's Coast are like wine—some years are good; some are lousy. During a good season, plenty of light, fluffy snow blankets the dark, rocky coast and offers a profound peace and tranquillity. The muffling qualities of fresh snow can bring a thunderous silence to the region, and the hiss and pop of a wood fire at a coastal inn can sound like an overwrought symphony. What's more, the sea is typically at its most turbulent during the winter, and can put on a spectacular show during a heavy blizzard. During these winters, coastal vacations can be unforgettable—nothing beats cross-country skiing on fresh snow at the edge of the pounding surf.

During the other winters, the lousy ones, the wet sea winds bring a nasty melange of rain and sleet. In 1998 a destructive ice storm wreaked havoc on trees (you'll see broken trunks and branches almost everywhere) and citizens, stranding over half of Maine's homes without power for up to 2 weeks. It's bone-numbing cold, and bleak, bleak, bleak.

Ergo, visiting the coast in the winter can be a high-risk venture. It's best to come prepared for hunkering down with a long book or a jigsaw puzzle at a comfortable inn. If the weather cooperates and provides crisp weather and new-fallen snow, consider it an added bonus.

Where to go? Beach towns like York Beach and Ogunquit and tourist destinations like Boothbay Harbor tend to be shuttered and melancholy in the winter. Intrepid winter travelers are better off heading to places with more substantial year-round communities and a good selection of year-round lodging, like Kennebunkport, Portland, Camden, and Bar Harbor.

SPRING

Maine's spring seemingly lasts only a weekend or so, often appearing around mid-May but sometimes as late as June. One day the ground is muddy, the trees barren, and gritty snow is still collected in shady hollows. The next day, it's in the 80s, trees are blooming, and kids are jumping off the docks into the ocean. Travelers must be very crafty and alert if they want to experience Maine's spring. This is also known as mud season, and it's a time many innkeepers and restaurateurs close up for a few weeks for repairs or to venture someplace warm.

That said, April and May can offer superb days when a blue sky arches overhead and it's warm in the sun. And this may be the most peaceful time of year—a good season for solitary walks on the beach or to sit on rocky promontories with only seagulls for company. Just be aware that as soon as the sun slips behind a cloud or over the horizon, it'll quickly feel like winter again. Don't leave your parka or gloves behind if you venture here in spring.

THE MAINE COAST CALENDAR OF EVENTS

January
✪ **New Year's Portland.** Ring in the New Year with a smorgasbord of events and entertainment throughout downtown Portland.

Events for families are scheduled in the afternoon; adult entertainment including loads of live music kicks off later in the evening at numerous auditoriums, shops, and churches. One admission price buys entrance to all events. Call ☎ **207/772-6828.** December 31 and January 1.

February

- **U.S. National Toboggan Championship,** Camden. Hundreds of teams from around the country converge at the Camden Snowbowl to try their hand at the 400-foot wooden toboggan chute. Call ☎ **207/236-3438.** Early February.

March

- **Maine Boatbuilders Show,** Portland. More than 200 exhibitors and 9,000 boat aficionados gather as winter fades to make plans for the coming summer. It's a great place to meet boatbuilders and get ideas for your dream craft. Call ☎ **207/774-1067.** Late March.

- **Maine Maple Sunday.** Maple sugarhouses throughout the state open their doors to visitors. Call ☎ **207/287-3491.** Third Sunday in March.

April

- **Boothbay Harbor Fisherman's Festival.** Local fishermen display their talents in fish filleting, clam shucking, and even lobster eating. Enjoy seafood feasts, exhibits, games, and a Blessing of the Fleet on Sunday afternoon. Call ☎ **207/633-2353.** Second weekend of April.

June

- ✪ **Old Port Festival,** Portland. A daylong block party in the heart of Portland's historic district with live music, food vendors, and activities for kids. Call ☎ **207/772-2249** for information. Early June.

- **Bar Harbor Lobster Race.** Lobsters are the actual competitors in this unique event, which takes place in a custom-made saltwater tank with four lanes. Local businesses sponsor their favorite lobster, with proceeds going to the local YMCA. Call ☎ **207/288-5103.** Third weekend in June.

- **Great Kennebec Whatever Week,** Augusta. A community celebration to mark the cleaning up of the Kennebec River, culminating in a wacky race involving all manner of watercraft, some more seaworthy than others. Call ☎ **207/623-4559** for details. Late June.

July

- **Fourth of July Celebrations.** Parades, food, fireworks, and fes-
  tivities abound along the Maine Coast. Check local newspapers
  or contact chambers of commerce for details.
- **Summer Performance Series,** Portland. Relax and enjoy 50 free
  noontime performances in Portland's Downtown Parks. Music
  includes classical, folk, jazz, rock, country, and children's shows.
  Call ☎ 207-772-6828 for a complete listing.
- **Moxie Festival,** Lisbon Falls. A quirky community festival
  celebrating the soft drink that once outsold Coca-Cola. Call
  ☎ 207/783-2249. Early July.

August

- **Maine Lobster Festival,** Rockland. Fill up on the local harvest
  at this event marking the importance and delectability of Maine's
  favorite crustacean. Enjoy a boiled lobster or two, and take in the
  ample entertainment during this informal waterfront gala. Call
  ☎ 207/596-0376 or 800/562-2529. Early August.
- ✪ **Maine Festival,** Brunswick. A 3-day festival showcasing Maine-
  made arts and crafts, music, foods, and performers. Boisterous,
  fun, and filling. Call ☎ 207/772-9012. Early August.
- **York Days,** York Village. Enjoy a quintessential coastal Maine celebration complete with crafts, road races, parades, dances, concerts,
  fireworks, and much more. Call ☎ 207/363-1040. Early August.
- **Blueberry Festival,** Machias. A festival marking the harvest of the
  region's wild blueberries. Eat to your heart's content. Call
  ☎ 207/794-3543. Mid-August.
- **Blue Hill Fair,** Blue Hill. A classic country fair just outside one of
  Maine's most elegant villages. Call ☎ 207/374-9976. Late August.

September

- **Windjammer Weekend,** Camden. Come visit Maine's impressive fleet of old-time sailing ships, which host open houses
  throughout the weekend at this scenic harbor. Call ☎ 207/
  236-4404. Early September.
- ✪ **Common Ground Fair,** Unity. An old-time state fair with a
  twist: The emphasis is on organic foods, recycling, and whole-
  some living. Call ☎ 207/623-5515. Late September.

October

- **Fall Foliage Fair,** Boothbay. More than 100 exhibitors display
  their arts and crafts at the Railroad Village; plenty of festive food-
  stuffs and live music too. Call ☎ 207/633-4924. Early October.
- **Fall Festival,** Camden. This 2-day event includes more than 90

artists and craftsmen, children's activities, food, and entertainment. Call ☎ **207/236-4404.** Early October.

November

• **Victorian Holiday,** Portland. From late November until Christmas, Portland decorates its Old Port in a Victorian Christmas theme. Enjoy the window displays, take a free hayride, and listen to costumed carolers sing. Call ☎ **207/772-6828** for details.

December

• **Christmas Prelude,** Kennebunkport. This scenic coastal village greets Santa's arrival in a lobster boat, and marks the coming of Christmas with street shows, pancake breakfasts, and tours of the towns' inns. Call ☎ **207/967-3286.** Early December.

• **York Village Festival of Lights.** This beautiful festival displays an entire York Village and York Beach lit with Christmas lights, carolers, a parade, and much more. Call ☎ **207/363-4422.** Early December.

3 Enjoying the Great Outdoors

The Maine Coast is a fine destination for those who like their coastal vacations seasoned with adventure. While southern Maine has classic beach towns where the smell of salt air mixes with coconut oil and taffy, much of the rest of the Maine Coast is unruly and wild. In parts, it seems to share more in common with Alaska—you can see bald eagles soaring above and whales breaching below. In between these two archetypes, you'll find remote coves perfect for a rowboat jaunt, and isolated offshore islands accessible only by sea kayak.

The best places for coastal adventure are usually not the most obvious places—those tend to be crowded and more developed. You'll need to do a bit of homework to find the real treasures. A growing number of specialized guidebooks can help point visitors in the right direction; some of the best are mentioned below. And don't overlook another great resource: the dozens of outdoor shops around the state, where the staff is often happy to send you in the right direction.

BEACHGOING

Swimming at Maine's ocean beaches is for the foolish and the hearty. The Gulf Stream, which prods warm waters toward the Cape Cod shores to the south, veers toward Iceland south of Maine and leaves the state's 4,600-mile coastline washed by the brisk Nova Scotia current, an offshoot of the Arctic Labrador Current. During the summer months, water temperatures along the south coast will top 60° during an especially warm spell where the water is shallow, but it's usually cooler than that. The average ocean temperature at Bar Harbor in summer is 54°; farther east in Passamaquoddy Bay it's 51°.

Maine's beaches are found mostly between Portland and the New Hampshire border. Northeast of Portland there are a handful of fine beaches—including popular **Reid State Park** and **Popham Beach State Park**—but rocky coast defines this territory for the most part. The southern beaches are beautiful, but rarely isolated. Summer homes occupy the low dunes in most areas; mid-rise condos give **Old Orchard Beach** a "mini-Miami" air. For my money, the best beaches are at **Ogunquit,** which boasts a 3-mile-long sandy strand, some of which has a mildly remote character, and **Long Sands Beach** at York, which has a festive, carnival atmosphere right along Route 1A.

Remember that in Maine, the term "sand beach" is not redundant. It simply distinguishes these from their more common cousins, the "pebble beach" and the "cobblestone beach." These probably don't require further definition, but you should be aware that some hyperbolic innkeepers might refer to a nearby pebble beach where closer examination shows the pebbles range in size from billiard balls to bowling balls.

If you love swimming but loathe shivering, head inland to the sandy beaches at Maine's wonderful lakes, where the water is tepid by comparison. A number of state and municipal parks offer access. Among the most accessible to the coast are **Sebago Lake State Park** (☎ 207/693-6613), about 20 miles northwest of Portland, the municipal **Pemaquid Beach Park** (☎ 207/677-2754) near Damariscotta, and **Swan Lake State Park** (☎ 207/525-4404), 6 miles north of Belfast. Small admission fees are charged at all three.

BICYCLING

Mount Desert Island and **Acadia National Park** are the premier coastal destinations for bikers, especially mountain bikers in search of scenic but easy-riding terrain. The 57 miles of well-maintained carriage roads in the national park offer superb cruising through thick forests and to the tops of rocky knolls with ocean views. No cars are permitted on these grass and gravel roads, so bikers and hikers have them to themselves. Mountain bikes can be rented in Bar Harbor. The Park Loop Road, while often crowded with slow-moving cars, offers one of the more memorable road-biking experiences in the state. The rest of Mount Desert Island is also good for road biking, especially on the quieter western half of the island.

In southern Maine, **Route 103** and **Route 1A** offer pleasant excursions for bikers along the coast. Offshore, bring your bike to the bigger islands for car-free cruising. **Vinalhaven** and **North Haven** in Penobscot Bay, and **Swan's Island** in Blue Hill Bay, are all popular destinations.

BIRD WATCHING

Bird watchers from southern and inland states should be able to lengthen their life lists along the Maine Coast, which attracts both migrating birds cruising the Atlantic flyway (it's warbler mania in spring!) and boasts populations of numerous native shorebirds, such as plovers (including the threatened piping plover), whimbrels, sandpipers, and dunlins. Gulls and terns are frequently seen; you'll see a surfeit of herring and great black-backed gull, along with the common tern; less frequently seen are Bonaparte's gull, laughing gull, jaeger, and the arctic tern. Far up the coast near Lubec, look for members of the alcid family, including razorbill and guillemot. Puffins (another alcid) nest on several offshore islands; tour boats to view puffins depart from Boothbay Harbor, Bar Harbor, and Jonesport. See chapter 4 for more information.

CAMPING

Car campers traveling the Maine Coast have plenty of choices, from well-developed private campgrounds to more basic state parks. **Acadia National Park** tends to be the biggest draw, but there's no shortage of other options on and near the coast.

Among the coastal state parks worthy of an overnight are **Lamoine State Park** (☎ 207/667-4778), which is convenient to Acadia National Park yet away from the thickest of the crowds, and remote **Cobscook Bay State Park** (☎ 207/726-4412), where most campsites are on the water, offering a great view of the massive 28-foot tides that slosh in and out. For more information about other state parks, contact the **Department of Conservation,** State House Station #22, Augusta, ME 04333 (☎ 207/287-3821). To make camping reservations at most state park campgrounds, call between January and August (☎ 207/287-3824 or 800/332-1501 in Maine).

Maine also has more than 200 private campgrounds spread throughout the state, many offering full hookups for RVs. For a guide to the private campgrounds, contact the **Maine Campground Owners Association,** 655 Main St., Lewiston, ME 04240 (☎ 207/

782-5874). Campsites get booked quickly for summer weekends, so try to call ahead for reservations.

CANOEING

The state's best canoeing tends to be far inland and deep in the woods, but day paddlers can find good trips at several lakes along the coast, or in some of the protected bays. A fine day's paddle may be had anywhere along the **Damariscotta–Pemaquid River Canoe Trail,** a 40-mile flatwater loop that tracks some of the ancient Indian trails. Contact **Pemaquid River Canoe Rental** (☎ 207/563-5721) for information on the trail and canoe rentals.

For a low-key afternoon with a paddle, head to **Long Pond** on Mt. Desert Island, where canoes may be rented by the hour. Two excellent sources for detailed canoeing information statewide are the *AMC River Guide: Maine* and *Quiet Water Canoe Guide: Maine,* both published by the Appalachian Mountain Club, 5 Joy St., Boston, MA 02108.

FISHING

Deep-sea fishing charters are available at many of the harbors along the Maine Coast, with options ranging from inshore fishing expeditions for stripers and bluefish, to offshore voyages in search of shark, cod, and pollock. Prices range from $25 per person for day trips to $395 to charter an offshore boat for the day. Visitor information centers and chambers of commerce listed in this guide will be able to match you up with the right boat to meet your needs.

For freshwater fishing not too far from the Downeast coast, **Grand Lake Stream** is a popular and historic destination. Located deep in the woods of Washington County, close to the border with Canada, the area has a rich heritage as a fisherman's settlement, and a number of camps and outfitters cater to the serious angler, especially those in search of landlocked salmon, smallmouth bass, and brook trout. Among the classic fishing lodges in this area are **Weatherby's** (☎ 207/796-5558) and **Indian Rock Camps** (☎ 800/498-2821 or 207/796-2822).

Saltwater fishing requires no license. For freshwater fishing, nonresident **licenses** are $50 for the season, or $21 for 3 days. Seven- and 15-day licenses are also available. Fees are reduced for juniors (12 to 15); no license is required for those under 12. Licenses are available at many outdoor shops and general stores throughout the state, or by mail from the address below. For a booklet of fishing regulations, contact the **Department of Inland Fisheries and**

Wildlife, State House Station #41, Augusta, ME 04333 (☎ 207/
287-8000).

GOLFING

With six of its holes bordering Penobscot Bay, the golf course at the
Samoset Resort in Rockport (☎ 207/594-2511) is easily the state's
most dramatic. (It's also among the priciest, with greens fees running
$80 during peak season—if you can even get a reservation.) Other
notable courses along the coast (although not necessarily on the
water) are the historic **Kebo Valley Golf Club** (☎ 207/288-3000)
in the rolling hills outside of Bar Harbor; and Kennebunkport's
Cape Arundel Golf Club (☎ 207/967-3494), which is favored by
a certain ex-president when he's in town.

HIKING

Serious hiking—as opposed to strolling—is limited along the Maine
Coast. The most challenging and most rewarding trails are found at
Acadia National Park. Although the peaks top out at 1,530 feet, the
terrain may be more rugged than you might expect, and often leads
to blustery hilltops of granite and blueberry, offering exceptional
vistas of islands and sea. Another good destination for hilly coastal
hiking is Camden Hills State Park on the west shore of Penobscot
Bay.

Less demanding strolls may be found tucked all up and down the
coast, with many of these a matter of local knowledge. Two fine
pathways skirt the water in York (see chapter 2), and even in Portland you can saunter on well-maintained (and heavily used) pathways along about 5 miles of tidal waters. More inveterate explorers
should continue eastward along the coast to Washington County.
Hikes at Great Wass Island, near Cutler, and at West Quoddy Head
(and just over the border on Canada's Campobello Island) provide
a measure of remoteness and solitude that has been lost along much
of the rest of the Maine Coast.

More detailed information on hiking in the area may be found
in John Gibson's fine book, *50 Hikes in Southern and Coastal Maine*
(1996, Backcountry Publications).

SEA KAYAKING

Sea kayakers nationwide migrate to Maine in the summer for world-
class voyaging. The 3,500 miles of rocky coastline and the thousands
of offshore islands have created a wonderful sea kayaker's playground.
Paddlers can explore protected estuaries far from the surf, or test their

skills and determination with excursions across choppy, open seas to islands far offshore. It's a sport that can be extremely dangerous (the seas can turn on you in a matter of minutes), but can yield plenty of returns for those with the proper equipment and skills.

The nation's first long-distance "water trail" was created here in 1987 when the **Maine Island Trail** was established. This 325-mile waterway winds along the coast from Portland to Machias, and incorporates some 70 state and privately owned islands along the route. Members of the Maine Island Trail Association, a private nonprofit, are granted permission to visit and camp on these islands, as long as they follow certain restrictions (for example, don't visit designated islands during nesting season). The association seeks to encourage low-impact, responsible use of these natural treasures. A guidebook, published annually, provides descriptions of all the islands in the network and is free with association membership (note that the guide is available *only* to members). Membership is $40 per year (individual or family); contact the **Maine Island Trail Association,** P.O. Box C, Rockland, ME 04841 (☎ **207/596-6456** or 207/761-8225).

For novices, Maine has a number of kayak outfitters offering guided excursions ranging from an afternoon to a week. Recommended outfitters include the **Maine Island Kayak Co.,** 70 Luther St., Peaks Island, ME 04108 (☎ **207/766-2373**) and **Maine Sports Outfitters,** P.O. Box 956, Rockport, ME 04856 (☎ **800/244-8799** or 207/236-8797).

WINDJAMMING

An ideal way to combine time in the outdoors with relative luxury and an easy-to-digest education in maritime history is aboard a windjammer cruise on the coast. Maine boasts a sizeable fleet of vintage sailing ships that offer private cabins, meals, entertainment, and adventure. The ships range in size from 53 to 132 feet, and most are berthed in the region between Boothbay Harbor and Belfast. You choose your adventure: An array of excursions is available, from simple overnights to weeklong expeditions gunkholing among Maine's thousands of scenic islands and coves.

Several windjammer festivals and races are held along the Maine Coast throughout the summer; these are perfect events to shop for a ship on which to spend a few days. Among the more notable events are the **Windjammer Days** in Boothbay Harbor (late June) and the **Camden Windjammer Weekend** in early September. Contact the appropriate chamber of commerce for more information.

For more about windjamming, flip ahead to the "Rockland" section in chapter 5.

4 Tips for Travelers with Special Needs

FOR TRAVELERS WITH DISABILITIES   Prodded by the Americans with Disabilities Act, a growing number of inns and hotels have been retrofitting their rooms for travelers with disabilities. Most innkeepers are quite proud of their improvements—when I arrive for a site visit, they're invariably quick to show me their new rooms with barrier-free entrances, wheelchair-accessible showers, and fire alarms equipped with strobe lights. Outdoor recreation areas, especially on state and federal lands, are also providing trails and facilities for those who've been effectively barred in the past owing to seemingly small barriers.

Accessibility is improving regionwide, but improvements are far from universal. When in doubt, call ahead to ensure that you'll be accommodated.

Wilderness Inquiry, Fifth Street SE, Box 84, Minneapolis, MN 55414 (☎ **612/379-3858** or 800/728-0719) offers adventure-travel packages for disabled travelers nationwide, including a canoe trip on the Moose River in Maine.

FOR SENIORS   The Maine Coast is well suited for older travelers, with a wide array of activities for seniors and discounts often available. It's wise to request a discount at hotels or motels when booking the room, not when you arrive. An identification card from the **American Association of Retired Persons (AARP),** 601 E St., NW, Washington, DC 20049 (☎ 202/434-2277) can be invaluable in obtaining discounts.

Excellent programs for seniors are offered by **Elderhostel,** 75 Federal St., Boston, MA 02110 (☎ **617/426-7788**). These educational programs for people over 55 years old are reasonably priced, and include lodging and meals. Participants can study everything from the art of downhill skiing to the art of autobiography. The locations of these classes are often intriguing and dramatic.

FOR FAMILIES   Families rarely have trouble finding things to do with kids along the Maine Coast. The natural world holds tremendous wonder for the younger set—an afternoon exploring a tidepool can be a huge adventure. Older kids often like the challenge of learning to paddle a sea kayak in choppy seas, or playing video games at an arcade. And there's always the beach, which is usually good for hours of sunny diversion. Recommended destinations for families include the obvious—**Old Orchard Beach** and **Acadia National Park**—along with less so, like **Sebasco Harbor Resort** south of Bath, **Samoset Resort** in Rockport, and the rocky headland and nearby beach of **Pemaquid Point.**

Be aware that many inns cater to couples, and kids aren't exactly welcomed with open arms. Many inns don't allow kids, or strongly prefer only children over a certain age. Innkeepers will let you know when you make your reservation, but you should mention that you're traveling with kids. Anyway, it's often wise to mention that you're a family when booking a room; often you'll get accommodations nearer the game room or the pool, making everyone's life a bit easier.

Several specialized guides offer more detailed information for families on the go. Try *Frommer's New England with Kids,* and *Best Hikes with Children in Vermont, New Hampshire & Maine* by Cynthia and Thomas Lewis.

FOR GAY & LESBIAN TRAVELERS   Ogunquit on the south coast is an historic gay resort, a sort of very low-key Provincetown. (Unlike at Provincetown, straight visitors can visit here and not realize that there's a substantial gay population in summer.) Ogunquit features a lively bar-beach scene in the summer; in the winter the scene is decidedly more mellow. Several Ogunquit B&Bs are owned by gay entrepreneurs, who make gay visitors feel right at home.

Portland, Maine, has attracted many refugees, both gay and straight, who've fled the crime and congestion of Boston and New York. Portland hosts a sizeable gay pride festival early each summer that includes a riotous parade and a dance on the city pier, among other events. Contact the **Convention and Visitor's Bureau of Greater Portland** (☎ 207/772-5800 or 207/772-4994) to ask about festival dates for the upcoming year.

Portland's oldest gay club is **The Underground,** located at 3 Spring St. near the Old Port (☎ 207/773-3315). Half of the place is a tidy, friendly bar and hangout; the other half is a disco with pulsing lights and loud, urban music. Other places to visit are **Blackstones,** 6 Pine St. (☎ 207/775-2885), which has a low-key neighborhood bar feel to it, and **Sisters,** 45 Danforth (☎ 207/774-1505), which draws many of the city's lesbians.

5 Getting There

BY CAR   Reaching coastal Maine doesn't require much in the way of special knowledge. Coming from the south, take I-95, which parallels the southern Maine Coast before veering inland near

Brunswick. If you're headed to mid-coast Maine, take I-95 to Brunswick and follow Route 1 up to the coast. If you're driving to Camden or Belfast on western Penobscot Bay, you can avoid coastal traffic by taking the turnpike to Augusta, then connecting via Route 17 (to Camden) or Route 3 (to Belfast).

Those heading directly to Acadia National Park will find it most expedient to follow interstates to Bangor, then Route 1A to Ellsworth, where you can connect to Route 3 onward to Mount Desert Island.

BY PLANE   Several commercial carriers serve Portland and Bangor. Airlines most commonly fly to these airports from New York or Boston, although direct connections from other cities, such as Chicago and Philadelphia, are also available. Many of the scheduled flights to northern New England from Boston are aboard smaller prop planes; ask the airline or your travel agent if this is an issue for you.

Portland is served by regularly scheduled flights on **Delta/Business Express** (☎ 800/638-7333; www.delta-air.com), **Continental** (☎ 800/525-0280; www.flycontinental.com), **US Airways** (☎ 800/428-4322; www.usairways.com), **United** (☎ 800/241-6522; www.ual.com), **Pine State** (☎ 207/353-6334), and **Northeast Airlines** (☎ 800/983-3247).

Several smaller coastal airports in the region are served by feeder airlines and charter companies, including Rockport and Bar Harbor (actually, it's Trenton, which is just across the causeway from Mount Desert Island). Contact **Colgan Air** (☎ **800/272-5488** or 207/596-7604; www.colganair.com).

Many travelers headed for Maine find they pay less and have a wider choice of flight times by flying into Boston's Logan Airport, or into Manchester, NH, which recently was added as an outpost of budget-friendly **Southwest Airlines** (☎ **800/435-9792;** www.iflyswa.com). Boston and Manchester are both about 2 hours by car from Portland.

BY BUS   Express bus service is well-run if a bit spotty in northern New England. You'll be able to reach the major cities and tourist destinations by bus, along with a handful of coastal towns and villages. Tickets are quite reasonable—about $12 one way from Boston to Portland—and taking the bus requires no advance planning.

Two major bus lines serve coastal Maine: **Vermont Transit Lines** (☎ **800/451-3292** or 800/642-3133), which is affiliated with Greyhound; and **Concord Trailways** (☎ **800/639-3317**). Concord Trailways buses tend to be a bit more luxurious (and a few dollars more expensive) than Vermont Transit, and often provide videos and music piped through headphones en route.

BY TRAIN   Rail service from Boston to Portland and possibly beyond was originally slated to begin in 1994, but wrangling over track upgrades and other issues has severely delayed the process. At press time, it looked mildly hopeful for a return to service sometime in 1999 or 2000. For an update, contact Amtrak at ☎ **800/ 872-7245;** www.amtrak.com.

6 Getting Around

BY CAR

The Portland and Bangor airports (see "Getting There," above) both host national car-rental chains. Some handy phone numbers are **Avis** (☎ 800/331-1212), **Budget** (☎ 800/527-0700), **Enterprise** (☎ 800/325-8007), **Hertz** (☎ 800/654-3131), **National** (☎ 800/ 227-7368), **Rent-A-Wreck** (☎ 800/535-1391), and **Thrifty** (☎ 800/367-2277). You might also find independent car-rental firms in some of the cities and bigger towns; contact the local chambers of commerce for the names of such agencies.

Don't underestimate the size of the Maine Coast—Kittery to Eastport (the easternmost city in the United States) is 293 miles. Driving times can be longer than you'd expect due to narrow roads and zigzagging peninsulas, not to mention high-season traffic.

In the summer, I-95 leading from Boston to Maine is often sluggish on Friday afternoons and evenings, and Route 1 along the coast can also back up for miles as tourists bottleneck where they cross two-lane bridges spanning tidal rivers. To avoid the worst of the tourist traffic, try to stay put on weekends and big summer holidays; if your schedule allows it, take an extra day off work, it'll pay handsome dividends in lowered blood pressure.

If you're a connoisseur of backroads and off-the-beaten-track exploring, the **Maine Atlas and Gazaetter,** produced by DeLorme Mapping (☎ 888/227-1656) in Yarmouth, is an invaluable purchase. It offers an extraordinary level of detail, right down to logging roads and canoe launch sites. DeLorme's atlases are available at many local book and convenience stores, or at the company's headquarters and map store in Yarmouth, a few minutes north of Portland (Exit 17 off I-95).

BY PLANE

Contact **Colgan Air** (☎ **800/272-5488** or 207/596-7604) for information on scheduled flights to Rockland and Bar Harbor.

Quoddy Air (☎ **207/853-0997**), based in Eastport, offers charter service to airports in and around Downeast Maine.

BY BUS

See the "Getting There" section, above, for information about bus lines serving the Maine Coast.

FAST FACTS: The Maine Coast

AAA   The club's Maine headquarters (☎ **207/780-6900**) is in Portland and can help members with trip planning and discount tickets to events and attractions. Call ☎ **800/222-4357** for membership information.

Emergencies   In the event of fire, crime, or medical emergency, dial ☎ 911.

Liquor Laws   The legal age to consume alcohol in Maine is 21, and hard liquor is sold through state-run stores as well as "agency stores," which are often found as sections in some of the larger supermarkets. Beer and wine are available in grocery and convenience stores. Purchasing is strictly regulated; even those clearly over the age of consent may be asked to show ID.

Maps   Free road maps can be requested at official tourist information centers. For more detailed coverage, consider purchasing a DeLorme atlas of the state (see "By Car" under "Getting Around," above).

Newspapers/Magazines   Almost every small town seems to have a daily or weekly newspaper covering events and happenings of the area. These are good sources of information for small-town events and dinner specials at local restaurants—the day-to-day things that slip through the cracks at the tourist bureaus. These are also great sources of local color.

The state's two main daily papers are the *Bangor Daily News,* which covers the northern and eastern parts of the state, and the *Portland Press Herald,* which covers the rest. The *Press Herald* maintains an active Web site (**www.portland.com**), which is handy for getting a sense of the state before you arrive.

Taxes   The sales tax in Maine is 6%, but increases to 7% for accommodations and meals. At press time, the legislature was considering rolling back the general sales tax to 5%.

2

The South Coast

*M*aine's southern coast runs roughly from the state line at Kittery to Portland, and is the destination of the great majority of travelers into the state (including many day-trippers from the Boston area). While it will take some doing to find privacy and remoteness here, you'll turn up at least two excellent reasons for a detour: the long beaches that are the region's hallmark, and the almost tactile sense of history in the coastal villages.

Thanks to quirks of geography, nearly all of Maine's sandy beaches are located in this 60-mile stretch of coastline. It's not hard to find a relaxing sandy spot, whether you prefer dunes and the lulling sound of the surf or the carny atmosphere of a festive beach town. The waves are dependent on the weather—during a good Northeast blow (especially prevalent in spring and fall) they pound the shores and threaten beach houses built decades ago. During the balmy days of midsummer the ocean can be as gentle as a farm pond, with barely audible waves lapping timidly at the shore.

One thing all beaches share in common: They're washed by the frigid waters of the Gulf of Maine. Except among the very young, who seem immune to blood-chilling temperatures, swimming sessions here tend to be very brief and often accompanied by shrieks, whoops, and agitated hand-waving. The beach season itself is also brief and intense, running from July 4th to Labor Day. Before and after, beach towns lapse into a lazy slumber.

On foggy or rainy days, plan to search out the South Coast's rich history. More than 3 centuries ago the early European newcomers first settled here, only to be driven out by hostile Native Americans, who had been pushed to the brink by treaty-breaking British settlers and prodded by the mischievous French. Settlers later re-established themselves, and by the early 19th century the southern Maine Coast was one of the most prosperous regions in the nation. Shipbuilders constructed brigantines and sloops, and Maine ship captains plied the Eastern Seaboard, the Caribbean, and far beyond. Merchants and traders constructed vast warehouses along the rivers in which to store their goods. Many handsome and historic homes near the coast today attest to the region's former prosperity.

A second wave of settlers arrived in the mid- to late-19th century, when wealthy city dwellers from Boston and New York sought respite from the summer heat and congestion by fleeing to Maine's coast. They built shingled estates (which they coyly called "cottages") with views of Atlantic. After the turn of the century, aided by trolleys and buses, wealthy rusticators were followed by the emerging middle class, who built bungalows near the shore and congregated at oceanside boarding houses to splash in the waves.

1 Kittery & the Yorks

Driving into Maine from the south, as most visitors do, the first town you'll come to is Kittery. Kittery was once famous nationally for its naval yard (it's still operating), but regionally at least Kittery is now better known for the dozens of factory outlets that cluster here. (Why they chose to spring up here and not a couple of miles away in sales-tax-free New Hampshire remains an enduring mystery.) Maine has the second highest number of outlet malls in the nation (only California has more), and Kittery is home to a good many of them.

"The Yorks," just to the north, are comprised of three towns that share a name but little else. In fact, it's rare to find three such well-defined and diverse New England archetypes in such a compact area. York Village is redolent with early American history and architecture. York Harbor reached its zenith during America's late Victorian era, when wealthy urbanites constructed rambling cottages at the ocean's edge. York Beach has a turn-of-the-century beach town feel, with loud amusements, taffy shops, a modest zoo, and small gabled summer homes set in crowded enclaves near the beach.

ESSENTIALS
GETTING THERE

Kittery is accessible from I-95 or Route 1, with exits well marked. The Yorks are reached most easily from Exit 1 of the Maine Turnpike. From the exit, look for Route 1A just south of the turnpike exit. This route connects all three York towns.

VISITOR INFORMATION

Travelers entering the state on I-95 can stock up on travel information for the region and beyond at the **Kittery Information Center**

(☎ 207/439-1319), located at a well-marked rest area. Open 8am to 6pm in summer, 9am to 5pm year-round, it's amply stocked with brochures, and the helpful staff can answer most questions.

The **York Chamber of Commerce,** P.O. Box 417, York, ME 03909 (☎ 207/363-4422), operates an attractive, helpful information center at 571 Rte. 1, a short distance from the turnpike exit. It's open 9am to 5pm daily (until 6pm Fridays). A trackless trolley (a bus retrofitted to look like an old-fashioned trolley) regularly links all three York towns and provides a convenient way to explore without having to scare up parking spots at every stop. Hop the trolley at one of the well-marked stops for a 1-hour narrated tour ($3), or disembark along the way and explore by foot ($1.50 for a partial trip).

EXPLORING & SHOPPING IN KITTERY

Kittery's consumer mecca is 4 miles south of York on Route 1. Some 120 **factory outlets** flank the highway, scattered among more than a dozen strip malls. Name-brand retailers include Champion, Anne Klein, Old Navy, Harry & David, Sunglass Hut, Tommy Hilfiger, Mikasa, J. Crew, Izod, Bose, and Black and Decker. The area can be tough to navigate in peak season owing to the four lanes of heavy summer traffic and capricious restrictions on turns. Information on current outlets is available from ☎ 888/548-8379, or on the web at www.thekitteryoutlets.com.

Departing from downtown Kittery (south of the outlet zone), an attractive route north to York follows winding Route 103. (Perfect for a drive, it's a bit busy and narrow for a bike ride.) The road passes through the historic village of Kittery Point, where homes seem to be located just inches from the roadway, and past two historic forts (both in parks open to the public). Look for the **Lady Pepperell House** on your right at the first left elbow in the road. The handsome cream-colored Georgian home was built in 1760, and is considered one of the most elegant of its kind in the nation. (Not open to the public.)

Just before coming into the village of York, keep an eye on your left near the marshes and tidal inlets for the Wiggly Bridge (see "Walks Along the Water," below).

DISCOVERING LOCAL HISTORY

Old York Historical Society. South Side Rd., York. ☎ 207/363-4974. $6 adults, $2.50 children 6 to 16 (includes admission to all buildings). Tues–Sat 10am–5pm; Sun 1–5pm. (Last tour leaves at 4pm.) Closed Oct through May.

John Hancock is famous for his oversized signature on the Declaration of Independence, his tenure as governor of Massachusetts, and the insurance company named after him. What's not so well known is his earlier checkered past as a businessman. Hancock was the proprietor of Hancock Wharf, a failed enterprise that's but one of the intriguing historic sites in York Village, a fine destination for those curious about early American history.

First settled in 1624, York Village has several early homes open to the public. Tickets are available at any of the properties, but a good place to start is **Jefferds Tavern,** across from the handsome **old burying ground.** Changing exhibits here document various facets of early life. Next door is the **School House,** furnished as it might have been in the last century. A 10-minute walk along lightly traveled Lindsay Road will bring you to **Hancock Wharf,** which is next door to the **George Marshall Store.** Also nearby is the **Elizabeth Perkins House** with its well-preserved Colonial Revival interiors.

The two don't-miss buildings in the society's collection are the intriguing **Old Gaol,** built in 1719 with its now-musty dungeons for criminals and debtors. The jail is the oldest surviving public building in the United States. Just down the knoll from the jail is the **Emerson-Wilcox House,** built in the mid-1700s. Added to periodically over the years, it's a virtual catalog of architectural styles and early decorative arts.

WALKS ALONG THE WATER

Two local strolls will allow visitors to stretch their legs and get the cobwebs out of their heads.

York Harbor and York Village are connected by a quiet pathway that follows a river and passes through gently rustling woodlands. **Fisherman's Walk** departs from below Edward's Harborside Inn, near the Stage Neck Inn. (There's limited parking at tiny York Harbor Beach.) Follow the pathway along the river, past lobster shacks and along lawns leading up to grand shingled homes. Cross Route 103 and walk over the **Wiggly Bridge** (said to be, not implausibly, the smallest suspension bridge in the world), then head into the woods. You'll soon connect with a dirt lane; follow this and you'll emerge at Lindsay Road near Hancock Wharf (see above). Depending on your pace, the entire walk is about a mile and will take a half hour to 45 minutes.

Also departing from near York Harbor Beach is the **Cliff Walk,** a trail that follows rugged terrain along rocky bluffs and offers sweeping views of the open ocean and glimpses of life in some of the town's more grand cottages. The far end of this trail was destroyed by forceful ocean waves some years back; you'll have to retrace your steps back to the beach. The pathway has also been the subject of recent disputes between the town and landowners seeking to limit access to their properties. Check signs for any new restrictions before you set off.

BEACHES

York Beach actually consists of two beaches—**Long Sands Beach** and **Short Sands Beach**—separated by a rocky headland and a small island capped by scenic **Nubble Light.** Both offer plenty of room for sunning and Frisbees when the tide is out. When the tide is in, they're both a bit cramped. Short Sands fronts the town of York Beach with its candlepin bowling and video arcades. It's the better bet for families traveling with kids who have short attention spans. Long Sands runs along Route 1A, across from a profusion of motels, summer homes, and convenience stores. Parking at both beaches is metered (50¢ per hour).

Public restrooms are available at both beaches; other services, including snacks, are provided by local restaurants and vendors.

WHERE TO STAY

For basic accommodations, try York Beach, which has a proliferation of motels and guest cottages facing Long Sands Beach. Even with this abundance, however, it's advisable to reserve ahead during prime season. And don't expect any real bargains in midsummer, even among the most basic of motels. Among those offering basic accommodations on or very near the beach are **The Anchorage Inn** (☎ **207/363-5112**), **Sea Latch Motor Inn** (☎ **800/441-2993** or 207/363-4400), and the **Sunrise Motel** (☎ **800/242-0750** or 207/363-4542).

IN KITTERY

Gundalow Inn. 6 Water St., Kittery, ME 03904. ☎ **207/439-4040.** 6 units. Mid-May to Oct $110–$125 double; Nov to mid-May $80–$90. Rates include full breakfast. 2-night minimum stay on holiday weekends. DISC, MC, V. Children under 16 accepted by special arrangement.

Innkeepers Cevia and George Rosol converted this 1889 home in 1990, and they did a superb job of it. The rooms are tastefully restored and furnished with eclectic antiques, including vintage 1930s iron bedsteads. A first-floor common room and a small front porch allow guests to unwind with grace after a day's exertions. You can walk about a half-mile across the bridge to Portsmouth, New Hampshire. Breakfasts are notable for their delectability and generous portions, and typically include blueberry-lemon soup, scones, and pancakes, along with regional fare like smoked salmon or codfish cakes.

IN YORK

Dockside Guest Quarters. Harris Island (P.O. Box 205), York, ME 03909. ☎ **207/363-2868.** Fax 207/363-1977. www.docksidegq.com. E-mail: info@docksidegq.com. 25 units (2 with shared bathroom). TV. Mid-June to early Sept $69–$174 double. 2-night minimum stay July–Sept. DISC, MC, V. Closed weekdays Nov–May. Drive south on Rte. 103 from Rte. 1A in York Harbor; after bridge over York River, turn left and follow signs.

David and Harriet Lusty established this quiet retreat in 1954, and recent additions (mostly new cottages) haven't dulled any of the friendly, maritime flavor of the place. Situated on an island connected to the mainland by a small bridge, the inn occupies nicely landscaped grounds, which are shady with maples and white pines. Five of the rooms are in the main house, built in 1885, but the bulk of the accommodations are in small, town-house-style cottages constructed between 1968 and 1974. These are simply furnished, bright, and airy, and all have private decks that overlook the entrance to York Harbor. (Several rooms also offer woodstoves.)

Dining: The inn operates a locally popular restaurant on the property, serving traditional New England meals like broiled halibut, baked stuffed lobster, and braised lamb. Entrees are $13 to $17.

Facilities: Rowboats, 13-foot *Boston Whaler*, badminton, croquet, ocean swimming.

Union Bluff Hotel. Beach St. (at the north end of Short Sands Beach), York Beach, ME 03910. ☎ **207/363-1333,** or 800/833-0721 out of state. www.unionbluff.com. 61 units. A/C TV TEL. Summer $98–$148 double; early fall $68–$88 double; spring and late fall $58–$78 double; winter $48–$68 double. $208 suite in season; $158 off-season. AE, DISC, MC, V.

Viewed from Short Sands Beach, the Union Bluff Hotel, with its stumpy turrets, dormers, and prominent porches, has the look and feel of an old-fashioned beach hotel. So it's a bit of a surprise to learn it was built in 1989 (the fifth hotel to rise on this site since the late 1800s). Inside is a generic-modern building with most amenities. Rooms have oak furniture, wall-to-wall carpeting, and small refrigerators. There's a comfortable and quiet deck on the top floor for getting away from it all (alas, no ocean view). Step outside and you're virtually at the beach and the Fun-O-Rama arcade with its candlepin bowling and banks of video games. (It can be noisy in the evening if your room faces this direction.) A newly acquired motel next door added 21 rooms to the mix, and these are furnished simply. Stick to the main inn for the better views; the best rooms are the suites on the top floor, which offer beach vistas from sitting areas in the turrets.

Dining: On the ground floor there's a locally popular lounge and a restaurant; both are open only during the warmer months. The restaurant features American and Italian specialties, including pasta, burgers, and steamed lobsters.

WHERE TO DINE
IN KITTERY

Bob's Clam Hut. Rte. 1, Kittery. ☎ **207/439-4233.** Reservations not accepted. Sandwiches $1.50–$2.95; dinners $3.95–$18.45. AE, MC, V. Sun–Thurs 11am–9pm, Fri–Sat 11am–9:30pm; shorter hours off-season. Located just north of the Kittery Trading Post. FRIED FISH.

Set amid the factory outlets of Route 1, Bob's may be the only place within miles that still has a gravel driveway. Since 1956 this spot has managed to retain an old-fashioned flavor while serving up heaps of fried clams and other diet-busting enticements with great efficiency. Order at the front window, get a soda from a vending machine, then stake out a table inside or on the deck with a Route 1 view while waiting for your number to be called. The food is surprisingly light, cooked in cholesterol-free vegetable oil, and the onion rings are especially good.

Chauncey Creek Lobster Pier. Chauncey Creek Rd., Kittery Point. ☎ **207/439-1030** or 207/439-9024. Reservations not accepted. Lobsters priced to market; other items $1.50–$8.95. Daily 11am–8pm (until 7pm during shoulder seasons); open Tues–Sun only after Labor Day. Closed Columbus Day to Mother's Day. Located between Kittery Point and York on Rte. 103; watch for signs.

It's not on the wild, open ocean, but Chauncey's remains one of the most scenic lobster pounds in the state, not the least because the Spinney Family, which has been selling lobsters here since the 1950s, takes such obvious pride in their place. You reach the pound by walking down a wooden ramp to the water's edge, where a broad deck and plenty of brightly painted picnic tables await. (If it's too crowded, order your meal to go and head to Gerrish Island State Park, just down the road.)

Lobster, served hot and fresh, is the specialty, of course, but they also offer up steamed mussels (in wine and garlic) and clams. This is an à la carte place—buy a bag of potato chips and sodas while waiting for your lobsters to cook. There's a BYOB policy, and you can bring in any other food you want provided they don't sell it here. Afterwards, wash up at the outdoor sink (labeled "finger bowl") on the deck.

IN THE YORKS

✪ **Cape Neddick Inn Restaurant.** 1233 Rte. 1, Cape Neddick. ☎ **207/363-2899.** Reservations recommended. Main courses $16–$28. DISC, MC, V. Summer daily 5:30–9:30pm; Sunday brunch 11:30am–3pm (winter only). Call for off-season hours. REGIONAL/AMERICAN.

This fine inn has offered some of the consistently best dining in southern Maine since 1979, and continues to do so under new ownership. Located in an elegant structure on a relatively quiet stretch of Route 1, the Cape Neddick Inn has an open, handsome dining area that mixes traditional and modern. The old comes in the cozy golden glow of the room. The modern is the artwork, which changes frequently and showcases some of the region's better painters and sculptors.

The creative menu changes seasonally to make the most of local products. There's an extensive selection of appetizers, including a lobster roll with wasabi, and applewood-smoked seafood (smoked on premises) served tossed in an apple-cider vinaigrette on Rhode Island johnnycakes. Depending on the season, main courses might include cod wrapped in smoked bacon and served on cabbage, or grilled rack of pork with firecracker shrimp on saffron basmati rice.

Goldenrod Restaurant. Railroad Rd. and Ocean Ave., York Beach. ☎ **207/363-2621.** www.thegoldenrod.com. Breakfast $2.10–$5.25; lunch and dinner entrees $1.75–$7.50. MC, V. Memorial Day to Labor Day daily 8am–10pm (until 9pm in June); Labor Day–Columbus Day Weds–Sun 8am–3pm. Closed Columbus Day to Memorial Day. FAMILY-STYLE.

This beach-town classic is the place for local color with your breakfast or lunch   it's been a summer institution in York Beach since it first opened in 1896. It's easy to find: Look for visitors on the sidewalk gawking through plate glass windows at the ancient taffy machines hypnotically churning out taffy in volume, enough (63 tons a year) to make busloads of dentists very wealthy. The restaurant is behind the taffy and fudge operation, and is low on frills and long on atmosphere. Diners sit on stout oak furniture around a stone fireplace, or at the marble soda fountain. There are dark beams overhead and the sort of linoleum floor you don't see much anymore. Breakfast offerings are the standards: omelets, waffles, griddle cakes, and bakery items. Lunch is equally predictable

American fare (soups, club sandwiches, hamburgers, hot dogs), but well presented. As for dinner, you'd probably be better served heading to someplace more creative.

2 Ogunquit

Ogunquit is a bustling beachside town that's attracted vacationers and artists for more than a century. While notable for its abundant and elegant summer resort architecture, Ogunquit is most famous for its 3½-mile white-sand beach, which is backed by grassy dunes. The beach serves as the town's front porch, and everyone drifts over there at least once a day when the sun is shining.

Ogunquit's fame as an art colony dates to around 1890, when Charles H. Woodbury arrived and declared the place an "artist's paradise." He was followed by artists such as Walt Kuhn, Elihu Vedder, Yasuo Kuniyoshi, and Rudolph Dirks, who was best known for creating the "Katzenjammer Kids" comic strip.

In the current century, the town found quiet fame as a destination for gay travelers, at a time when being gay was not something acknowledged in polite society. Ogunquit has retained its appeal for gay travelers through the years, and visitors often find themselves at local enterprises run by gay entrepreneurs. However, few travel here to boisterously celebrate their sexuality, as is the case in Provincetown, Mass., another historic gay beach town. It's more like an understated family resort, where a good many family members just happen to be gay.

One's first impression of the town is apt to be of teeming crowds on foot and in cars. Despite its architectural gentility and the overall civility of the place, the town can feel overrun with tourists during the peak summer season, especially on weekends. The crowds are part of the allure for some Ogunquit regulars.

Those hoping to avoid the close company of others might consider other destinations along the coast, or at the least come early or late in the season. If you arrive early in the morning, you can hike a bit and stake out one of the more remote sections of the town's famous beach, which is long enough to allow most of the teeming masses to disperse.

ESSENTIALS
GETTING THERE

Ogunquit is located on Route 1 between York and Wells. It's accessible from either Exit 1 or Exit 2 of the Maine Turnpike.

VISITOR INFORMATION

The **Ogunquit Welcome Center,** P.O. Box 2289, Ogunquit, ME 03907 (☎ **207/646-5533** or 207/646-2939), is on Route 1 south of the village center. It's open daily 9am to 5pm Memorial Day through Columbus Day (until 8pm during the peak summer season) and weekdays during the off-season. On the web, head to **www.ogunquit.org**.

GETTING AROUND

The village of Ogunquit is centered around an awkward three-way, no-stop-signs intersection that seems fiendishly designed to cause massive traffic foul-ups in summer. Parking in and around the village is also tight and relatively expensive (expect to pay $6 per day or more). As a result, Ogunquit is best seen on foot or by bike.

A number of trackless trolleys (with names like Dolly and Ollie— you get the idea) run all day long from mid-May through Columbus Day between Perkins Cove and the Wells town line to the north, with detours to the sea down Beach and Ocean streets. The cost is 50¢ per boarding; the driver can't make change. It's well worth the small expense to avoid the hassles of driving and parking.

EXPLORING THE TOWN

The village center is good for an hour or two of browsing among the boutiques, or sipping a cappuccino at one of the several coffee emporia.

From the village you can walk a mile to scenic Perkins Cove along **Marginal Way,** a mile-long oceanside pathway once used for herding cattle to pasture. Earlier in this century, the land was bought by a local developer who deeded the right-of-way to the town. The pathway, which is wide and well-maintained, departs across from the Seacastles Resort on Shore Road. It passes tide pools, pocket beaches, and rocky, fissured bluffs, all of which are worth exploring. The seascape can be spectacular (especially after a storm), but Marginal Way can also be spectacularly crowded during fair-weather weekends. To elude the crowds, I recommend heading out in the very early morning.

Perkins Cove, accessible either from Marginal Way or by driving south on Shore Road and veering left at the Y intersection, is a small, well-protected harbor that seems custom-designed for a photo opportunity. As such, it attracts visitors by the busload, carload, and boatload, and is often heavily congested. A handful of galleries, restaurants, and T-shirt shops catering to the tourist trade occupy a cluster of quaint buildings between the harbor and the sea. An intriguing pedestrian drawbridge is operated by whomever happens to be handy, allowing sailboats to come and go.

Perkins Cove is also home to a handful of deep-sea fishing and tour boat operators, who offer trips of various durations. Try the **Deborah Ann** (☎ **207/361-9501**) for whale watching (two tours daily), or the **Ugly Anne** (☎ **207/646-7202**) for deep-sea fishing.

One last bit of advice: If crowds and tourist traps make you break out in a rash, steer well clear of Perkins Cove.

Not far from the cove is **The Ogunquit Museum of American Art,** 183 Shore Rd. (☎ **207/646-4909**), one of the best small art museums in the nation. Set back from the road in a grassy glen overlooking the rocky shore, the museum's spectacular view initially overwhelms the artwork as visitors walk through the door. But stick around a few minutes—the changing exhibits in this architecturally engaging modern building of cement block, slate, and glass will get your attention soon enough, since the curators have a track record of staging superb shows and attracting national attention. (Be sure to note the bold, underappreciated work of Henry Strater, the Ogunquit artist who founded the museum in 1953.) A 1,400-square-foot wing opened in 1996, adding welcome new exhibition space. The museum is open July 1 to September 30 from 10:30am to 5pm Monday through Saturday, and 2 to 5pm on Sunday. Admission is $4 for adults, $3 for seniors and students, and children under 12 are free.

For evening entertainment, head to the **Ogunquit Playhouse,** Route 1 (☎ **207/646-5511**), a 750-seat summer stock theater that has garnered a solid reputation for its careful, serious attention to stagecraft. The theater has entertained Ogunquit since 1933, attracting noted actors such as Bette Davis, Tallulah Bankhead, and Gary Merrill. Stars of recent seasons have included Gavin McLeod and Kitty Carlisle Hart.

BEACHES

Ogunquit's main beach is more than 3 miles long, and width varies greatly with the tides. There are three paid parking lots (around $2 per hour) along its length. The most popular access point is at the foot of Beach Street, which connects to Ogunquit Village. The beach ends at a sandy spit, where the Ogunquit River flows into the sea; facilities here include changing rooms, bathrooms, and a handful of informal restaurants. It's also the most crowded part of the beach.

A Kid's-Eye View of Ogunquit

I love to go to Ogunquit. Most kids do. I come up here every summer with my family and have a great time every year. There is so much to do here. I can go to the beach, I can go to Perkins Cove, I can go mini-golfing, I can go on a lobstering boat, whale watches, deep-sea fishing, and the like. I really like to go to the beach. The waves are big in Ogunquit, and they are good for surfing, body boarding, and bodysurfing. After a storm, they get really big, and it's fun just to jump around in them.

Another thing I love to do is eat lobster. I think that half the fun is cracking it. It takes a lot of work, though. First you have to crack the claws in several places, then pick the meat out. Then you wrench the tail off and pull the meat out, but you usually don't get all of it because the guts stick to the meat.

Riding on the trolleys is a lot of fun, too. They all have different names that rhyme with trolley, like Molly, Dolly, or Rolly. It's hard to memorize all the names that there are.

In my opinion, any kid who goes to Ogunquit and has a bad time there is far too difficult to please. I think it is a wonderful place to go.

—*By Billy Brink, age 10*

Less congested options are at **Footbridge Beach** (turn on Ocean Avenue off Route 1 north of the village center) and **Moody Beach** (turn on Eldridge Avenue in Wells). Restrooms are maintained at all three beaches.

A ROAD TRIP TO LAUDHOLM FARM

A short drive north of Ogunquit, just above the beach town of Wells, is **Laudholm Farm** (☎ 207/646-1555), an historic saltwater farm owned by the nonprofit Laudholm Trust since 1986. The 1,600-acre property was originally the summer home of 19th-century railroad baron George Lord, but has been used for estuarine research since taken over by the trust. The farm has 7 miles of trails through diverse ecosystems, which range from salt marsh to forest to dunes. A visitor center in the regal Victorian farmhouse will get you oriented. Tours are available, or you can explore the grounds on your own. Parking costs $5 in summer; it's free the rest of the year. There's no admission charge to the grounds or visitor center. The farm is open daily 8am to 5pm; the visitor center is open 10am to 4pm Monday to Saturday, and noon to 4pm on Sunday.

The farm is reached by turning east on Laudholm Farm Road at the blinking light just north of Harding Books. Bear left at the fork, then turn right into the farm's entrance.

WHERE TO STAY

Beachmere Inn. Beachmere Rd., Ogunquit, ME 03907. ☎ **800/336-3983** or 207/646-2021. Fax 207/646-2231. www.beachmereinn.com. 53 units. A/C TV TEL. Peak season $110–$195, mid-season $75–$140, off-season $65–95. Rates include continental breakfast. 3-night minimum stay in summer. Closed mid-Dec to Apr.

Run by the same family since 1937, the Beachmere Inn sprawls across a grassy hillside (the inn occupies about 4 acres) and nearly every room has a view northward up Ogunquit's famous beach. Guests choose from two buildings. The Beachmere Victorian dates to the 1890s and is all turrets and porches. Among the 28 guest rooms is #26, which has a wraparound private deck with a million-dollar view, and a cozy turret sitting area. Next door is the dated but fun Beachmere South, a two-story motel-like structure done up in 1960s modern style, featuring concrete slathered with a stucco finish. The rooms are spacious (some are mini-suites), interestingly angled, and all have private balconies or patios and great views. The beach is a short walk away via the Marginal Way pathway. When these rooms are filled, guests are offered rooms in the Bullfrog Cottage nearby. The five units are darker, lack views, and are less impressively furnished, but are spacious and popular with families.

Two or three couples traveling as a group (no kids under 8) should inquire about Hearthstone, a wonderful 1921 house on a side street above the inn that has three bedrooms, a modern kitchen, a barbecue house, a stunning reading room, and a manicured yard. There's no ocean view, but it's a beautiful spot and for a group it's well priced at $295 per night ($125 in the off-season).

Grand Hotel. 108 Shore Rd. (P.O. Box 1526), Ogunquit, ME 03907. ☎ **207/646-1231.** www.thegrandhotel.com. E-mail: info@thegrandhotel.com. 28 suites (including 5 penthouses). A/C TV TEL. Peak season $140–$190 double, mid-season $105–$170, off-season $65–$125. Ask about spring and fall packages. Rates include continental breakfast. 2- or 3-night minimum stay on weekends and in peak season. AE, DISC, MC, V. Closed early Nov to early Apr.

The modern Grand Hotel, built in 1990, seems a bit ill at ease in Victorian Ogunquit. Constructed in a vaguely Frank Lloyd Wright–inspired style, the hotel centers around a three-story atrium and consists of 30 two-room suites. All rooms have refrigerators and VCRs (tapes may be rented at $4.50 each). The modern, tidy guest rooms have a generic, chain-hotel character, but all have private decks on which to enjoy the woodsy Maine air. The five top-floor penthouses are airier and brighter, with cathedral ceilings and Duraflame-log fireplaces. The hotel is located on busy Shore Road, and is about a 10-minute walk to the beach. Other nice touches: Parking is underground and connected to the rooms by elevator, and there's a small indoor pool.

Marginal Way House. Wharf Lane (P.O. Box 697), Ogunquit, ME 03907. ☎ **207/646-8801** or 207/363-6566 in winter. 30 units (1 with private bathroom down the hall). A/C TV. Peak season $86–$175 double, shoulder seasons $42–$143 double. 2-night minimum stay on holiday weekends. MC, V. Closed late Oct to mid-Apr. Pets allowed off-season.

If you travel for vistas, this is your place. Even if your room lacks a sweeping ocean view (and that's unlikely), you've got the run of the lawn and the guest house porch, both of which overlook Ogunquit River to the beach and the sea beyond. This attractive compound centers around a four-story, mid-19th-century guest house, with summery, basic rooms that feature white painted furniture. Room 7 is the best, with a private porch and canopy and a killer view. The guest house is surrounded by four more-or-less modern outbuildings, which lack charm but feature motel-style rooms that are clean, comfortable, and very, very bright. The whole affair is situated on a large, grassy lot on a quiet cul-de-sac. It's hard to believe that you're smack in the middle of Ogunquit, with both the beach and the village just a few minutes' walk away. All rooms have refrigerators; for longer stays one- and two-bedroom efficiencies are available.

Nellie Littlefield House. 9 Shore Rd., Ogunquit, ME 03907. ☎ **207/646-1692.** 8 units. A/C TV TEL. Peak season $140–$195, mid-season $90–$140, off-season $75–$120. Rates include full breakfast. 2-night minimum stay on weekends; 3 nights on holidays. DISC, MC, V. Closed late Oct to Apr. Children over 12 accepted.

This 1889 home stands impressively at the edge of Ogunquit's compact commercial district; the prime location and the regal Queen Anne architecture are the main draws. The updated and carpeted rooms feature a mix of modern and antique reproduction furnishings, and several have refrigerators. Four rooms to the rear have private decks, but views are limited, mostly of the unlovely motel next door. The most spacious room? The third-floor J.H. Littlefield suite, with two TVs and a Jacuzzi. The most unique? The circular Grace Littlefield room, located in the upper turret and overlooking the street. The basement features a compact fitness room with modern equipment.

WHERE TO DINE

Just north of Ogunquit in the town of Wells is **Congdon's Dough-nuts,** 1090 Post Rd. (☎ **207/646-4219**), a local institution since 1955. The old-fashioned, irregularly shaped donuts are of the antique sort that explode wonderfully in soft busts of powdered sugar when you bite into them, leaving a tracery of white on your shirt. It's the way donuts used to be.

✪ **Arrows.** Berwick Rd. ☎ **207/361-1100.** Reservations strongly recommended. Main courses $29.95–$32.95. MC, V. July–Aug Tues–Sun 6–9:30pm; May and Columbus Day to Thanksgiving Fri–Sun 6–9:30pm; June and Sept to Columbus Day Wed–Sun 6–9:30pm. Closed after Thanksgiving to Apr. Turn uphill at the Key Bank in the village; the restaurant is 1.9 miles on the right. NEW AMERICAN.

When owner/chefs Mark Gaier and Clark Frasier opened Arrows in 1988, they quickly put Ogunquit on the national culinary map. They've done so by not only creating an elegant and intimate atmosphere in a pleasant country setting, but by serving up some of the freshest, most innovative cooking in New England. The emphasis is on local products; the salad greens are grown in gardens on the grounds, and much of the rest is grown or raised nearby. The food transcends traditional New England, and is deftly prepared with exotic twists and turns. Frasier lived and traveled for a time in Asia, and his Far Eastern experiences tend to influence the menu, which changes nightly. Among the more popular recurrent dishes is the homemade prosciutto (hams are strung up around the restaurant to cure in the off-season) served with pears, toasted pumpkin seeds, and olive oil. The bento box includes marinated lamb brochettes, orange cabbage, and "strange flavored eggplant"; the grilled beef tenderloin is spiced with a Szechuan peppercorn marinade. The wine list is top-rate. Arrows isn't for the timid of wallet, but certainly will make for a special evening.

Aunt Marie's. Rte. 1 (north of town). ☎ **207/646-9144.** Breakfast $2.85–$5.75, lunch $3.95–$7.95. AE, DISC, MC, V. Daily 7am–2pm. Closed late Oct to Apr. BREAKFAST JOINT.

Located on a cluttered stretch of Route 1 with its view of the ocean blocked by graceless condos, Aunt Marie's is still the best spot for breakfast any time of the day. Don't expect your taste buds to be titillated; do expect to leave very full. Fearless of fat and feeling hungry? Try the Bucks Port Pie, which consists of a sausage and cheese omelet served atop french fries and beans and slathered with hollandaise sauce.

Barnacle Billy's & Barnacle Billy's Etc. Perkins Cove. ☎ **207/646-5575.** www.barnbilly.com. Reservations not accepted. Lunch $3.65–$11.95, dinner $10.95–$18.95. AE, MC, V. Daily 11am–9pm. Closed Nov to mid-Apr. SEAFOOD.

This pair of side-by-side restaurants under the same ownership are a bit like brothers, one of whom became a fisherman, the other an executive. The original Barnacle Billy's, a local landmark since 1961, is a place-your-order-take-a-number-and-wait-on-the-deck-style restaurant with the usual nautical decor and pine furniture inside. Its younger and fancier sibling next door has valet parking, sit-down service, and shows somewhat better breeding.

In both places, you're paying for pretty much the same thing: an unobstructed view of Perkins Cove. At the original Barnacle Billy's, that means the food is at the high end of the price range for what you get. It's best to stick to simple fare, like chowder or boiled lobster. The prices are steeper but the value better next door, where the service seems less weary. Entrees include a variety of broiled, fried, and grilled seafood, along with a selection of poultry and meat.

✪ **Hurricane.** Oarweed Rd., Perkins Cove. ☎ **207/646-6348** or 800/ 649-6348 (Me. & N.H. only). Reservations recommended. Lunch items mostly $7–$14; dinner main courses $15–$30. AE, DC, DISC, MC, V. Mon–Sun 11:30am–3:30pm, Sun–Thurs 5:30–9:30pm, Fri–Sat 5:30–10:30pm (closed 9:30 weekends in winter). NEW AMERICAN.

Tucked away amid the T-shirt kitsch of Perkins Cove is one of southern Maine's classier dining experiences. The plain shingled exterior of the building, set along a curving, narrow lane, doesn't even hint at what you'll find inside. The narrow dining room is divided into two smallish halves, but soaring windows overlooking the Gulf of Maine lend a sense that the place is larger than it actually is. During a storm you feel as if you're on the prow of an embattled ship.

Hurricane's menu is often in flux, but it's known for consistently creative concoctions, like the appetizer of deviled Maine lobster cakes served with a tangy fresh salsa. Main courses include a delectable lobster cioppino, and a baked salmon and brie baklava with a Key-lime bearnaise. Added bonus: Hurricane makes the best martinis in town.

98 Provence. 104 Shore Rd. (P.O. Box 628), Ogunquit, ME 03907. ☎ **207/ 646-9898** or 207/646-7350. Fax 207/641-8786. www.98provence.com. Reservations recommended. Main courses $14.95–$24.95, Table d'Hote (appetizer, main course, and dessert) $21.95. Wed–Mon 5:30–9:30pm. FRENCH.

This relatively new entry to Ogunquit's dining scene has been garnering raves, and rightly so. It's a charming spot, if a bit on the precious side. Candlelight reflects off the warm wood interior and infuses the surroundings with a romantic glow; tables are covered with two layers of Provençal-style linens, lace curtains hang at the windows, and colorful china almost, but not quite, distracts one from the delicious food. Chef Pierre relies on fresh, local ingredients to create such dishes as terrine of lobster delicately flavored with mandarin orange. You might want to start with the *soupe de Pecheur* (mussels, shrimp, scallops, and fish in a fresh fennel broth) or terrine of foie gras. Unless you enjoy your food on the extremely rich and heavy side, avoid the overdone snails in puff pastry with a hazelnut and Pernod butter. The main courses could almost be sung to the tune of "Old MacDonald's Farm" as virtually every animal is represented, from medallion of Provimi veal and roasted beef tenderloin, to grilled lamb chops, roasted Mallard duck breast, and goat cheese raviolis with rabbit stew. For those who like their meat wilder, there's Maine venison with a wild-berry sauce. Poached salmon and a fish of the day round out the choices.

3 The Kennebunks

"The Kennebunks" consist of the villages of Kennebunk and Kennebunkport, both situated along the shores of small rivers. The region was first settled in the mid-1600s and flourished after the American Revolution, when ship captains, shipbuilders, and prosperous merchants constructed the imposing, solid homes. The Kennebunks are famed for their striking historic architecture and expansive beaches. Leave time to explore both.

While summer is the busy season along the coast, winter has its charms: The grand architecture is better seen through leafless trees. When the snow flies, guests find solace by retreating to a spot in front of a fire at one of the inviting inns.

ESSENTIALS
GETTING THERE

Kennebunk is located off Exit 3 of the Maine Turnpike. Kennebunkport is 3.5 miles southeast of Kennebunk on Port Road (Route 35).

VISITOR INFORMATION

The **Kennebunk-Kennebunkport Chamber of Commerce,** P.O. Box 740, Kennebunk, ME 04043 (☎ **800-982-4421** or 207/967-0857), can answer your questions year-round by phone or at their offices on Route 9 next to Meserve's Market. The **Kennebunkport Information Center** (☎ **207/967-8600**) is off Dock Square (next to Ben & Jerry's) and is open daily throughout the summer and fall.

EXPLORING KENNEBUNK

Inland Kennebunk thrives in the shadow of better-known Kennebunkport, where George and Barbara Bush summer. Downtown is a dignified, old-fashioned, small commercial center of white clapboard and brick, with stores that sell things real people really need. It's far enough from the summer swirl of the beach towns to feel more like the year-round community it is, even in August.

The **Brick Store Museum,** 117 Main St. (☎ **207/985-4802**), hosts shows of historical art and artifacts throughout the summer, switching to contemporary art in the off-season. The museum is housed in a historic former brick store (that is, a store that once sold bricks), along with three adjacent buildings. Admission is $5 adults, $2 children 8 to 17, free for children under 8. Open Tuesdays through Saturdays 10am to 4:30pm.

Tom's of Maine (☎ **207/985-3874**), a toothpaste maker, is also headquartered here. Tom and Kate Chappell sell their all-natural toothpaste and other personal-care products worldwide, but are almost as well known for their green, socially conscious business philosophy. Tom's factory outlet sells firsts and seconds of its own products (some at a terrific markdown), as well as a selection of other natural products. The shop is at Lafayette Center, a sturdy industrial building converted to shops and offices on Storer Street, near the corner of Main Street.

When en route to or from the coast, be sure to note the extraordinary historic homes that line Route 35 (called Port Road near the shore, Summer Street near downtown). This includes the much-photographed, over-the-top **Wedding Cake House,** at 104 Summer St. Local lore claims that this Federal-style house was festooned with gingerbread by a guilt-ridden ship captain, who left for the sea before his bride could enjoy a proper wedding cake. The house is privately owned, but can be enjoyed from the outside. (An adjoining gift shop is open to the public.)

EXPLORING KENNEBUNKPORT

Kennebunkport is the summer home of former President George Bush, whose family has retreated here in summer for much of this century. Given that, it has the tweedy, upper-crust feel one might expect. This historic village, whose streets were laid out during days of travel by foot and horse, is subject to monumental traffic jams around the town center, called **Dock Square.** If the municipal lot off the square ($2 per hour) is full, head north on North Street a few minutes to the free long-term lot and catch the trolley back into town. Or walk—it's a pleasant 10 or 15 minutes from the lot to Dock Square.

Dock Square has a comfortable wharf-like feel to it, with low buildings of mixed vintages and styles (you'll find mansard, gabled, and hip roofs side by each), but the flavor is mostly clapboard and shingles. The boutiques in the area are attractive, and many feature creative artworks and crafts. But Kennebunkport's real attraction is found in the surrounding blocks, where the side streets are lined with one of the nation's richest assortments of early American homes. The neighborhoods are especially ripe with examples of Federal-style homes; many have been converted to bed-and-breakfasts (see "Where to Stay," below).

A MUSEUM ON A ROLL

✪ **The Seashore Trolley Museum.** Log Cabin Rd., Kennebunkport. ☎ 207/967-2800. www.gwi.net/trolley/. $7 adults, $4.50 children 6–16, $6 seniors, $22 family. Open daily May to mid-Oct (10am–5:30pm during July and Aug; call for shoulder-season hours); weekends only through the end of Nov. Closed Dec–Apr. Head north from Kennebunkport on North St.; look for signs.

A short drive north of Kennebunkport on Log Cabin Road is one of the quirkiest and more engaging museums in the state. The Seashore Trolley Museum, a place with an excess of character, is well worth a visit. This scrapyard-masquerading-as-a-museum ("world's oldest and largest museum of its type") was founded in 1939 to preserve a disappearing way of life, and today the collection contains more than 200 trolleys from around the world, including specimens from Glasgow, Moscow, San Francisco, and Rome. (Of course, there's also a streetcar named Desire from New Orleans.)

About 40 of the cars still operate, and the admission charge includes rides on a 2-mile track. The other cars, some of which still contain turn-of-the-century advertising, are on display outdoors and in vast storage sheds. A good museum inspires awe and educates its visitors so deftly that they may not realize until they're driving away

Reaching the Beach

A word about beach parking: Finding a spot is often difficult, and all beaches require a parking permit, which may be obtained at the town offices or from your hotel. You can avoid parking hassles by renting a bike and leaving your car behind at your inn or hotel. A good spot for rentals is **Cape Able Bike Shop** (☎ **207/967-4382** or 800/220-0907), which rents three-speeds (all you'll need here) for $10 a day or $40 per week. The bike shop is on North Street north of Kennbunkport at Arundel Road. Some inns (like The Colony) will rent bikes to guests; others have free bikes for guests to use. Ask when you reserve a room.

The local trolley (bus) makes several stops in and around Kennebunkport and also serves the beaches. The fare is $6 per person per day, and includes unlimited trips.

how much they've learned about getting around in a pre-car America.

BEACHES

The coastal area around Kennebunkport is home to several of the state's finest beaches.

Southward across the river (technically this is Kennebunk, although it's much closer to Kennebunkport) are **Gooch's Beach** and **Kennebunk Beach.** Head eastward on Beach Street (from the intersection of routes 9 and 35) and you'll soon wind into a handsome colony of eclectic shingled summer homes (some improbably grand, some modest). The narrow road twists past sandy beaches and rocky headlands. The area can be frightfully congested when traveling by car in the summer; avoid the local version of gridlock by exploring on foot or bike.

Goose Rocks Beach is north of Kennebunkport off Route 9 (watch for signs), and is a good destination for those who like their crowds light, and prefer beaches to beach scenes. You'll find an enclave of beach homes set amid rustling oaks just off a fine sand beach. Just offshore is a narrow barrier reef that has historically attracted flocks of geese—which in turn lent their name to the beach.

WHERE TO STAY

Bed-and-breakfasts are legion but motels are few in Kennebunkport. The one exception is the **King's Port Inn** (☎ 800/286-5767 or 207/967-4340), located at the junction of routes 9 and 35. It's within walking distance of everything in the village, and comfortable if basic. (Ask about the new Jacuzzi suites for a bit more luxury.) The 32 rooms cost $89 to $175 in summer, and start at $69 in the winter. A breakfast buffet is included.

A unique choice for budget accommodations is the **Franciscan Guest House,** Beach Street (☎ **207/967-2011**), a former dormitory on the 200-acre grounds of the St. Anthony's Monastery. The 60 rooms are basic and clean and have private baths; guests can stroll the attractive riverside grounds or walk over to Dock Square, about 10 minutes away. Rooms are $55 to $66. No credit cards; open mid-June to mid-September.

Expensive

✪ **Captain Lord.** Pleasant and Green sts. (P.O. Box 800), Kennebunkport, ME 04046. ☎ **207/967-3141.** Fax 207/967-3172. www.captainlord.com. E-mail: captain@biddeford.com. 16 units. A/C TEL. Summer–fall $159–$349 double; winter and spring midweek from $99, weekends from $125. Rates include full breakfast. 2-night minimum stay on weekends and holidays year-round; some holidays 3-night minimum. DISC, MC, V. Children 10 and over accepted.

It's simple: This is the best building in Kennebunkport, in the best location, and furnished with the best antiques. The Captain Lord is one of the most architecturally distinguished inns anywhere, housed in a pale-yellow Federal-style home that peers down a shady lawn toward the river. The adjective "stately" is laughably inadequate.

When you enter the downstairs reception area, you'll know immediately that you've transcended the realm of "wannaB&Bs." This is the genuine article, with grandfather clocks and Chippendale highboys—and that's just the front hallway. Off the hall is a comfortable common area with piped-in classical music and a broad brick fireplace. Head up the elliptical staircase to the guest rooms, which are furnished with splendid antiques; 14 feature gas-burning fireplaces. If you're really looking to spoil yourself, book the first-floor Captain's Suite with king-sized canopy bed, audio system, TV/VCR, whirlpool, exercise equipment, and shower with a multijet hydro-massage spa. The only complaint I've heard about this place is that it's too nice, too perfect, too friendly. That evidently puts some people on edge.

✪ **The Colony Hotel.** Ocean Ave. (about a mile from Dock Square; P.O. Box 511), Kennebunkport, ME 04046. ☎ **800/552-2363** or 207/967-3331. Fax 207/967-8738. www.thecolonyhotel.com/maine. E-mail: info-me@ thecolonyhotel.com. 125 units in 4 buildings. TEL. July–Aug $185–$355 double, including breakfast and dinner; call for off-season rates. 2-night minimum stay on weekends and holidays in main hotel. Closed mid-Oct to mid-May. AE, MC, V. Pets accepted.

The Colony is one of the handful of oceanside resorts that have pre-
served the classic New England vacation experience intact. This
gleaming white Georgian Revival (built in 1914) lords over the
ocean and the mouth of the Kennebunk River. The three-story main
inn has 105 rooms, most of which have been updated. The rooms
are bright and cheery, simply furnished with summer cottage
antiques. Rooms in two of the three outbuildings carry over the
rustic elegance of the main hotel; the exception is the East House,
a 1950s-era motor hotel at the back edge of the property with 20
charmless motel-style rooms.

Guest rooms lack TVs in the main inn, and that's by design. The
Boughton family, which has owned the hotel since 1948, encour-
ages guests to leave their rooms in the evening and socialize
downstairs in the lobby, on the porch, or at the shuffleboard court,
which is lighted for nighttime play. A staff naturalist leads guided
coastal ecology tours Saturday mornings in July and August.

Dining: The massive, pine-paneled dining room seats up to 400,
and guests are assigned one table throughout their stay. Dinners
begin with a relish tray, but quickly progress to a more contemporary
era with creative regional entrees. On Fridays there's a lobster
buffet, and Sunday a jazz brunch. Lunch is served poolside, and a
pub menu is available for those seeking lighter fare. The dining room
is open to outsiders, with entrees priced $10 to $22. Live music is
offered in the Marine Room lounge on weekends.

Amenities: Bike rental, putting green, game room, library, heated
saltwater pool, small beach, conference rooms, poolside sundeck,
cocktail lounge, gift shop, free refreshments in lobby, room service,
social director, free newspaper, safe deposit boxes. Health club
3 miles away for $6 fee.

Maine Stay Inn and Cottages. 34 Maine St. (P.O. Box 500), Kennebunkport,
ME 04046. ☎ **800/950-2117** or 207/967-2117. Fax 207/967-8757.
www.mainestayinn.com. E-mail: innkeeper@mainestayinn.com. 17 units. A/C
TV. Summer-foliage season $145–$225 double, late fall–spring $85–$200
double. Rates include full breakfast. 2-night minimum stay on weekends;
3 nights on major holiday weekends. AE, MC, V.

Innkeepers Carol and Lindsay Copeland have maintained a strong
sense of history in this 1860 home as they've ushered it into the current era. Guest room decor might best be described as traditional-
without-going-overboard-to-be-authentic. The common room is
comfortably furnished; be sure to note the exceptionally fine staircase in the main hall. The cottages, arrayed along the property's

perimeter, are equally appealing. While constructed in the 1950s, they've been updated with small kitchens, and many have gas or wood fireplaces. The inn is happy to accommodate children in cottage rooms (minimum age is 6 in the main building), and there's a small playground on the edge of the lawn. Feeling stressed? Four rooms have Jacuzzis.

The Tides Inn. Goose Rocks Beach, Kennebunkport, ME 04046. ☎ **207/967-3757.** 22 units (4 share 2 bathrooms). Peak season $165–$225 double with private bathroom (from $110 off-season); $105 with shared bathroom (from $85 off-season). Closed mid-Oct to mid-May. 3-night minimum stay in peak season (mid-June through Labor Day and all weekends). AE, MC, V.

This is the best bet in the region for a quiet getaway. Located just across the street from Goose Rocks Beach, the Tides Inn is a yellow clapboard and shingle affair dating from 1899 that retains a seaside boarding house feel while providing up-to-date comfort. (Past guests have included Teddy Roosevelt and Arthur Conan Doyle.) The rooms tend toward the small side, but are comfortable and you can hear the lapping of surf from all of them. Among the brightest and most popular rooms are #11, #15, #24, and #29, some of which have bay windows and all of which have ocean views. The parlor has old wicker, TV, and chess for those rainy days. The pub is cozy and features a woodstove and dartboard.

Dining/Diversions: The Belvedere Room offers upscale traditional dining in a Victorian setting with options such as rack of lamb, shellfish ragout, filet mignon, and boiled lobster. Entrees are $16.95 to $27.95. Less elaborate meals, including salads, burritos, and burgers ($4.50 to $10.25), are served in the pub. Breakfast is also offered, but not included in room rates.

✪ **White Barn Inn.** Beach St. (¼ mile east of junction of routes 9 and 35; P.O. Box 560), Kennebunkport, ME 04046. ☎ **207/967-2321.** Fax 207/967-1100. www.whitebarninn.com. E-mail: innkeeper@whitebarninn.com. 24 units. A/C TEL. $160–$250 double, suites $350–$420. Rates include continental breakfast and afternoon tea. 2-night minimum stay on weekends; 3 nights on holiday weekends. AE, MC, V.

The White Barn Inn pampers its guests like no other place in Maine. Upon checking in, guests are shown to one of the inn's parlors and offered sherry or brandy while valets in crisp uniforms gather luggage and park the cars. A tour of the inn follows; then guests are left to their own devices. They can avail themselves of the inn's free bikes (including a small fleet of tandems) to head to the beach, or walk across the street and wander the quiet, shady pathways of

St. Anthony's Franciscan Monastery. The rooms are individually decorated in a refined country style that's elegant without being obtrusive.

The inn has an atmosphere that's distinctly European, and the emphasis is on service. I'm not aware of any other inn of this size that offers as many unexpected niceties: robes, fresh flowers in the rooms, bottled water, and turn-down service at night. Nearly half the rooms have wood-burning fireplaces.

Dining: See "Where to Dine," below.

Amenities: Concierge, room service (breakfast only), free newspaper, in-room massage, twice-daily maid service, valet parking, guest safe, afternoon tea, outdoor heated pool, bicycles, nearby ocean beach, conference rooms, sundeck.

Moderate

Captain Jefferds Inn. 5 Pearl St. (P.O. Box 691), Kennebunkport, ME 04046. ☎ **800/839-6844** or 207/967-2311. www.captainjefferdsinn.com. E-mail: capjeff@captainjefferdsinn.com. 16 units. $105–$240, including full breakfast. MC, V. 2-night minimum stay on weekends July–Oct and holidays. Dogs accepted by advance reservation ($20 additional).

This 1804 Federal home surrounded by other historic homes was fully done over in 1997, and the new innkeepers have done a superb job in coaxing out the historic feel of the place while giving each room a unique personality. Fine antiques abound throughout, and guests will need some persuading to come out of their wonderful rooms once they've settled in. Among the best are Manhattan, with a four-poster bed, fireplace, and beautiful afternoon light; and Assissi, with a restful indoor fountain and rock garden (sounds weird, but it works). The wide price range reflects the varying room sizes, but even the smallest rooms—like Katahdin—are comfortable and well beyond merely adequate. Bright common rooms on the first floor offer alluring lounging space; an elaborate breakfast is served before a fire on cool days, and on the terrace when summer weather permits.

Sundial Inn. 211 Beach Ave., Kennebunk Beach, ME 04043. ☎ **207/967-3850.** Fax 207/967-4719. E-mail: sundial@lamere.net. 34 units. Peak season $111–$195 double; mid-season $90–$185; late fall $70–$140; winter $68–$15. Rates include continental breakfast. 3-night minimum stay in peak season; 4 nights for ocean view. AE, DC, DISC, MC, V. Children over 13 accepted.

This is a good bet if you have your heart set on being in Kennebunk Beach. The inn was built in 1891 but has been extensively modernized and expanded. The rooms are all carpeted and aspire to a motel-like feel, although historic touches and Victorian accenting break the mold. The main draw is the lovely porch, where you can look out at the pebble beach across the road and idly watch bikers and in-line skaters pass by.

WHERE TO DINE

Those in mind of a quick lobster have a couple of options in the Kennebunkport area, although the prices tend to be a bit dearer than at other casual lobster spots further along up the coast. **Nunan's Lobster Hut** (☎ 207/967-4362) on Route 9 north of Kennebunkport at Cape Porpoise is a classic lobster shack, and is often crowded with diners clamoring for a basic boiled lobster dinner. No reservations and no credit cards; Nunan's is open daily for dinner, starting at 5pm in summer.

A bit farther along at 15 Pier Rd. is **Cape Porpoise Lobster Co.** (☎ 800/967-4268 or 207/967-4268), a compact, informal spot overlooking the sparkling water. There's limited outside dining, but most everything comes on Styrofoam plates, so beware of rogue winds that strive to dump your meal on your lap. The best bets are the straightforward boiled lobsters and lobster rolls. No reservations; credit cards accepted. Open for lunch and dinner daily in season.

Federal Jack's Restaurant and Brew Pub. Lower Village (south bank of Kennebunk River), Kennebunkport. ☎ **207/967-4322.** www.shipyard.com. Lunch $5.25–$12.95; main dinner courses $6.25–$21.95. AE, DISC, MC, V. Daily 11:30am–10pm. PUB FARE.

This light, airy, and modern restaurant is in a retail complex of recent vintage that sits a bit uneasily amid the scrappy boatyards lining the south bank of the Kennebunk River. From the second-floor perch (look for a seat on the spacious deck in warm weather), you can gaze across the river toward the shops of Dock Square. The menu includes hamburgers, steamed mussels, and pizza, and everything is quite well prepared. Watch for specials like the grilled crab and havarti sandwich. Don't leave without sampling the Shipyard ales, lagers, and porters brewed downstairs, which are among the best in New England. (Brewery tours available.) Consider the ale sampler, which provides tastes of various brews. Non-tipplers can enjoy a zesty homemade root beer.

Grissini. 27 Western Ave., Kennebunkport. ☎ **207/967-2211.** Reservations encouraged. Main courses $9.95–$15.95. AE, MC, V. Daily 5:30–9:30pm, (limited hours and days in the off-season; call first). TUSCAN.

Opened by the same folks who run the White Barn Inn, Grissini is a handsome trattoria that offers good value. The mood is rustic

Italian writ large: Italian advertising posters line the walls of the soaring, barnlike space, and burning logs in the oversized fireplace take the chill out of a cool evening. In fact, everything seems oversized, including the plates, flatware, and water goblets. The meals are also luxuriously sized and nicely presented, and include a wide range of pastas and pizza, served with considerable flair. (The linguini tossed with seafood is simple, filling, and tasty.) The desserts are competent, not stellar, and include old friends like creme caramel and tiramisu.

Seascapes. 77 Pier Rd., Cape Porpoise, Kennebunkport. ☎ **207/967-8500.** Reservations recommended. Entrees $19–$25. Daily 12:30–2:30pm and 5–9pm (open until 10pm Fri and Sat in peak season). Closed late Oct–Apr. UPSCALE NEW ENGLAND.

A tony restaurant with a wonderful ocean view, Seascapes is decorated in what might be termed traditional country-club bamboo, with a few creative touches like rustic handpainted table settings. It's fancy but not overly fussy, a popular spot with regular visitors to the coast (it opened in 1988) yet with food several notches above the tired and true. All the fish is fresh (excepting shrimp), and all the breads and desserts are made on premises. The menu offers traditional favorites like grilled sirloin with scallion mashed potatoes, along with more adventurous dishes like grilled swordfish with smoked corn, avocado, and black-bean salsa. The favorites among the regulars? Christina's shrimp (served with feta cheese and Kalamata olives), and the pan-roasted bass fillet.

✪ **White Barn Inn.** Beach St., Kennebunkport. ☎ **207/967-2321.** Reservations recommended. Fixed-price dinner $62. AE, MC, V. Daily 6–9pm. Closed 2 weeks in Jan. REGIONAL/NEW AMERICAN.

The setting is magical. The restaurant (attached to an equally magical inn, see "Where to Stay," above) is housed in an ancient, rustic barn with a soaring interior. (The furnace runs nearly full time in winter to keep the space comfortable.) There's a copper-topped bar off to one side, rich leather seating in the waiting area, a pianist setting the mood, and an eclectic collection of country antiques displayed in the hay loft above. On the tables are floor-length tablecloths, and the chairs feature imported Italian upholstery that recalls early Flemish tapestries. The service is impeccable, although those accustomed to more informal settings might find it overly attentive.

The excellent menu changes frequently, but depending on the season you might start with a lobster spring roll with daikon, carrots, snow peas, and cilantro, then graduate to a crab-glazed poached fillet of halibut on sweet-pea puree, or pan-seared veal and venison on bacon-roasted butternut squash. Among the more popular dishes is the Maine lobster on homemade fettuccini with cognac corral butter sauce. Anticipate a meal to remember. The White Barn won't let you down.

3

Portland

*P*ortland is Maine's largest city, and easily one of the more attractive and livable small cities on the East Coast. Actually, Portland feels more like a large town than a small city. Strike up a conversation with a resident, and you're likely to get an earful about how easy it is to live here. You can buy superb coffee, see great movies, and get delicious pad thai to go (Portland has several Thai restaurants). Yet it's still small enough to walk from one end of town to the other, and postal workers and bank clerks know your name soon after you move here. Despite its outward appearance of being an actual metropolis, Portland has a population of just 65,000, or roughly half that of Peoria, Ill.

Like most successful downtowns, Portland has been forced to reinvent itself every couple of generations as economic and cultural trends overturn the old paradigms. The city was a center for maritime trade in the 19th century, when a forest of ship masts obscured the view of the harbor. It's been a manufacturing hub, with locomotive factories, steel foundries, and fish-packing plants. It's been a mercantile center with impressive downtown department stores and a slew of wholesale dealers.

Today, as the sprawling, could-be-anywhere mall area of South Portland siphons off much of the local economic energy, the city is bent on reshaping downtown as a tourist destination and regional center for the arts. The newest attraction, a public market featuring Maine-grown fresh foods and flowers, opened in the summer of 1998; plans for a $50 million modern aquarium are underway; and talk of a new convention center periodically erupts. The verdict is still out on whether this current reincarnation will ultimately succeed. But unlike other deteriorating downtowns nationwide, today Portland has few vacant storefronts. Office space is in short supply, and there's a sort of brisk urban vitality that's eluded other cities many times its size.

1 Orientation

GETTING THERE

Portland is off the Maine Turnpike (I-95). Coming from the south, downtown is most easily reached by taking Exit 6A, then following

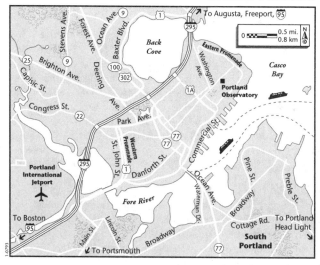

I-295 to downtown. Exit at Franklin Street and follow this eastward until you arrive at the waterfront at the Casco Bay Lines terminal. Turn right on Commercial Street and you'll be at the lower edge of the Old Port. Continue on a few blocks to the visitor's center (see below).

Concord Trailways (☎ **800/639-3317** or 207/828-1151) and **Vermont Transit** (☎ **800/537-3330** or 207/772-6587) offer bus service to Portland from Boston and Bangor. The Vermont Transit bus terminal is located at 950 Congress St. Concord Trailways, which is a few dollars more expensive, usually offers movies and headsets on its trips. The Concord terminal is inconveniently located on Sewall Street (a 35-minute walk from downtown), but has plenty of free parking and is served by local buses from nearby Congress Street ($1 fare).

The **Portland International Jetport** is served by regularly scheduled flights on several airlines, including **Delta/Business Express** (☎ 800/638-7333), **Continental** (☎ 800/525-0280), **US Airways** (☎ 800/428-4322), **United** (☎ 800/241-6522), **Pine State** (☎ 207/353-6334), and **Northeast Airlines** (☎ 800/983-3247). The small and easily navigated airport is located just across the Fore River from downtown, although ongoing construction and tight parking can be frustrating at times. Metro buses ($1) connect the airport to downtown; cab fare runs about $12.

VISITOR INFORMATION

The **Convention and Visitor's Bureau of Greater Portland,** 305 Commercial St., Portland, ME 04101 (☎ **207/772-5800** or 207/772-4994), stocks a large supply of brochures and is happy to dispense information about local attractions, lodging, and dining. The center is open in summer weekdays 8am to 6pm and weekends 10am to 5pm; hours are shorter during the off-season. Ask for the free "Greater Portland Visitor Guide" with map.

Casco Bay Weekly is a free alternative paper distributed Thursdays at many downtown stores and restaurants. It's a good bet for perusing listings of performers at area clubs and other upcoming events.

CITY LAYOUT

The city of Portland is divided into two areas: on-peninsula and off-peninsula. (There are also the islands, but more on that below.) Most travelers are destined for the compact peninsula, which is home to the downtown and where most of the city's cultural life and much of its commercial action takes place.

Viewed from the water, Portland's peninsula is shaped like a sway-backed horse, with the Old Port in the belly near the waterfront, and the peninsula's two main residential neighborhoods (Munjoy Hill and the West End) on the gentle rises overlooking downtown. These two neighborhoods are connected by Congress Street, Portland's main artery of commerce. The western stretch of Congress Street (roughly between Monument Square and State Street) is home to Portland's emerging Arts District, where you can find a handsome art museum, several theaters, the campus of the Maine College of Art (located in an old department store), an L.L. Bean outlet, and a growing number of restaurants and boutiques.

GETTING AROUND
PARKING

Parking is notoriously tight in the Old Port area, and the city's parking enforcement notoriously efficient. Several parking garages are convenient to the Old Port, with parking fees less than $1 per hour.

SPECIAL EVENTS

New Year's/Portland (☎ 207/772-9012) rings in January with a smorgasbord of events and entertainment throughout downtown Portland. Events for families are scheduled in the afternoon; entertainment more oriented for adults—including loads of live music—kicks off later in the evening at numerous locales, including auditoriums, shops, and churches. The emphasis is on enjoying New Year's without alcohol. One admission fee buys entrance to all events.

The **Old Port Festival** (☎ 207/772-6828) takes place in early June when tens of thousands of revelers descend upon the historic Old Port section to herald the arrival of summer. Several blocks of the Old Port are blocked to traffic, and the throngs order food and buy goods from street vendors. Several stages provide entertainment, ranging from kids' sing-alongs to raucous blues. Admission is free.

2 Exploring the City

Any visit to Portland should start with a stroll around the historic **Old Port.** Bounded by Commercial, Congress, Union, and Pearl streets, this several-square-block area near the waterfront contains the city's best commercial architecture, a plethora of fine restaurants, a mess of boutiques, and one of the thickest concentrations of bars you'll find anywhere. (The Old Port tends to transform as night lengthens, with the crowds growing younger and rowdier.) The narrow streets and intricate brick facades reflect the mid-Victorian era during which most of the area was rebuilt following a devastating fire in 1866. Leafy, quaint **Exchange Street** is the heart of the Old Port, with other attractive streets running off and around it.

Just outside the Old Port, don't miss the **First Parish Church** at 425 Congress St., an uncommonly beautiful granite meeting house with an impressively austere interior that's changed little since it first opened its doors in 1826. A few doors down the block is Portland's **City Hall,** at the head of Exchange Street. Modeled after New York's City Hall, Portland's seat of government was built of granite in 1909. It houses the Merrill Auditorium, the city's premier venue for concerts and Broadway roadshows. In a similarly regal vein is the **U.S. Custom House** at 312 Fore St. During business hours feel free to wander inside to view the elegant woodwork and marble floors dating back to 1868.

If you're hungry after a morning of shopping and strolling check out the newly-opened **Portland Public Market** at 25 Preble St., one-half block west of Monument Square. The market features 30 vendors selling fresh foods and flowers, much of which is Maine grown. The architecturally distinctive building houses fishmongers, butchers, fresh fruit dealers, and a seafood cafe. It's a much-recommended spot for a quick snack, or just to sit and watch Portland pass by. The market's open year-round Monday to

Saturday 9am to 6pm and Sunday 10am to 5pm. Call ☎ **207/ 228-2000** for more information.

Flanking the Old Port on the two low hills are the downtown's main residential areas. Drive eastward on Congress Street up and over Munjoy Hill and you'll come to the **Eastern Promenade,** a 68-acre hillside park with broad, grassy slopes extending down to the water and superb views of Casco Bay and its islands. Along the base of the park you'll find the Eastern Prom Pathway, which wraps along the waterfront between the Casco Bay Lines ferry terminal near the Old Port and the East End Beach. The pathway is suitable for walking or biking, and offers wonderful views across the harbor and its constant boat traffic out toward the islands. The easiest place to park is at the bottom of the hill near the beach and boat ramp. Atop Munjoy Hill, above the Eastern Promenade, is the **Portland Observatory,** a quirky shingled tower dating from 1807 and once used to signal which ships were coming into port. It was closed indefinitely for extensive repairs and restorations in 1995; call for an update (☎ **207/774-5561**).

On the other end of the peninsula is the **Western Promenade.** (Follow Spring Street westward to Vaughan; turn right and then take your first left on Bowdoin Street.) This narrow strip of lawn atop a forested bluff has views across the Fore River, which is lined with less-than-scenic light industry, to the White Mountains in the distance. It's a great spot to watch the sun set. Around the Western Prom are some of the grandest and most imposing houses in the city. A walk through the neighborhood reveals a wide array of architectural styles, from Italianate to Shingle to Stick.

THE TOP ATTRACTIONS: FROM LIGHTHOUSES TO LONGFELLOW

Children's Museum of Maine. 142 Free St. (next to the Portland Museum of Art). ☎ **207/828-1234.** Admission $5; children under 1 free. MC, V. Summer Mon–Sat 10am–5pm, Sun noon–5pm; closed Mon and Tues fall through spring.

The centerpiece exhibit of the Children's Museum is the camera obscura, a room-sized "camera" located on the top floor of this stout, columned downtown building next to the art museum. Children gather around a white table in a dark room, where they see magically projected images that include cars driving on city streets and boats plying the harbor. The camera obscura never fails to enthrall, and it provides a memorable lesson in the workings of a lens— whether in a camera or an eye.

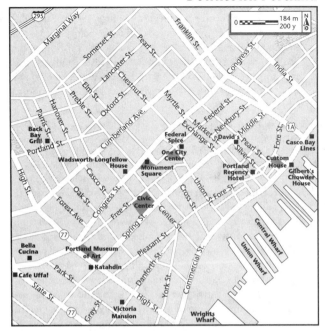

But there's plenty more to do here, from running a supermarket checkout counter to sliding down the firehouse pole or piloting a mock space shuttle from a high cockpit. Leave time for lunch at the cafe, where you can order up a peanut butter and jelly sandwich, a tall glass of milk, and an oatmeal cookie.

✪ **Portland Head Light and Museum.** Fort Williams Park, 1000 Shore Rd., Cape Elizabeth. ☎ **207/799-2661.** www.portlandheadlight.com. Grounds free; museum admission $2 adults, $1 children 6–18. Park grounds open daily year-round sunrise to sunset (until 8:30pm in summer); museum open daily June–Oct 10am–4pm; open weekends only in spring and late fall. From Portland, follow State St. across the Fore River and continue straight on Broadway. At second light, turn right on Cottage Rd., which soon becomes Shore Rd.; follow until you arrive at the park, on your left.

Just a 10-minute drive from downtown Portland, this 1794 lighthouse is one of the most picturesque in the nation. (You'll probably recognize it from its cameo role in numerous advertisements and calendars.) The light marks the entrance to Portland Harbor, and was occupied continuously from its construction in 1791 until 1989, when it was automated and the graceful keeper's house converted to a small museum focusing on the history of navigation. The lighthouse itself is still active and thus closed to the public, but visitors can stop by the museum, browse for lighthouse-themed gifts at the gift shop, wander the park grounds, and watch the sailboats and cargo ships come and go. The park has a pebble beach, grassy lawns with ocean vistas, and picnic areas well-suited for informal barbecues.

Portland Museum of Art. 7 Congress Sq. (corner of Congress and High sts.). ☎ **207/775-6148.** www.portlandmuseum.org. E-mail: pma@maine.rr.com. Admission $6 adults, $5 students and seniors, $1 children 6–12; free Fri 5–9pm. July to mid-Oct Sat–Wed 10am–5pm and Thurs–Fri 10am–9pm; Mid-Oct to June Tues–Wed and Sat–Sun 10am–5pm, Thurs–Fri 10am–9pm.

This bold, modern museum was designed by I. M. Pei Associates in 1983, and displays selections from its own fine collections along with a parade of touring exhibits. The museum is particularly rich in American artists who had a connection to Maine, including Winslow Homer, Andrew Wyeth, and Edward Hopper, and has fine displays of early American furniture and crafts. The museum shares the Joan Whitney Payson Collection with Colby College (the college gets it one semester every other year). The collection features wonderful European works by Renoir, Degas, and Picasso. Guided tours are offered daily at 2pm, and at 6pm on Thursday. A cafe serves light fare.

Victoria Mansion. 109 Danforth St. ☎ **207/772-4841.** $5 adults, $2 children under 18. May–Oct Tues–Sat 10am–4pm, Sun 1–5pm; tours offered at quarter past and quarter of each hour. Closed Nov–Apr, except for holiday tours from the end of Nov to mid-Dec. From the Old Port, head west on Fore St. and veer right on Danforth St. at light near Stonecoast Brewing; proceed 3 blocks to the mansion, which is at the corner of Park St.

Widely regarded as one of the most elaborate Victorian brownstone homes in existence, this mansion (also known as the Morse-Libby House) is a remarkable display of high Victorian style. Built between 1859 and 1863 for a Maine businessman who made a fortune in the New Orleans hotel trade, the towering, slightly foreboding home is a prime example of the Italianate style once in vogue. Inside, it appears that not a square inch of wall space was left unmolested by craftsmen or artisans (11 painters were hired to create the murals). The decor is ponderous and somber, but it offers an engaging look at a bygone era. A gift shop sells Victorian-themed gifts and books.

Wadsworth Longfellow House and Center for Maine History. 489 Congress St. ☎ **207/879-0427.** www.mainehistory.com. Gallery and Longfellow house tour $5 adults, $1 children under 12. Gallery only $2 adults, $1 children. Longfellow House and gallery open June–Oct daily 10am–4pm; gallery only Oct–June Wed–Sat noon–4pm.

The Maine Historical Society's "history campus" includes three widely varied buildings in the middle of downtown Portland. The austere brick Wadsworth-Longfellow House dates to 1785 and was built by Gen. Peleg Wadsworth, father of noted poet Henry Wadsworth Longfellow. It's furnished in an authentic early-19th-century style, with many samples of Longfellow family furniture on display. Adjacent to the home is the Maine History Gallery, located in a garish post-modern building. Changing exhibits explore the rich texture of Maine history.

ON THE WATER

The 3.5-mile **Back Cove Pathway** loops around Portland's Back Cove, offering attractive views of the city skyline across the water, glimpses of Casco Bay, and a bit of exercise. The pathway is the city's most popular recreational facility; after work in summers, Portlanders flock here to walk, bike, jog, and windsurf (there's enough water $2^{1}/_{2}$ hours before and after high tide). Part of the pathway shares a noisy bridge with I-295 and it can be a bit fulsome at a dead low tide, but when tides and weather cooperate it's hard to find a more lovely spot than the pathway along Baxter Boulevard.

The main parking lot is located across from Shop 'n Save Plaza at the water's edge. Take Exit 6 (Forest Avenue north) off I-295; turn right at the first light on Baxter Boulevard; at the next light turn right again and park in the lot ahead on the left.

Casco Bay Lines. Commercial and Franklin sts. ☎ **207/774-7871.** Fares vary depending on the run, but are generally $5.25–$15 round trip. Frequent departures 6am–midnight.

Six of the Casco Bay islands have year-round populations and are served by scheduled ferries from downtown Portland. (Most of these are part of the city of Portland; the exception is Long Island, which broke away in a secession bid.) The ferries offer an inexpensive way to view the bustling harbor and get a taste of Maine's islands. Trips range from a 20-minute (one-way) excursion to Peaks Island (the closest thing to an island suburb with 1,200 year-round residents), to the $5^{1}/_{2}$-hour cruise to Bailey Island (connected by bridge to the mainland south of Brunswick) and back. All of the islands are well-suited for walking; Peaks Island has a rocky back shore that's easily accessible via the island's paved perimeter road (bring a picnic lunch). Cliff Island is the most remote of the bunch, and has a sedate turn-of-the-century island retreat character.

Eagle Island. Eagle Island Tours, Long Wharf (Commercial St.). ☎ **207/774-6498.** $15 adults, $9 children under 9 (plus state park fee of $1.50 adults, 50¢ children). One departure daily at 10am.

Eagle Island was the summer home of famed Arctic explorer and Portland native Robert E. Peary, who claimed in 1909 to be the first person to reach the North Pole. (His accomplishments have been the subject of exhaustive debates among Arctic scholars, some of whom insist he inflated his claims.) In 1904 Peary built a simple home on a remote, 17-acre island at the edge of Casco Bay; in 1912 he added flourishes in the form of two low stone towers. After his death in 1920 his family kept up the home, then later donated it to the state, which has since managed it as a state park. The home is open to the public, maintained much the way it was when Peary lived here. Island footpaths through the scant forest allow exploration to the open, seagull-clotted cliffs at the southern tip. Eagle Tours offers one trip daily from Portland. The 4-hour excursion includes a $1^1/2$-hour stopover on the island.

SHOPPING

Aficionados of antique and secondhand furniture stores love Portland. Good browsing may be had on Congress Street. Check out the stretches between State and High streets in the arts district, and from India Street to Washington Avenue on Munjoy Hill. About a dozen shops of varying quality (mostly low-end) can be found in these two areas.

For new items, the Old Port, with its dozens of boutiques and storefronts, is well worth browsing. It's especially strong in contemporary one-of-a-kind clothing that's a world apart from generic stuff you'll find at a mall. Artisan and crafts shops are also well represented.

Abacus American Crafts. 44 Exchange St. ☎ **207/772-4880.**

A wide range of bold, inventive crafts of all variety—from furniture to jewelry—is displayed on two floors of this centrally located shop. Even if you're not in a buying frame of mind, this is a great place for browsing.

Take Me Out to the Ball Game

Whether you're a baseball fanatic, or simply like spending warm summer nights sitting outside eating hot dogs, you'll probably enjoy an evening watching the Portland Sea Dogs. The Sea Dogs are the Double-A team affiliated with the 1997 World Champion Florida Marlins. The team plays from April to Labor Day at Hadlock Field, a small stadium near downtown that retains an old-time feel despite aluminum benches and other updating. Games are geared toward families, with lots of entertainment between innings and a selection of food that's a couple of notches above basic hot dogs and hamburgers. (Try the tasty french fries and grilled sausages.)

Getting tickets can sometimes be a problem—the more popular weekend and night games often sell out well in advance. Pick a date and call ☎ **800/936-3647** or 207/874-9300 for reservations. If a game's sold out, don't despair. General-admission tickets are often for sale out in front of the main gate by folks who bought too ambitiously back in the spring; they're almost always sold at face value ($4 to $6). If you buy general-admission seats, plan to arrive at least a half-hour early so you don't end up way down the left field line.

Amaryllis. 41 Exchange St. ☎ **207/772-4439.**

Portland's original funky clothing store, Amaryllis offers unique clothing for women that's as comfortable as it is casually elegant. The colors are rich, the patterns unique, and some items are designed by local artisans.

Fibula. 50 Exchange St. ☎ **207/761-4432.**

Original, handcrafted jewelry by Maine's top designers is beautifully displayed at this tasteful shop in the heart of the Old Port. There's also a collection of loose gemstones on display.

Green Design Furniture. 267 Commercial St. ☎ **207/775-4234.**

This inventive shop sells a line of beautiful, Mission-inspired furniture that disassembles for easy storage and travel. These beautiful works are creatively crafted of cherry.

L.L. Bean Factory Store. 542 Congress St. ☎ **207/772-5100.**

Sporting goods retailer L.L. Bean opened its first downtown factory outlet here in 1996. Look for last year's fashions, returns, and slightly damaged goods, along with a small selection of first-run, full-price items.

Maine Potters Market. 376 Fore St. ☎ **207/774-1633.**

Maine's largest pottery collective has been in operation for nearly 2 decades. You can select from a variety of styles; shipping is easily arranged.

The Whip and Spoon. 161 Commercial St. ☎ **800/937-9447** or 207/774-4020.

Look for great kitchen gadgets, Maine-made food products, and the city's best selection of wine (including a Maine blueberry variety).

3 Where to Stay

Two sizeable downtown hotels stand out against the skyline. The **Holiday Inn by the Bay,** 88 Spring St. (☎ 207/775-2311), offers great views of the harbor from about half the rooms, along with the usual chain-hotel creature comforts. Peak-season rates are approximately $140 double. The **Radisson Eastland,** 157 High St. (☎ 207/775-5411), is Portland's most venerable old hotel, and features two restaurants, a dated rooftop lounge, and a spacious lobby imbued with an old-world elegance. The rooms, however, are overdue for a makeover. Summer rates start at $99 double and climb to $150.

Budget travelers may choose to seek accommodations near the Maine Mall in South Portland and off the Maine Turnpike near Westbrook—two areas that are patently charmless, but offer reasonable access to the attractions of downtown (about 10 minutes away), and are close to the airport. Try **Days Inn** (☎ 207/772-3450) or **Coastline Inn** (☎ 207/772-3838) near the mall, or the **Super 8 Motel** (☎ 207/854-1881) or **Susse Chalet** (☎ 207/774-6101) off turnpike Exit 8.

The Danforth. 163 Danforth St., Portland, ME 04102. ☎ **800/991-6557** or 207/879-8755. Fax 207/879-8754. www.visionwork.com/danforth. E-mail: danforth@maine.rr.com. 10 units. A/C TV TEL. $115–$225 double. Rates include continental breakfast. Discounts available in the off-season. AE, MC, V. Pets accepted.

Located in an exceptionally handsome brick home constructed in 1821, The Danforth has been something of a work in progress since it first opened in 1994 with just two guest rooms. But it's fast closing in on its ultimate goal of becoming one of Portland's most elegant small inns. (The Pomegranate is the other.) The guest rooms are handsomely decorated, many in rich and vibrant tones. The inn's extra touches are exceptional, from working fireplaces in most guest rooms to the richly paneled basement billiards room and the direct-line phones in the rooms. Especially appealing is Room 1 with a sitting room and private second-floor deck, and Room 2 with high ceilings and superb morning light; rooms 5 and 6 are smaller, housed in the old servants' wing. The inn is located at the edge of the Spring Street Historic District, and is within 10 minutes' walk of downtown attractions.

Amenities: Newspaper delivery, in-room massage, billiards room, bicycle rental, access to in-town health club.

✪ **Pomegranate Inn.** 49 Neal St., Portland, ME 04102. ☎ **800/356-0408** or 207/772-1006. Fax 207/773-4426. 8 units. A/C TV TEL. Summer–fall $135–$175 double, winter–spring $95–$135 double. Rates include full breakfast. 2-night minimum stay on summer weekends; 4 nights at Christmas and Thanksgiving. AE, DISC, MC, V. On-street parking. From the Old Port, take Middle St. (which turns into Spring St.) to Neal St. in the West End (about 1 mile); turn right and proceed to inn. Children 16 and over accepted.

This is Portland's most stunning B&B, and one of the best in northern New England. Housed in a handsome, dove-gray 1884 Italianate home in the architecturally distinctive Western Prom neighborhood, the interiors are wondrously decorated with whimsy and elegance—a combination that can be fatally cloying if attempted by someone without impeccably good taste. Look for the bold and exuberant wall paintings by a local artist, and the wonderfully eclectic antique furniture collected and tastefully arranged by owner Isabel Smiles. If you have the chance, peek into some of the unoccupied rooms—they're all different, with painted floors and boisterous faux-marble woodwork. Most rooms have gas fireplaces; the best of the lot is in the carriage house, which has its own private terrace, kitchenette, and fireplace.

Portland Regency Hotel. 20 Milk St., Portland, ME 04101. ☎ **800/727-3436** or 207/774-4200. Fax 207/775-2150. www.theregency.com. 95 units. A/C MINIBAR TV TEL. Summer $199–$249 double; off-season $159–$219 double. AE, CB, DC, DISC, MC, V.

The Regency boasts the city's premier hotel location—a cobblestone courtyard in the middle of the trendy Old Port—and it's one of the more architecturally striking and well-managed hotels in the state. Housed in a historic brick armory, the hotel offers a number of moderately sized, modern guest rooms nicely appointed and furnished with all the expected upscale amenities like hair dryers, irons, and ironing boards. The one complaint I've heard is about the noise: The interior guest room walls are a bit thin, so noise travels from room to room, and on weekends the revelry in the Old Port streets can penetrate even the dense brick exterior walls.

Dining: The hotel is home to The Armory Restaurant, which serves breakfast, lunch, and dinner. Dinners include traditional favorites like steak au poivre and surf and turf, with entree prices ranging from $16 to $25.

Amenities: Limited room service, valet parking, dry cleaning (Monday to Friday), baby-sitting (with prior notice), valet parking ($5), courtesy car to airport, safety deposit boxes, Jacuzzi, sauna, fitness club, conference rooms, aerobics classes.

West End Inn. 146 Pine St., Portland, ME 04102. ☎ **800/338-1377** or 207/772-1377. 6 units (1 with detached bathroom). A/C TV. $89–$169 double. Rates include full breakfast. AE, MC, V. Parking on street.

This brick, mansard-roofed 1871 duplex sits in one of Portland's more distinguished residential neighborhoods. And the innkeepers have done a fine job making this urban town house into a welcoming retreat. The downstairs parlor features gold-leaf detailing on the ceiling, leather furniture, and Asian antiques. The guest rooms on two upstairs floors have canopy beds and are nicely decorated with bold wallpaper and antiques. The inn is well situated for walks in the West End and the Western Prom.

4 Where to Dine

More than anything else, Portland is a city of creative cheap eats. In addition to the places listed under the "Inexpensive" category below, you'll find great fare at **Granny's Burritos,** 420 Fore St. (☎ **207/761-0751**), filling homemade noodles at the cafeteria-style **Fresh Market Pasta,** 43 Exchange St. (☎ **207/773-7146**), and classic breakfasts served all day to hungry fishermen and well-scrubbed college kids alike at **Becky's Diner,** 390 Commercial St. (☎ **207/773-7070**).

Barbecue lovers migrate to the greater India Street area (between the Old Port and Munjoy Hill), where they find three slow-cook joints, all of which serve quite good meats and more: **Norm's Bar BQ,** 43 Middle St. (☎ **207/774-6711**), **BBQ Bob's,** 147 Cumberland Ave. (☎ **207/871-8819**) and—my favorite—**Uncle Billy's Bar-B-Que,** located at 69 Newbury St. (☎ **207/871-5631**).

EXPENSIVE

Portland is also noted for its profusion of excellent restaurants featuring grilled foods. The city's chefs know how to do it right, with most emphasizing fresh local seafood. All four restaurants in the "expensive" category offer outstanding wood-grilled fare, along with other selections for those in the mood for something else.

✪ **Back Bay Grill.** 65 Portland St. ☎ **207/772-8833.** Reservations encouraged. Main courses $17.50–$24.95. AE, DC, DISC, MC, V. Mon–Thurs 5:30–9:30pm, Fri and Sat 5:30–10:30pm. NEW AMERICAN.

Back Bay Grill offers an upscale, contemporary ambience in a rather downscale neighborhood near the main post office. There's light jazz in the background, and bold artwork that goes several steps beyond merely atmospheric. The kitchen has been serving up some of Maine's most innovative meals for more than a decade, and has developed a loyal following. Diners might launch an evening with house-cured gravlax on tuna carpaccio, or Maine crab cakes with a curry oil. Main dishes include creative pastas (for example, herbed goat cheese ravioli), along with more ambitious meals like sautéed halibut and a chorizo-saffron sauce, or herbed rack of lamb with figs and basil. If you're looking to sate your craving for lobster and expense is no object, there's a lobster tasting menu available on limited nights (call first) that includes four creative lobster dishes (such as lobster on asparagus risotto with a carrot-ginger jus) at a cost of $62 per person.

David's. 164 Middle St. ☎ **207/773-4340.** Reservations recommended on weekends. Main courses $14–$20. AE, DISC, MC, V. Daily 11am–4pm and 5–9:30pm (until 10:30pm Fri–Sat). GLOBAL/FUSION.

David's is appointed in a sort of contemporary hunt-club motif on two levels, with limited outside dining in summer on a sort of elevated sidewalk cafe. Downstairs is darker and more formal; upstairs is sprightlier and has a pubbier feel. (There's also a raw bar on the second level.) The menu is creative, and the fare consistently among the best-prepared in Portland. Entrees might include a shiitake ravioli topped with an applewood-grilled chicken breast, or haddock stuffed with a salmon and scallop mousse and topped with a lemon-dill cream sauce.

✪ **Fore Street.** 288 Fore St. ☎ **207/775-2717.** Reservations recommended. Main courses $11.95–$21.95. AE, MC, V. Sun–Thurs 5:30–10pm, Fri–Sat until 10:30pm. CONTEMPORARY GRILL.

During the long summer evenings, light floods in through the huge sets of windows at this loftlike space; later at night, it takes on a more intimate glow with soft lighting against the brick walls and buttery wooden floors. But the place always bustles—dead center is the sprawling open kitchen filled with a team of chefs busy with stoking the wood-fired brick oven and grilling fish. And though the menu is constantly in play, grilled foods remain the specialty. You might start with the grilled calamari served with tomatoes and wild mushrooms or wood-fired pesto pizzetta, then move on to the baked halibut or turnspit-roasted Maine rabbit. There's always a selection of wonderfully grilled meats, including steak, chicken, duckling, or fresh fish steaks. Meals are consistently excellent here, and disappointments are rare.

MODERATE

Bella Cucina. 653 Congress St. ☎ **207/828-4033.** Reservations recommended. Main courses $9–$17. AE, CB, DISC, MC, V. Daily 5pm–10pm. RUSTIC ITALIAN.

Situated in one of Portland's less elegant commercial neighborhoods, Bella Cucina sets an inviting mood with rich colors, soft lighting, and pinpoint spotlights over the tables that carve out alluring islands of light. The eclectic menu changes frequently but dances deftly between rustic Italian and regional, with options like a robust ciopinno with haddock and lobster, and a melange of veal, pork, and chicken served with a prosciutto and mushroom ragout. Three or four vegan entrees are always on hand. About half the seats are kept open for walk-ins, so take a chance and stop by even if you don't have reservations. There's a good selection of wines, and free parking evenings behind Joe's Smoke Shop.

Café Uffa! 190 State St. ☎ **207/775-3380.** Reservations not accepted. Breakfast $3–$6.25, dinner $7.50–$14.95. MC, V. Wed–Fri 7–11am and 5:30–10pm, Sat 8–12am and 5:30–10pm, Sun 9am–2pm. MULTIETHNIC/SEAFOOD.

If you're looking to stretch your dollar while enjoying a fine meal, Uffa consistently manages to impress with its well-prepared fare. The specialty is fish grilled to perfect tenderness over a wood-stoked fire (the salmon is especially good), with wonderful dishes including cracked-pepper-crusted swordfish with shiitake mushrooms. There's no meat on the menu, but you will find pastas and other non-seafood options. With its mismatched chairs, last-week's-flea-market decor, and high ceilings, Uffa attracts a young crowd with its aggressively informal styling. Sunday brunches are also superb, but there's often a line to get in.

Cotton Street Cantina. 10 Cotton St. ☎ **207/775-3222.** Reservations not accepted. Lunch items $6–$8, dinner main courses $9–$16. Mon–Thurs 11:30am–2:30pm and 5–9:30pm, Fri 11:30am–2:30pm and 5–10:30pm, Sat 5–10:30pm, Sun 5–9:30pm. LATINO/CARIBBEAN.

Located on a side street at the south edge of the glittery Old Port (it's just off Fore Street), this festive and funky spot opened in 1997 in an old taxi garage. There's a bubbling indoor fountain, two levels of seating, and loads of atmosphere thanks to a liberal use of galvanized steel. The food that emerges from the open first-floor kitchen draws on the whole of Latin America and the Caribbean for inspiration, and the kitchen is fond of smoked peppers, cilantro, and citrus. Alas, consistency is not the strong suit here: The food can be very good; it can also disappoint on an off-night. Likewise with service, which can be painfully slow at times. If you have an unlucky night, take solace in the bar, which stocks an impressive assortment of rums and tequilas.

Katahdin. 106 High St. ☎ **207/774-1740.** Reservations not accepted. Main courses $9.95–$15.95. DISC, MC, V. Tues–Thurs 5–9:30pm, Fri–Sat until 10:30pm. CREATIVE NEW ENGLAND.

Katahdin is a lively, often noisy spot that prides itself on its eclectic cuisine. Artists on slim budgets dine on the nightly blue plate special, which typically features something basic like meat loaf or pan-fried catfish. Wealthy business folks one table over dine on more delicate fare, like the restaurant's noted crab cakes. Other recommended specialties include pan-seared oysters for an appetizer, and grilled sea scallops with a spicy lime vinaigrette or London broil marinated in a ginger, scallion, and garlic mix. Sometimes the kitchen nods, but for the most part it's good food at very reasonable prices. Reservations aren't accepted, but there's a bar in the dining room where you can enjoy Portland's best martini while waiting for a table.

INEXPENSIVE

Federal Spice. 225 Federal St. ☎ **207/774-6404.** Reservations not accepted. Main courses $2.50–$6. No credit cards. Mon–Sat 11am–9pm. WRAPS/GLOBAL.

This is Portland's best bet for a quick, cheap, and filling nosh. Located beneath a parking garage (it's just off Temple Street), Federal Spice is a breezy, informal spot with limited dining inside and a few tables outside. You'll find quesadillas, salads, and soft tacos here, along with the well-regarded wraps, which are stuffed full of inventive, taste-bud-awakening stuffings (the curried coconut chicken is among the best). The yam fries are excellent, and go nicely with just about everything on the menu.

Gilbert's Chowder House. 92 Commercial St. ☎ **207/871-5636.** Reservations not accepted. Chowders $2.25–$9.50, sandwiches $1.75–$9.95, main courses $6–$18.95. Mon–Thurs 11am–10pm, Fri–Sat 11am–11pm, Sun noon–9pm (closed earlier in winter). CHOWDER/SEAFOOD.

Gilbert's is an unprepossessing waterfront spot that's nautical without being too cute. Angle for the outdoor tables overlooking a parking lot and the working waterfront; sometimes it smells pleasantly nautical, sometimes unpleasantly so. The chowders are flavorful if a bit pasty. If you're looking to bulk up, consider getting your chowder in a bread bowl. Other meals include fried clams and haddock sandwiches, and a mess of other seafood available broiled or fried. There's also a basic lobster dinner, which includes corn on the cob and a cup of clam chowder. Limited microbrews are on tap; the homemade cheesecake makes a fitting dessert.

Seng's 2. 921 Congress St. ☎ **207/879-2577.** No reservations. Main courses $5–$9.95. No credit cards. Open daily 11am–10pm. THAI.

Portland's most authentic Thai food is found in a small, rather dingy spot in a cheerless part of town near the bus station. Don't come here expecting atmosphere—unless you're a connoisseur of fluorescent lights. Come here expecting a big pile of good food at great prices. The spicy pad thai has developed a cult following among knowledgeable Portlanders. The curries are tangy, as are the hot basil leaves with chicken, beef, or tofu. Everything is available to go. It's close to the Hadlock Field, so consider an early dinner followed by a night of minor-league baseball.

✪ **Silly's.** 40 Washington Ave. ☎ **207/772-0360.** Lunch and dinner $1.25–$6.50; pizza $5.95–$16.90. MC, V. Mon–Sat 10am–10pm; closed Sun. ECLECTIC/TAKE-OUT.

Silly's is the favored cheap-eats joint among even jaded Portlanders. Situated on an aggressively charmless urban street, the interior is informal, bright, and spunky, with a fine selection of mismatched 1950s-era dinettes and funky-retro accessories. The menu is creative and the selections tasty. A lot of the meals are served in hubcap-sized pita bread (the shish kebab roll-up is especially delicious), the pizza is superb, and there's beer on tap. Don't overlook the great mound of french fries, or the huge old-fashioned milk shakes and malts.

5   Portland After Dark

Portland is lively in the evenings, especially on summer weekends when the testosterone level in the Old Port seems to rocket into the stratosphere with young men and women prowling the dozens of bars and spilling out onto the streets.

BARS, PUBS & CLUBS

Among the bars favored by locals are **Three-Dollar Dewey's** at the corner of Commercial and Union streets (try the great fries), **Gritty McDuff's Brew Pub** on Fore Street near the foot of Exchange Street, and **Brian Ború,** slightly out of the Old Port on Center Street. All three bars are casual and pubby, with guests sharing long tables with new companions.

Beyond the active Old Port bar scene, a number of clubs offer a mix of live and recorded entertainment throughout the year. There's been considerable upheaval and turmoil among clubs and club owners in recent years; check the free alternative paper, *Casco Bay Weekly,* for current venues, performers, and show times.

Among the more reliable spots for live music is **Stone Coast Brewing Co.,** 14 York St. (☎ **207/773-2337**), a sizeable brewpub in an old brick cannery at the edge of the Old Port. Downstairs there's a no-smoking bar and restaurant overlooking the brewery. Upstairs is "The Smoking Room," with pool tables, dart lanes, sales of hand-rolled cigars, and live music. Music features local acts, as well as touring bands like 10,000 Maniacs, Better Than Ezra, and J Geils. Cover charges range from $1 to $20, but is typically $3 to $5 for local and regional acts.

PERFORMING ARTS

Portland Stage Company. Portland Performing Arts Center, 25A Forest Ave. ☎ **207/774-0465.** Tickets $18–$30.

The most slick and professional of the Portland theater companies, Portland Stage offers crisply produced productions staring local and imported equity actors in a handsome, second-story theater. About a half-dozen shows are staged throughout the season, which usually runs from October into May. Check the newspaper or call to inquire about special summer shows.

FILM

The Movies (10 Exchange St.; ☎ **207/772-9600**) offers a frequently changing lineup of foreign and domestic independent films, along with that greatest rarity of theater treats: reasonably priced popcorn and snacks.

It's small, many of the seats are uncomfortable, and the sound can be spotty at times, but you'll be able to see many films here that are hard to find even on videotape.

6 Side Trips

OLD ORCHARD BEACH

About 12 miles south of Portland is the unrepentantly honky-tonkish beach town of Old Orchard Beach, which offers considerable stimulus for most of the senses. This venerable Victorian-era resort is famed for its amusement park, pier, and long, sandy beach, which attracts sun worshippers from all over. Be sure to spend time and money on the stomach-churning rides at the beachside amusement park of **Palace Playland** (☎ **207/934-2001**), then walk on the 7-mile-long beach past the mid-rise condos that sprouted in the 1980s like a scale-model Miami Beach.

The beach is broad and open at low tide; at high tide, space to plunk your towel down is at a premium. In the evenings, teens and young adults dominate the town's culture, spilling out of the video arcades and cruising the main strip. For dinner, do as the locals do and buy hot dogs and pizza and cotton candy; save your change for the arcades.

Old Orchard is just off Route 1 south of Portland. The quickest route is to leave the turnpike at Exit 5, then follow I-195 and the signs to the beach. Don't expect to be alone here: Parking is tight, and the traffic can be horrendous during the peak summer months.

SEBAGO LAKE & DOUGLAS HILL

Maine's second-largest lake is also its most popular. Ringed with summer homes of varying vintages, many dating from the early part of this century, Sebago Lake attracts thousands of vacationers to its cool, deep waters.

You can take a tour of the outlying lakes and the ancient canal system between Sebago and Long lakes on the **Songo Queen,** a faux-steamship berthed in the town of Naples (☎ **207/693-6861**). Or just lie in the sun along the sandy beach at bustling **Sebago Lake State Park** (☎ **207/693-6613**) on the lake's north shore (the park is off Route 302; look for signs between Raymond and South Casco). The park has shady picnic areas, a campground, a snack bar, and lifeguards on the beach (entrance fee charged). It can be uncomfortably crowded on sunny summer weekends; it's best on weekdays.

Bring food and charcoal for barbecuing at the shady picnic areas off the beach. The park's campground has a separate beach and is at a distance from the day-use area, and is less congested during good weather. It books up early in the season, but you might luck into a cancellation if you need a spot to pitch your tent.

To the west of the lake, the rolling wooded uplands hold some surprises. For a low-key excursion, head to the **Jones Museum of Glass and Ceramics** (☎ **207/787-3370**), a place that captivates even visitors who have little interest in either. Housed in a beautiful old farm building near a compound of summer homes, the museum has hundreds of pieces of old and contemporary glass displayed in highly professional exhibits. The museum is just off Route 107 south of Sebago (the town, not the lake), on the lake's west side, and is conscientious about posting signs directing you there; watch for them. It's open 10am to 5pm Monday through Saturday May to mid-November (1 to 5pm only on Sunday). Admission is $5 for adults, $3 for students, children under 12 free.

A short hop up the hill from the museum is **Douglas Mountain,** whose summit is capped with a medieval-looking 16-foot stone tower. The property is open to the public; the summit is reached via an easy one-quarter mile trail from the parking area. Look for wild berries in late summer.

✪ SABBATHDAY LAKE SHAKER COMMUNITY

Route 26 from Portland to Norway is a speedy highway past new housing developments and through hilly farmland. At one point the road pinches through a cluster of stately historic buildings that stand proudly beneath towering shade trees. That's the Sabbathday Lake Shaker Community (☎ **207/926-4597**), the last active Shaker community in the nation. The half-dozen or so Shakers living here today still embrace their traditional beliefs and maintain a communal, pastoral way of life. The bulk of the community's income comes from the sale of herbs, which have been grown here since 1799.

Tours are offered daily in summer except on Sundays (when visitors are invited to attend Sunday services). Docents provide tours of the grounds and several of buildings, including the graceful 1794 meetinghouse. Exhibits in the buildings showcase the famed furniture handcrafted by the Shakers, and include antiques made by Shakers at other U.S. communes. You'll learn plenty about the Shaker ideology with its emphasis on simplicity, industry, and celibacy. After your tour, browse the gift shop for Shaker herbs and teas. Tours last either 1 hour ($5 adult, $2 children 6 to 12) or 1 hour and 45 minutes ($6.50 adult, $2.75 children). Open daily except Sunday Memorial Day to Columbus Day from 10am to 4:30pm. The last tour is at 3:30pm.

The Shaker village is about 45 minutes from Portland. Head north on Route 26 (Washington Avenue in Portland). The village is 8 miles from Exit 11 (Gray) of the Maine Turnpike.

FERRIES TO NOVA SCOTIA

A trip to northern New England can serve as a springboard for an excursion to Atlantic Canada. The most hassle-free way to link the two is by ferry. Two ferries connect Yarmouth, Nova Scotia with Maine, saving hours of driving time and providing a relaxing mini-cruise along the way.

The *Scotia Prince* departs each evening from Portland for an 11-hour crossing to Nova Scotia, arriving early in the morning. The ship is bustling with activity, from its cafe and restaurant to casino and glitzy floor show in the lounge. When the party winds down, you can retire to a cabin for a good night's sleep, awakening for breakfast before disembarking in Nova Scotia. Day cabins are available on the return trip, but you'll save some money sitting in the lounge or relaxing on a deck chair and watching for whales.

High season one-way adult fares are $80 (children 5 to 14 traveling with adults are half-price), with additional fares for a car ($98) or cabin ($32 to $98). Ask about package deals, which often include hotel stays in Nova Scotia. For more information, contact **Prince of Fundy** (☎ **800/341-7540** or 207/775-5611).

In the summer of 1998, a brand-new high-speed ferry began service between Bar Harbor with Yarmouth. The *Cat* is the fastest car ferry in North America, and makes the crossing in about $2^{1}/_{2}$ hours (compared to 6 hours aboard the old *Bluenose* ferry). The 300-foot-long jet-powered catamaran has a top speed of 50 miles per hour, and can carry 900 passengers and 240 cars. The *Cat* departs twice daily in summer from Bar Harbor (at 8am and 3:30pm). Fares are $45 per adult one way, $20 for children 5 to 12. Cars are $45. For more information, contact **Bay Ferries** (☎ **888/249-7245**). The ride is usually smooth, but the process of getting the kinks worked out has been bumpy. During its inaugural summer, the ferry suffered a series of mechanical and operational difficulties (including a low-speed collision with a fishing boat off foggy Nova Scotia, which killed the fisherman). The future of the high-speed service was uncertain at press time; it's best to call ahead to confirm details.

4

Freeport to Port Clyde

*V*eteran Maine travelers contend this part of the coast is fast losing its native charm—it's too commercial, too developed, too much like the rest of the United States. The grousers do have a point, especially regarding Route 1's roadside, but get off the main roads and you'll find pockets where you can catch glimpses of another Maine. Among the sights backroad travelers will stumble upon are quiet inland villages, dramatic coastal scenery, and a rich sense of history, especially maritime history.

The best source of information for the region in general is found at the **Maine State Information Center** (☎ **207/846-0833**) just off Exit 17 of I-95 in Yarmouth. This state-run center is stocked with hundreds of brochures and free newspapers, and is staffed with a helpful crew that can provide information on the entire state, but is particularly well-informed about the mid-coast region.

1 Freeport

If Freeport were a mall (and that's not a far-fetched analogy), L.L. Bean would be the anchor store. It's the business that launched Freeport, elevating its status from just another town off the interstate to one of the two outlet capitals of Maine (the other is Kittery). Freeport still has the form of a classic coastal village, but it's a village that's been largely taken over by the national fashion industry. Most of the old homes and stores have been converted to upscale shops, and now sell name-brand clothing and housewares. Banana Republic occupies an exceedingly handsome brick Federal-style home; even the McDonald's is in a tasteful, understated Victorian farmhouse—you really have to look for the golden arches.

While a number of more modern structures have been built to accommodate the outlet boom, strict planning guidelines have managed to preserve much of the local charm, at least in the village section. Huge parking lots off Main Street are hidden from view, making this one of the more aesthetically pleasing places to shop.

But even with these large lots, parking can be scarce during the peak season, especially on rainy summer days when every cottage-bound tourist between York and Camden decides that a trip to Freeport is a winning idea. Bring a lot of patience, and expect teeming crowds if you come at a busy time.

ESSENTIALS

GETTING THERE

Freeport is on Route 1, but is most commonly reached via I-95 from either Exit 19 or 20.

VISITOR INFORMATION

The **Freeport Merchants Association,** P.O. Box 452, Freeport, ME 04032 (☎ **800/865-1994** or 207/865-1212), publishes a map and directory of businesses, restaurants, and overnight accommodations. The free map is available widely around town at stores and restaurants, or you can contact the association to have them send you one.

SHOPPING

At last count, Freeport had more than 100 retail shops between Exit 19 of I-95 at the far lower end of Main Street and Mallett Road, which connects to Exit 20. Shops have recently begun to spread south of Exit 19 toward Yarmouth. If you don't want to miss a single shopping opportunity, get off at Exit 17 and head north on Route 1. As at many other outlet centers, bargains vary from extraordinary to "huh?", so plan on racking up some mileage if you're intent on finding great deals. Among national chains with a presence in Freeport are The Gap, Anne Klein, Levi's, Boston Traders, Patagonia, The North Face, Nike, J. Crew, Timberland, Coach, Maidenform, and many others.

Stores in Freeport are typically open daily 9am to 9pm during the busy summer season.

Cuddledown of Maine. 231 U.S. Rte. 1 (between exits 17 and 19, near Subway). ☎ **207/865-1713.** www.cuddledown.com.

Down pillows are made right in this shop, which carries a variety of European goose-down comforters in all sizes and weights. Look also for linens and home furnishings.

J.L. Coombs Shoe Outlet. 15 Bow St., and 278 Rte. 1 (between exits 17 and 19). ☎ **207/865-4333.**

A Maine shoemaker since 1830, J.L. Coombs today carries a wide assortment of imported and domestic footwear at its two Freeport shops, including a good selection of those favored by teens and college kids, like Doc Marten, Ecco, and Mephisto. There's also outerwear by Pendleton and Jackaroos.

✪ L.L. Bean. Main and Bow sts. ☎ **800/341-4341.** www.llbean.com.

Monster outdoor retailer L.L. Bean traces its roots to the day Leon Leonwood Bean decided that what the world really needed was a good weatherproof hunting shoe. He joined a watertight gum shoe with a laced leather upper. Hunters liked it. The store grew. An empire was born.

Today L.L. Bean sells millions of dollars worth of clothing and outdoor goods to customers nationwide through its well-respected catalogs, and it continues to draw hundreds of thousands through its door. This modern, multilevel store is the size of a regional mall, but tastefully done with its own indoor trout pond and lots of natural wood. L.L. Bean is open 365 days a year, 24 hours a day (note the lack of locks or latches on the front doors) and it's a popular spot even in the dead of night, especially in summer and around holidays. Selections include Bean's own trademark clothing, along with home furnishings, books, shoes, and plenty of outdoor gear for camping, fishing, and hunting. A 2-minute walk away is the L.L. Kids store, with goods for the younger set.

In addition to the main store, L.L. Bean stocks an outlet shop with a relatively small but rapidly changing inventory at discount prices. It's in a back lot between Main Street and Depot Street—ask at the front desk of the main store for walking directions. L.L. Bean also has outlets in Portland, Ellsworth, and North Conway, N.H.

Maine Bear Factory. 294 U.S. Rte. 1. ☎ **207/846-1570.**

Kids love this place. Teddy bears are made on the premises, and kids can even make their own bears, choosing the perfect eyes and nose before sending it to the stuffing machine.

Mangy Moose. 112 Main St. ☎ **207/865-6414.**

A cute souvenir shop with a twist: Virtually everything in the place is moose-related. There are moose hackey sacks, moose wine glasses, moose trivets, moose cookie cutters, and, of course, moose T-shirts. And much more. The merchandise is a notch above the stuff you'll find in other tourist-oriented shops.

Maxwell's Pottery Outlet. 47 Main St. ☎ **207/865-1144.**

Maxwell's offers a good selection of practical and fancy pottery, candlestick holders, and other household accouterments. Prices are reasonable.

EXPLORING FREEPORT

While Freeport is nationally known for its outlet shopping, that's not all it offers. Just outside of town you'll find a lovely pastoral landscape, picturesque country walks, and scenic drives that make for a handy retreat from all that spending.

Head by car east on Bow Street (down the hill from the L.L. Bean's main entrance), and wind around for 1 mile to the sign for **Mast Landing Sanctuary** (☎ 207/781-2330). Turn left, then turn right in $^1/_{10}$ of a mile into the sanctuary parking lot. A network of trails totaling about 3 miles criss-crosses through a landscape of long-ago eroded hills and mixed woodlands; streams trickle down to the marshland estuary. The 140-acre property is owned by the Maine Audubon Society and is open to the public until dusk.

Back at the main road, turn left and continue eastward for 1.4 miles, then turn right on Wolf Neck Road. Continue 1.7 miles, then turn left for one-half mile on a dirt farm road. **Wolfe's Neck Farm,** owned and operated by a non-profit trust, has been experimenting with ways to produce beef without chemicals, and sells its own line of chemical-free meat. All this happens to take place at one of the most scenic coastal farms in Maine (it's especially beautiful near sunset). Stop at the gray farmhouse and pick up some tasty frozen steaks or flavorful hamburger. (Open Monday through Friday 1 to 6pm, Saturday 9am to 3pm; ☎ 207/865-4469).

Continue south on Wolf Neck Road and you'll soon come to 233-acre **Wolf Neck Woods State Park** (☎ 207/865-4465). This compact, attractive park has quiet woodland trails that run through forests of white pine and hemlock, past estuaries, and along the rocky shoreline of the bay. Be sure to find Googins Island and look for the osprey nest on it. This is a good destination for enjoying a picnic brought from town.

WHERE TO STAY

Freeport is blessed with more than 600 guest rooms, ranging from quiet B&Bs with three rooms to chain motels with several dozen. Reservations are strongly recommended during the peak summer season.

Harraseeket Inn. 162 Main St., Freeport, ME 04032. ☎ **800/342-6423** or 207/865-9377. www.stayfreeport.com. E-mail: harraseeke@aol.com. 84 units. A/C TV TEL. Summer and fall $165–$265 double; spring and early summer $130–$250; winter $100–$235. All rates include breakfast buffet. Take Exit 20 off I-95 to Main St. AE, DC, DISC, MC, V.

The Harraseeket Inn is a large, thoroughly modern hotel 2 blocks north of L.L. Bean. It's to the inn's credit that you could easily drive down Main Street and not notice it. A late-19th century home is the soul of the hotel, but most of the rooms are in later additions built in 1989 and 1997. Guests can relax in the well-regarded dining room, in the common room with the baby grand player piano, or in the homey Broad Arrow Tavern with its wood-fired oven and grill. The guest rooms are on the large side and tastefully done, with quarter-canopy beds and a nice mix of contemporary and antique furniture. All have hair dryers and coffee makers, about a quarter have gas or wood-burning fireplaces, and more than half feature single or double whirlpools.

Dining: There are two restaurants on the premises. The Maine Dining Room offers New American dining with an emphasis on local ingredients; entree prices are $13 to $26. The Broad Arrow Tavern has a more informal setting with a less ambitious menu, which includes an array of pizzas and pasta; entrees range from $10 to $21.

Amenities: Concierge, limited room service, dry cleaning, laundry service, safe deposit boxes, indoor heated lap pool, business center, conference rooms.

Isaac Randall House. 5 Independence Dr., Freeport, ME 04032. ☎ **800/ 865-9295** or 207/865-9295. Fax 207/865-9003. 12 units (1 with private hallway bathroom). A/C TEL. $100–$135 double peak season, $70–$100 off-season. Located $^1/_2$ mile south of the L.L. Bean store on Rte. 1. 2-night minimum stay on holiday and midsummer weekends. DISC, MC, V.

Freeport's first bed-and-breakfast, the Isaac Randall House, is located in an 1823 farmhouse that's been refurbished with a dozen handsome guest rooms, all with private bathroom, and four with gas fireplaces. The most charming of the bunch is the "Pine" room, built in an adjoining ell with rustic barn boards and decorated in a Southwestern motif. (It also features a unique antique copper tub.) The least desirable are the two smaller, modern rooms in an addition in back, and a dark "Loft" room upstairs. Breakfast is served in a homey country kitchen with a Glenwood stove and ticking Regulator clock. The inn is well situated for exploring Freeport; its main disadvantage is its location sandwiched between busy Route 1 and I-95. The sound of traffic is never far away.

Kendall Tavern. 213 Main St., Freeport, ME 04032. ☎ **800/341-9572** or 207/865-1338. 7 units. $100–$125 double peak season, $75–$95 off season. Rates include full breakfast. AE, DISC, MC, V.

If you want to be out of the bustle of town but not too far from the shopping, this is a good choice. This handsome B&B is in a cheerful yellow farmhouse on 3.5 acres at a bend in the road a half mile north of the center of Freeport. The rooms are all plushly carpeted and appointed with comfort in mind. Everything is decorated in a bright and airy style, with framed posters on the walls and a mix of antique and new furniture. Though the rooms facing Route 1 (Main Street) may be a bit noisier than the others, the traffic isn't likely to be too disruptive. There's a piano in one of the two downstairs parlors, and a sizeable hot tub in a spacious private room in the back.

Maine Idyll Motor Court. 325 Rte. 1, Freeport, ME 04032. ☎ **207/ 865-4201.** 20 cottages. TV. $44–$70 double (2- and 3-bedroom cottages $68–$90). No credit cards (checks accepted). Closed early Nov to late April. Pets accepted.

The 1932 Maine Idyll Motor Court is a Maine classic—a cluster of 20 cottages scattered about a grove of beech and oak trees. Each has a tiny porch, wood-burning fireplace (birch logs provided), TV, modest kitchen facilities (no ovens), and time-worn furniture. The cabins are not lavishly sized, but are comfortable and spotlessly clean. If you need a phone, you're out of luck—the cabins lack them, and there's no pay phone on the premises (the owners are good about letting guests use the office phone if they're in a pinch). The only interruption to an idyll here is the omnipresent sound of traffic: I-95 is just through the trees on one side, Route 1 on the other side. Get past the drone, though, and you'll find very good value for the money here.

WHERE TO DINE

For a quick and simple meal, you might head down Mechanic Street (near the Mangy Moose at 112 Main St.) to the **Corsican Restaurant** (9 Mechanic St.; ☎ 207/865-9421) for a 10-inch pizza, calzone, or king-sized sandwich. A favored spot for quick, reasonably priced lunch close to L.L. Bean is the **Falcon Restaurant** (8 Bow St.; ☎ **207/865-4031**).

Gritty McDuff's. Lower Main St., Freeport. ☎ **207/865-4321.** Reservations not accepted. Main courses $5.50–$12.95. AE, DISC, MC, V. Daily 11:30am– 11pm. BREWPUB.

Spacious, informal and air-conditioned in summer, Gritty's is an offshoot of Portland's first and most successful brewpub. It's located a short drive south of the village center, and is best known for its fine and varied selection of craft beers. The pub offers a wide ranging bar menu for both lunch and dinner, with few standout offerings but decent, consistent fare. The burgers and stone-oven pizzas are reliable; pub classics like shepherd's pie and barley-coated fish also tend to be popular. During the busy summer season the kitchen and waitstaff can get a bit overwhelmed; bring your patience and a newspaper.

Harraseeket Lunch & Lobster. Main St., South Freeport. ☎ **207/865-4888.** Reservations not accepted. Lobsters market price (typically $8–$11). No credit cards. Open daily 11:30am to 8:30pm. Closed mid-Oct to May 1. From I-95 take Exit 17 and head north on Rte. 1; turn right on S. Freeport Rd. at the huge Indian statue; continue to stop sign in South Freeport; turn right to waterfront. From Freeport take South St. (off Bow St.) to Main St. in South Freeport; turn left to water. LOBSTER POUND.

Located at a boatyard on the Harraseeket River about 10 minutes' drive from Freeport's main shopping district, this lobster pound is an especially popular destination on sunny days—although with its heated dining room, it's a worthy destination anytime. Order a crustacean according to how hungry you are (from 1 lb on up), then take in the river view from the deck while waiting for your number to be called. Be prepared for big crowds; a good alternative is to come in late afternoon between the crushing lunch and dinner hordes.

Jameson Tavern. 115 Main St. ☎ **207/865-4196.** Reservations encouraged. Main courses, tap room $5.25–$9.95; dining room lunch $5.25–$10.95, dinner $10.95–$19.95. AE, DC, DISC, MC, V. Tap room daily 11am–11pm; dining room daily 11am–2pm and 5–10pm. AMERICAN.

Located in a handsome, historic farmhouse literally in the shadow of L.L. Bean (it's just north of the store), the Jameson Tavern touts itself as the birthplace of Maine. In 1820 the papers were signed here legally separating Maine from Massachusetts. Today, it's a dual restaurant under the same ownership. As you enter the door you can head left to the historic tap room, a compact, often crowded spot filled with the smell of fresh-popped popcorn. (You're best off outside on the brick patio if the weather's good.) Meals here include fare like crab-cake burgers, lobster croissants, and a variety of build-your-own burgers. The other part of the house is the dining room, which is more formal in a country-colonial sort of way; and the food is more sedate and gussied up, with an emphasis on steak and hearty fare. (This isn't a spot for dieters.) While not overly creative, the meals in both the dining room and tap room will hit the spot if you've worked up one of those fierce hungers peculiar to marathon shopping adventures.

2   Brunswick & Bath

Brunswick and Bath are two handsome and historic towns that share a strong commercial past. Many travelers heading up Route 1 pass through both towns eager to reach the areas with higher billing on the marquee. That's a shame, for both are well worth the detour to sample the sort of slower pace that's being lost elsewhere.

Brunswick was once home to several mills along the Androscoggin River; these have since been converted to offices and the like, but Brunswick's broad Maine Street still bustles with activity. (Idiosyncratic traffic patterns can lead to snarls of traffic in the late afternoon, when local businesses let out.) Brunswick is also home to Bowdoin College, one of the nation's most respected small colleges. The school was founded in 1794, offered its first classes 8 years later, and has since amassed an illustrious roster of prominent alumni, including Nathaniel Hawthorne, Henry Wadsworth Longfellow, Franklin Pierce, and Arctic explorer Robert E. Peary. Civil War hero Joshua Chamberlain served as president of the college after the war.

Eight miles to the east, Bath is pleasantly situated on the broad Kennebec River, and is a noted center of shipbuilding. The first U.S-built ship was constructed downstream at the Popham Bay colony in the early 17th century; in the years since, shipbuilders have constructed more than 5,000 ships hereabouts. Bath shipbuilding reached its heyday in the late 19th century, but the business of shipbuilding continues to this day. Bath Iron Works is one of the nation's preeminent boatyards, constructing and repairing ships for the U.S. Navy. The scaled-down military has left Bath shipbuilders in a somewhat tenuous state, but it's still common to see the steely gray ships in the dry dock (the best view is from the bridge over the Kennebec), and the towering red-and-white crane (topped by a lighted Christmas tree in December) moving supplies and parts around the yard.

ESSENTIALS
GETTING THERE

Brunswick and Bath are both on Route 1. Brunswick is accessible via Exits 22 and 23 off I-95. If you're bypassing Brunswick and heading north up Route 1 to Bath or beyond, continue up I-95 and exit at the "coastal connector" exit in Topsham, which avoids some of the slower traffic going through Brunswick.

VISITOR INFORMATION

The **Bath-Brunswick Region Chamber of Commerce,** 59 Pleasant St., Brunswick, ME 04011 (☎ **207/725-8797** or 207/443-9751), offers information and lodging assistance Monday to Friday 8:30am to 5pm from its offices near downtown Brunswick. The chamber also staffs an information center 10am to 7pm daily in summer on Route 1 between Brunswick and Bath.

FESTIVALS

In early August look for posters for the ever-popular ✪ **Maine Festival** (☎ **207/772-9012**), which takes place at Thomas Point Beach between Brunswick and Bath. What started as a sort of counterculture celebration of Maine people and crafts has evolved and grown to a hugely popular mainstream event. Performers from throughout Maine gather at this pretty coveside park (it's a private campground the rest of the summer), and put on shows from noon past dark throughout the first weekend in August. Displays of crafts, artwork, and the products of small Maine businesses are also on display. An admission fee is charged.

WHAT TO SEE AND DO
IN BRUNSWICK

Bowdoin Museum of Art. Walker Art Building, Bowdoin College. ☎ **207/725-3275.** Free admission. Tues–Sat 10am–5pm, Sun 2–5pm.

This stern, neo-classical building on the Bowdoin campus was designed by the prominent architectural firm of McKim, Mead, and White. While the collections are small, they include a number of exceptionally fine paintings from Europe and America, along with early furniture and artifacts from classical antiquity. The artists include Andrew and N.C. Wyeth, Marsden Hartley, Winslow Homer, and John Singer Sargent. The older upstairs galleries have soft, diffused lighting from skylights high above; it feels a bit as if you're underwater. The basement galleries, which feature rotating exhibits, are modern and spacious.

Peary-MacMillan Arctic Museum. Hubbard Hall, Bowdoin College. ☎ **207/725-3416.** Free admission. Tues–Sat 10am–5pm, Sun 2–5pm.

While Admiral Robert E. Peary (class of 1887) is better known for his accomplishments (he "discovered" the North Pole at age 53 in 1909), Donald MacMillan (class of 1898) also racked up an impressive string of achievements in Arctic research and exploration. You can learn about both men and the wherefores of Arctic exploration in this altogether manageable museum on the Bowdoin campus. The front room features mounted animals from the Arctic, including some impressive polar bears. A second room outlines Peary's historic 1909 expedition, complete with excerpts from Peary's journal. The last room includes varied displays of Inuit arts and crafts, some historic, some modern. This compact museum can be visited in about 20 minutes or so; the art museum (see above) is just next door.

IN BATH

Maine Maritime Museum and Shipyard. 243 Washington St. ☎ **207/ 443-1316.** Admission $8 adults, $5.50 children 6–17, $24 family. Open daily 9:30am–5pm.

You don't have to be a ship aficionado to enjoy the Maine Maritime Museum and Shipyard. But those who do love boats love it here and are hard to drag away. This contemporary museum on the shores of the Kennebec River (it's just south of Bath Iron Works) features a wide array of displays and exhibits related to the boatbuilder's art. The location is appropriate—it's sited at the former shipyard of Percy and Small, which built some 42 schooners in the late 19th and early 20th century. The centerpiece of the museum is the handsomely modern Maritime History Building. Here, you'll find changing exhibits of maritime art and artifacts. (There's also a gift shop with a great selection of books about ships.) The 10-acre property houses a fleet of additional displays, including an intriguing exhibit on lobstering and a complete boat-building shop. Kids enjoy the play area (they can search for pirates from the crow's nest of the play boat). Be sure to wander down to the docks on the river to see what's tied up, or to inquire about river cruises (extra charge).

WHERE TO STAY

Brunswick Bed & Breakfast. 165 Park Row, Brunswick, ME 04011. ☎ **800/ 299-4914** or 207/729-4914. www.brunswickbnb.com. E-mail: info@ brunswickbnb.com. 8 units. A/C TEL. $87–$125 double, including full breakfast. MC, V. Closed January. Children 6 and over accepted.

This handsome B&B is located in downtown Brunswick facing the green, and is within walking distance to Bowdoin College, area theaters, and restaurants along Maine Street. The rooms in this Federal-style home with wraparound porch are quite spacious, and are furnished serviceably in a sort of country-modern style, some with wingback or wicker chairs, and all with attractive quilts; ask for one of the brighter, cheerier corner rooms. There's a TV downstairs in the common room; in-room telephones allow only outgoing calls.

Grey Havens. Seguinland Rd., Georgetown Island, ME 04548. ☎ **207/ 371-2616.** Fax 207/371-2274. 13 units (2 with private hall bathrooms). $100–$205 double including continental breakfast. Closed mid-Nov to early Apr. From Rte. 1, head south on Rte. 127 and then follow signs for Reid State Park; watch for inn on left. MC, V. Children under 7 not accepted.

On Georgetown Island southeast of Bath, Grey Havens is worth seeking out if you're yearning for a place to idly watch the ocean while you unwind. This graceful, 1904 shingled home with prominent turrets sits on a high, rocky bluff overlooking the sea. Inside, it's all richly mellowed pine paneling, and a spacious common room where you can relax in cozy chairs in front of the cobblestone fireplace while listening to classical music. The guest rooms are simply but comfortably furnished. In the turret rooms, the managers have even placed binoculars to help guests better monitor the comings and goings on the water. There's a premium for the oceanfront rooms and they're worth it, but if you want to save a few dollars, ask for one with a private bathroom just across the hall. Guests have the run of the old kitchen and can use the inn's canoe and bikes to explore the outlying area. One caveat: The inn has been only lightly modernized, which means rather thin walls. If you have loud neighbors, you'll learn more about their lives than you may care to know.

Sebasco Harbor Resort. Rte. 217, Sebasco Estates, ME 04565. ☎ **800/ 225-3819** or 207/389-1161. Fax 207/389-2004. www.sebasco.com. E-mail: info@sebasco.com. 115 units. TEL. July to Labor Day $186–$326 double; early June $146–$298; Sept–Oct $156–$306. All rates include breakfast and dinner. 15% service charge additional. AE, DISC, MC, V. 2-night minimum stay on weekends. Closed late Oct to early May. South from Bath 11 miles on Rte. 209; look for Rte. 217 and signs for Sebasco.

Sebasco is a grand old seaside resort under new and vigorous management that's fighting a generally successful battle against time and irrelevance. It's a self-contained resort of the sort that flourished 50 years ago, and today is being rediscovered by families. Some guests have been coming here for 60 years and love the timelessness of it; newcomers are starting to visit now that much of it has benefited from a facelift.

The 664-acre grounds remain the real attraction—guests enjoy sweeping ocean views, a lovely seaside pool, and great walks around well-cared-for property. The guest rooms, it should be noted, are adequate rather than elegant, and may seem a bit short of the mark given the high prices charged. Most lack a certain style—especially the 40 rooms in the old inn, which are dated, and I don't mean that in a good way. (The small wooden decks on many rooms are a plus, though.) Better are the quirky rooms in the octagonal Lighthouse Building—rooms #12 and #20 have some of the best views in the state. Most (not all) rooms have TVs; ask first if it's important to you. If you're coming for more than 2 days, it's probably best to book a cottage, which come in all sorts and sizes.

Dining/Diversions: The Pilot House Dining Room is airy, contemporary, and the best place to enjoy the sunsets. You'll find white linens and a jackets-recommended-for-men policy; the menu is contemporary resort style, with dishes like grilled swordfish with a pesto butter, and prime rib with a Parmesan Yorkshire pudding. The dining room is open to the public ($28 fixed price). Another restaurant, Ledges, is a more informal spot downstairs that serves from a lighter menu.

Amenities: Swimming in outdoor saltwater pool and ocean, 9-hole golf course, tennis courts, hot tub, sauna, health club, bay cruises, canoe and kayak rentals, shuffleboard, snack bar, children's center and programs, video games, candlepin bowling, movies, nature trails, sailing lessons, bike rentals. Popham Beach is 5 miles away.

WHERE TO DINE

Both downtown Brunswick and downtown Bath offer plenty of casual places to dine, ranging from burgers to barbecue and better. For informal fare, it's hard to go wrong at these streetside cafes and restaurants. The two places I've listed below are 20 minutes or so southeast of Bath, but are featured because they're both so distinctive they're well worth the detour.

Five Islands Lobster Co. Rte. 127, Georgetown. ☎ **207/371-2990.** Reservations not accepted. $5–$8 per lobster, 75¢ for corn on the cob. MC, V. Daily 11am–8pm in July and Aug; shorter hours during the off-season. Closed Columbus Day to Mother's Day. LOBSTER POUND.

The drive alone makes this lobster pound a worthy destination. It's located about 12 miles south of Route 1 down winding Route 127, past bogs and spruce forests with glimpses of azure ocean inlets. (Head south from Woolwich, which is just across the bridge from Bath.) Drive until you pass a cluster of clapboard homes, then keep going until you can't go any farther. Wander out to the wharf with its unbeatable island views and place your order.

This is a down-home affair, owned jointly by local lobstermen and the proprietors of Grey Havens, a local inn (see "Where to Stay," above). While you're awaiting your lobster, you can wander next door to the Love Nest Snack Bar for extras like soda or the killer onion rings (you get a huge basketful for $2.75). Gather up your grub and settle in at one of the wharf picnic tables, or head over to the grassy spots at the edge of the dirt parking lot. And bring some patience: Despite its edge-of-the-world feel, the lobster pound draws steady traffic and it can be crowded on weekends.

✪ **Robinhood Free Meetinghouse.** Robinhood Rd., Robinhood. ☎ **207/ 371-2188.** Reservations encouraged. Main courses $16–$23. AE, DISC, MC, V. Daily May–Oct 5:30–9pm. Call for off-season hours. FUSION.

Chef Michael Gagne is an ambitious fellow. His menu features between 30 and 40 entrees, and they're wildly eclectic—from Thai grilled vegetables to Wiener schnitzel to salmon en papiollote. Ordering from the menu almost seems like playing stump the chef: Let's see you make *this!*

And you know what? Gagne always hits his notes and rarely serves a mediocre meal. You just can't go wrong. Gagne has attracted legions of dedicated local followers, who appreciate the extraordinary attention paid to detail. Carbonated water and slices of citrus are served at every table. Foam baffles are glued discreetly to the underside of the seats to dampen the echoes in the sparely decorated, immaculately restored 1855 Greek Revival Meetinghouse. Even the sorbet served between courses is homemade. Eating here is not an inexpensive proposition, but it offers tremendous value for the price.

3 Harpswell Peninsula

Extending southwest from Brunswick and Bath is the picturesque Harpswell Peninsula. It's actually three peninsulas, like the tines of a pitchfork, if you include the islands of Orrs and Bailey, which are linked to the mainland by bridges. While close to some of Maine's larger towns (Portland is only 45 minutes away), the Harpswell Peninsula has a remote, historic feel with sudden vistas across meadows to the blue waters of northern Casco Bay. Toward the southern tips of the peninsulas, the character changes as clusters of colorful Victorian-era summer cottages displace the farmhouses found farther inland. Some of these cottages rent by the week, but savvy families book up many of them years in advance. Ask local real estate agents if you're interested.

There's no set itinerary for exploring the area. Just drive south from Brunswick on Route 24 or 123 until you can't go any farther, then backtrack for a bit and strike south again. Among the "attractions" worth looking for are the wonderful ocean and island views from **South Harpswell** at the tip of the westernmost peninsula (park and wander around for a bit), and the clever **Cobwork Bridge** connecting Bailey and Orrs islands. The hump-backed bridge was built in 1928 of granite blocks stacked in such a way that the strong tides could come and go and not drag the bridge out with it. No cement was used in its construction.

WHERE TO STAY

Driftwood Inn & Cottages. Washington Ave., Bailey Island, ME 04003. ☎ **207/833-5461,** or 508/947-1066 off-season. 18 double units, 9 single units, 6 cottages (most units share hallway bathrooms). $70–$75 double; weekly $345 per person including breakfast and dinner; cottages $475–$550 per week. No credit cards. Open late May to mid-Oct; dining room open late June to Labor Day.

The oceanside Driftwood Inn dates back to 1910 and is a coastal New England classic. A rustic summer retreat on 3 acres at the end of a dead-end road, the inn is a compound of four weathered, shingled buildings and a handful of housekeeping cottages on a rocky, oceanside property. The spartan rooms of time-aged pine have a simple turn-of-the-century flavor that hasn't been gentrified in the least. Most rooms share bathrooms down the hall, but some have private sinks and toilets. Your primary company will be the constant sound of surf surging in and ebbing out of the fissured rocks. The inn has an old saltwater pool and porches with wicker furniture to while away the afternoons; bring plenty of books and board games.

Dining: The dining room serves basic fare (roasts, fish, etc.) in a wonderfully austere setting overlooking the sea; meals are extra, although a weekly American plan is available. Dining is open to outside guests if you call ahead.

WHERE TO DINE

This is a great area to sample simple fare, like a bowl of chowder or a boiled lobster. One of the premier places for chowder off the beaten track is at the down-home ✪ **Dolphin Marina** (☎ **207/833-6000**) at Basin Point in South Harpswell. (Drive 12.2 miles south of Brunswick on Route 123, turn right at Ash Point Road near the West Harpswell School, then take your next right on Basin Point Road and continue to the end.) Find the boatyard and then wander inside the adjacent building, where you'll discover a tiny counter seating six and a handful of pine tables and booths with stunning views of Casco Bay. The fish chowder and lobster stew are reasonably priced and absolutely delicious, and the blueberry muffins are warm and have a crispy crown. The servers seem easily flummoxed at times, so bring some patience.

If you're in mind of a steamed lobster, several sprawling establishments specialize in delivering crustaceans fresh from the sea. On the Bailey Island side there's **Cook's Lobster House** (☎ **207/ 833-2818**), which has been serving up a choice of shore dinners since 1955. The restaurant has two decks for outdoor dining. Near Harpswell is the **Estes Lobster House** (☎ **207/833-6340**), which serves lobster (including an artery-clogging triple lobster plate for under $20) amid relaxed, festive surroundings.

4 Wiscasset & the Boothbays

Wiscasset is a lovely riverside town, and it's not shy about letting you know: "The Prettiest Village in Maine," is the boast on the sign at the edge of town and on many brochures. Whether or not you agree with this self-assessment, the town is attractive (although the sluggish and persistent line of traffic snaking through on Route 1 diminishes the charm), and makes a good stop for stretching legs, taking in an attraction or two, or grabbing a bite to eat en route to coastal destinations further east.

Boothbay Harbor, 11 miles south of Route 1 on Route 27 is another small and scenic town. This former fishing port was discovered in the last century by wealthy rusticators who built imposing seaside homes and retreated here in summer to avoid the swelter of the cities along the Eastern Seaboard.

Having embraced the tourist dollar, the harborfront village never really looked back, and in more recent years it has emerged as one of the premier destinations of travelers in search of classic coastal Maine. This embrace has had an obvious impact. The village has been discovered by bus tours, which has in turn attracted kitschy shops and a slew of mediocre restaurants that all seem to specialize in baked stuffed haddock.

If Boothbay Harbor is stuck in a time warp, it's Tourist Trap ca. 1974—bland and boxy motels hem in the harbor, and side-by-side boutiques hawk the same mass-market trinkets (Beanie Babies, T-shirts emblazoned with puffins). Despite it all, there's still an affable charm that manages to rise above the clutter and cheese, especially on foggy days when the horns bleat mournfully at the harbor's mouth.

ESSENTIALS
GETTING THERE

Wiscasset is on Route 1 midway between Bath and Damariscotta. Boothbay Harbor is south of Route 1 on Route 27. Coming from the west, look for signs shortly after crossing the Sheepscot River at Wiscasset.

VISITOR INFORMATION

Wiscasset lacks a tourist information booth, but a phone call to the **Wiscasset Regional Business Association** (☎ **207/882-9617**) should answer any questions you may have.

As befits a town where tourism is a major industry, Boothbay has three visitor information centers in and around town, reflecting the importance of the travel dollars to the region. At the intersection of Route 1 and Route 27 is a center that's open May through October and is a good place to stock up on brochures. A mile before you reach the village is the seasonal **Boothbay Information Center** on your right (open June to October). If you zoom past it or it's closed, don't fret. The year-round **Boothbay Harbor Region Chamber of Commerce,** P.O. Box 356, Boothbay Harbor, ME 04538 (☎ **207/ 633-2353**) is at the intersection of routes 27 and 96.

WHAT TO SEE & DO
IN WISCASSET

Aside from enjoying the town's handsome architecture and vaunted prettiness, there are several quirky, low-key attractions that will nicely break up a trip along the coast.

✪ Musical Wonder House. 18 High St. ☎ **207/882-7163.** $7.50 per room ($1 discount for seniors and children under 12). Late May to Labor Day daily 10am–5pm; call for off-season hours. Closed late Oct to late May.

Talk about your obsession! Danilo Konvalinka has been collecting music boxes both grand and tiny for decades, and nothing seems to delight him more than to play them for awestruck visitors. The collection includes massive and ancient music boxes that sound as resounding as an orchestra (an 1870 Girard music box from Austria), to the thinner, more ethereal sounds of the smaller contraptions. Music boxes are displayed (and played) in four rooms in a stately 1852 home; admission is charged by the room. It is quite pricey; if you're undecided whether it's worth it, try this: Visit the free gift shop and sample some of the coin-operated 19th-century music boxes in the adjoining hallway. Intrigued? Sign up for the next tour.

Castle Tucker. Lee and High sts. ☎ **207/882-7364.** $4 adults, $2 children. Tours leave on the hour noon–4pm Thurs–Sat; open July and Aug only.

This fascinating mansion at the edge of town overlooking the river was first built in 1807, then radically added to and altered in a more ostentatious style in 1860. The home remains more or less in the same state it was when reconfigured by cotton trader Capt. Richard Tucker; his descendent Janice Tucker still lives on the top floor. Tours of the lower floor are offered by the Society of New England Antiquities, which was given the house by Ms. Tucker in 1997. The detailing is exceptional and offers insight into the life of an affluent sea captain in the late 19th century. Be sure to note the extraordinary elliptical staircase and the painted plaster trim (it's not oak).

Maine Coast Railroad. Rte. 1 (just before the bridge). ☎ **800/795-5404** or 207/882-8000. $10 adults, $5 children 6–12, free for children under 5, $25 for families. Daily late June to mid-Sept 10am and 1pm; weekends only mid-Sept to mid-Oct 10am and 1pm.

Weary of Route 1 traffic? Hop on the Maine Coast Railroad and let somebody else do the driving while you put your feet up and enjoy the scenery. The 90-minute excursions are offered to either Bath or Newcastle, and both routes follow along forest and field, offering fleeting glimpses of the Maine of an earlier era. The railcars date from the 1930s.

EXPLORING THE BOOTHBAYS

Compact Boothbay Harbor, clustered along the water's edge, is ideal for exploring by foot. (The trick is parking, which in midsummer will require either persistence or the forking over of a few dollars.) Pedestrians naturally gravitate to the long, narrow footbridge across the harbor, first built in 1901, but it's more of a destination than a link—other than some restaurants and motels, there's really not much on the other side. The winding, small streets that weave through the town also offer plenty of boutiques and shops that cater to the tourist trade and offer decent browsing.

In addition to poking around town, a brief car excursion to **Ocean Point** is well worthwhile. Follow Route 96 southward from east of Boothbay Harbor, and you'll pass through East Boothbay before striking toward the point. The narrow road runs through piney forests before arriving at the rocky finger; it's one of the few Maine points with a road edging its perimeter, allowing wonderful ocean views. Bunches of colorful Victorian-era summer cottages bloom along the roadside like wildflowers.

Ocean Point makes for a good **bike loop,** as does a trip around **Southport Island,** which is connected to Boothbay Harbor via a bridge. Follow Route 238 around the island, stopping from time to time to enjoy the occasional sea views or to poke down gravel public roads. Mountain-bike rentals are available for $12 for a half day, $20 a full day, at Tidal Transit Kayak Co. (see below).

If dense fog or rain socks in the harbor, bide your time at the vintage **Romar Bowling Lanes** (☎ 207/633-5721). This log and shingle building near the footbridge has a harbor view and has been distracting travelers with the promise of traditional New England candlepin bowling since 1946. On rainy summer days, the wait for one of the eight lanes can be up to an hour. While you're waiting you can play pool and video games, or order a root beer float from the snack bar. It's not hard to find; you'll hear pins crashing, shrieks of victory, and howls of despair from various points around town.

Marine Resources Aquarium. McKown Point Rd., West Boothbay Harbor. ☎ **207/633-9542.** $2.50 adults, $2 children 5–18. Daily 10am–5pm. Closed after Columbus Day to just before Memorial Day.

Operated by the state's Department of Marine Resources, this compact aquarium offers context for life in the sea that surrounds Boothbay and beyond. You can view rare albino and blue lobsters, and get your hands wet at a 20-foot touch tank—a sort of petting zoo of the slippery and slimy. Parking is tight at the aquarium, which is located on a point across the water from Boothbay Harbor. A free shuttle bus (look for the Rocktide trolley) connects downtown with the aquarium and runs frequently throughout the summer.

BOAT TOURS

The best way to see the classic Maine coast around Boothbay is on a boat tour. Nearly two dozen tour boats berth at the harbor or nearby, offering a range of trips ranging from an hour's outing to a full-day excursion to Monhegan Island. You can even observe puffins at their rocky colonies far offshore.

Balmy Day Cruises (☎ 207/633-2284) runs several trips from the harbor, including an all-day excursion to Monhegan Island on the 65-foot *Balmy Days II* (this allows passengers about 4 hours to explore the island before returning—see the "Monhegan Island" section, below). The Monhegan trip is $29 (children $18). The company also offers harbor tours and 2-hour dinner cruises with onboard meals of chicken, lobster roll, and steamed lobster; harbor tours are $8.50, and dinner cruises are approximately $22. If you'd rather be sailing, ask about the 90-minute cruises on the *Bay Lady,* a 15-passenger Friendship sloop ($18).

Cap'n Fish's Scenic Nature Cruises (☎ **800/636-3244** or 207/633-3244) offers sightseeing trips of 1¹/₄ to 4 hours duration, including puffin and whale watches. The three boats in the fleet each carry between 130 and 150 passengers. In the strange-but-true department, the vessels are actually piloted by folks named Capt. Fish—John and Bob Fish, who both hail from a Boothbay family that's long messed about in boats in these parts. Prices range from $10 to $25 ($5 to $15 for children).

Windborne Cruises (☎ **207/882-1020**) sails from Smuggler's Cove Motel on Route 96, about 2 miles south of East Boothbay. Capt. Roger Marin is a great storyteller and captivates his temporary crew with local tales. The 40-foot *Tribute,* a handsome Block Island sailboat, accommodates just six passengers. Two-hour cruises depart at 11am and 3pm, and cost $25 per person. You can also charter the boat for a half day ($200) or full day ($375); both options include lunch.

The most personal way to see the harbor is via sea kayak. **Tidal Transit Kayak Co.** (☎ **207/633-7140**) offers morning, afternoon, and sunset tours of the harbor for $30 (sunset's the best bet). Kayaks may also be rented for $12 an hour, or $50 per day. Tidal Transit is open daily in summer (except when it rains) on the waterfront at 47 Townshend Ave. (walk down the alley).

WHERE TO STAY

Newagen Seaside Inn. Rte. 27 (P.O. Box 68), Cape Newagen, ME 04552. ☎ **800/654-5242** or 207/633-5242. E-mail: seaside@wiscasset.net. 26 units. $120–$200 double. Rates include breakfast. Closed late Sept—mid-June. Located on south tip of Southport Island; take Rte. 27 from Boothbay Harbor and continue on until the inn sign. MC, V.

This 1940s-era resort has seen more glamorous days, but it's still a superb small, low-key resort offering stunning ocean views and walks in a fragrant spruce forest. The inn is housed in a low, wide, white-shingled building that's furnished simply with country pine furniture. There's a classically austere dining room, narrow cruise ship–like hallways with pine wainscoting, and a lobby with a fireplace. The rooms are plain and the inn is a bit threadbare in spots, but never mind that. Guests flock here for the 85-acre oceanside grounds filled with decks, gazebos, and walkways that border on the magical. It's hard to convey the magnificence of the ocean views, which are some of the best of any Maine inn.

Dining: The handsome, simple dining room with ocean views offers a menu with traditional New England fare and a selection of more creative additions (entrees $10 to $25). Closed Tuesday for dinner.

Amenities: Freshwater and saltwater pools, badminton, horseshoes, tennis, sundeck, free use of rowboats.

Spruce Point Inn. Atlantic Ave. (P.O. Box 237), Boothbay Harbor, ME 04538. ☎ **800/553-0289** or 207/633-4152. www.sprucepointinn.com. E-mail: thepoint@sprucepointinn.com. 72 units. TV TEL. July–Aug $264–$396 double, shoulder seasons $150–$296. Rates include breakfast and dinner. 2-night minimum stay on weekends; 3 nights on holidays. AE, MC, V. Closed mid-Oct to Memorial Day. Turn seaward on Union St. in Boothbay Harbor; proceed 2 miles to the inn.

After years of quiet neglect, the inn has benefited greatly from a makeover that's been ongoing since the late 1980s. A number of new units were built in the late 1990s; they match the older buildings architecturally and blend in seamlessly. Those seeking modern resort facilities (Jacuzzis, carpeting, updated furniture) and just a bit of historic flavor will be delighted; however, those looking for historic authenticity may be disappointed. Fortunately, it's hard to imagine anyone being let down by the 15-acre grounds, situated on a rocky point facing west across the harbor.

Dining: Diners are seated in an elegant formal dining room (men are requested to wear jackets) and enjoy wonderful sunset views across the mouth of Boothbay Harbor. The menu features adaptations of traditional New England meals; try the signature cabbage and lobster soup with fresh dandelion. Entrees range from $15 to $25.

Amenities: Two outdoor pools (one heated), Jacuzzi, two outdoor clay tennis courts, fitness center, lawn games (shuffleboard, tetherball, etc.), sundeck, conference rooms, self-service Laundromat, concierge, dry cleaning, laundry service, in-room massage, baby-sitting, children's programs, safe, game room, free shuttle to Boothbay.

Five Gables Inn. Murray Hill Rd. (P.O. Box 335), East Boothbay, ME 04544. ☎ **800/451-5048** or 207/633-4551. www.maineguide.com/boothbay/5gables. 16 units. TEL. $100–$170 double. Rates include breakfast buffet. MC, V. Closed end of Oct to mid-May. Drive through East Boothbay on Rte. 96; turn right after crest of hill on Murray Hill Rd. Children 12 and over accepted.

The handsome Five Gables Inn was painstakingly restored just over a decade ago, and now sits proudly amid a small colony of summer homes on a quiet road above a peaceful cove. It's nicely isolated from the confusion and hubbub of Boothbay Harbor; the activity of choice here is to sit on the deck and enjoy the glimpses of the water through the trees. It's a good base for bicycling—you can pedal down to Ocean Point or in to town. It's also handy to the Lobsterman's Wharf for good, informal dining. The rooms are pleasantly appointed, and five have fireplaces that burn manufactured logs. The common room is nicely furnished in an upscale country style.

Topside. McKown Hill, Boothbay Harbor, ME 04538. ☎ **207/633-5404.** 25 units. TEL. July 1–Labor Day $65–$150 double (most rooms $85); May–June and Sept–Oct $50–$80 double. Rates include continental breakfast. Closed mid-Oct to mid-May. DISC, MC, V.

The old gray house on the hilltop looming over the dated motel buildings may bring to mind the Bates Motel, especially when a full moon is overhead. But get over that: Topside offers spectacular ocean views at a reasonable price from a quiet hilltop compound located right in downtown Boothbay. The inn itself—a former boarding house for shipyard workers—features several comfortable rooms, furnished with an odd mix of antiques and contemporary furniture. At the edge of the inn's lawn are two outbuildings housing basic motel units. These are on the small side, furnished simply and basically with dated paneling and some unfortunate furniture. (You definitely won't find this hotel profiled in *House Beautiful.*) Rooms #9 and #14 have the best views, but most offer a glimpse of the water, and many have decks or patios. All guests have access to the wonderful lawn and the killer views, and the Reed family, which owns and operates the inn, is accommodating and friendly.

WHERE TO DINE

Red's Eats. Water St. (Rte. 1 just before the bridge). ☎ **207/882-6128.** Sandwiches $1.75–$5.25; lobster rolls vary, but are typically around $11. No credit cards. Mon–Thurs 11am–11pm, Fri–Sat 11am–2am, Sun noon–6pm. Closed Oct–April. TAKE-OUT.

Red's is an innocuous roadside stand smack in downtown Wiscasset that's probably received more than its fair share of media ink about its famous lobster rolls. (They often crop up in "Best of Maine" surveys.) And they *are* good, consisting of moist chunks of chilled lobster placed in a roll served with a little mayo on the side. But be aware they're on the pricey end of the scale—you can find less expensive (although less meaty) versions elsewhere. The few tables behind the stand fill up quickly in summer, but you can walk a minute or two and be on a public riverfront deck, which has a better view anyway. One way to economize: Order one lobster roll and split it with a friend, then fuel up on the budget fare that dominates the rest of the menu (for example, "Cheeseburger Royale" for $2.35).

IN THE BOOTHBAYS

When wandering through Boothbay Harbor, watch for **"King" Brud and his famous hot-dog cart.** Brud started selling hot dogs in town in 1943, and he's still at it. Dogs are $1. He's usually at the corner of McKown and Commercial streets from 10am till 4pm from June through October.

Those wishing for innovative dining should also consider (in addition to Christopher's Boathouse, below) the dining rooms at Spruce Point Inn and Lawnmeer Inn, listed in "Where to Stay," above.

Boothbay Region Lobstermen's Co-op. Atlantic Ave., Boothbay Harbor. ☎ **207/633-4900.** Reservations not accepted. Sandwiches $1.25–$8.75; dinners $6.50–$9.95. No credit cards. Open daily May to mid-Oct 11:30am–8:30pm. By foot: cross footbridge and turn right; follow road for 1/3 mile to co-op. SEAFOOD.

"We are not responsible if the seagulls steal your food" reads the sign at the ordering window of this casual, harborside lobster joint. And that sets the tone pretty well. Situated across the harbor from downtown Boothbay, the lobstermen's co-op offers no-frills lobster and seafood. This is the best pick from among the cluster of usually dependable lobster-in-the-rough places that line the waterfront nearby. You order at a pair of windows, then pick up your meal and carry your tray to either the picnic tables on the dock or inside a garage-like two-story prefab building. Lobsters are priced to market (figure on $8 to $10), with extras like corn on the cob for 95¢. A bank of soda machines provides liquid refreshment. This is a fine place for a lobster on a sunny day, but it's uninteresting at best in rain or fog.

✪ **Christopher's Boathouse.** 25 Union St., Boothbay Harbor. ☎ **207/633-6565.** Reservations recommended during peak season. Main courses $16.75–$22.50. MC, V. Daily 5–9pm (until 9:30 Fri and Sat). CREATIVE AMERICAN/WOOD GRILL.

Christopher's opened in Boothbay Harbor in 1998 and offers a welcome change from the generally unexciting fare found elsewhere around town. Scenically located at the head of the harbor, the restaurant is open, bright, and modern, and a handful of lucky diners get a tremendous view up the harbor. (There's also outside deck dining when the weather is good.) The chef has a superb touch with spicy flavors, and deftly combines the expected with the unexpected (to wit: lobster and mango bisque with spicy lobster wontons). The meals from the wood grill are excellent, and include an Asian-spiced tuna with Caribbean salsa, and a barbecue-spiced flank steak. Christopher's is a popular destination in the summer months; make a reservation to avoid disappointment.

Lobsterman's Wharf. Rte. 96, East Boothbay. ☎ **207/633-3443.** Reservations accepted for parties of 6 or more only. Lunch from $4.50; dinner $13.25–$22.95 (mostly $14–$16). AE, MC, V. Daily 11:30am–midnight. Closed Nov to April. SEAFOOD.

Slightly off the beaten path in East Boothbay, the Lobsterman's Wharf is a comfortable, popular neighborhood bar, complete with pool table. The rarest of pubs, this is a place that's popular with the locals, but also serves up a good meal and knows how to make travelers feel at home. If the weather's cooperative, sit at a picnic table on the dock and admire the views of a spruce-topped peninsula across the Damariscotta River; tables inside are set amid a festive nautical decor. Entrees include a mixed-seafood grill, a barbecue shrimp and ribs platter, grilled swordfish with béarnaise, and fresh lobster offered four different ways.

5 Pemaquid Peninsula

The Pemaquid Peninsula is an irregular, rocky wedge driven deep into the Gulf of Maine. It's much less commercial and trinkety than the Boothbay Peninsula just across the Damariscotta River, and more inviting for off-the-beaten-track exploration. The inland areas are leafy with hardwood trees, and laced with narrow, twisting backroads that are perfect for bicycling. As you near the southern tip where small harbors and coves predominate, the region takes on a more remote, maritime feel. When the surf pounds Pemaquid Point's rugged, rocky shore at the extreme southern tip of the peninsula, this can be one of the most dramatic destinations in Maine.

ESSENTIALS
GETTING THERE

The Pemaquid Peninsula is accessible from the west by turning southward on Route 129/130 in Damariscotta, just off Route 1. (Stay on Route 130 to Pemaquid Point.) From the east, head south on Route 32 just west of Waldoboro.

VISITOR INFORMATION

The **Damariscotta Information Bureau,** P.O. Box 217, Damariscotta, ME 04543 (☎ **207/563-3175**), maintains an information
booth with spotty hours on Business Route 1 just up the hill from
the village (opposite the Baptist Church). It's been open lately
Thursday to Saturday 10am to 4pm, but it's best to call first.

For a free booklet containing information about the area,
write or call the **Damariscotta Region Chamber of Commerce,**
P.O. Box 13, Main Street, Damariscotta, ME 04543 (☎ **207/
563-8340**).

EXPLORING THE PEMAQUID PENINSULA

The Pemaquid Peninsula invites slow driving and frequent stops.
Start out by heading south on Route 129 toward Walpole from the
sleepy head-of-the-harbor village of Damariscotta. Keep an eye on
your left for the austerely handsome **Walpole Meeting House**, one
of three meeting houses built on the peninsula in 1772. (Only two
remain.) It's usually not open to the public, but services are held here
during the summer and the public is welcome.

Just north of the unassuming fishing town of South Bristol on
Route 129, watch for the **Thompson Ice Harvesting Museum**
(☎ **207/644-8551**). During winter's deep freeze (usually in
February), volunteers from around town carve out huge blocks of ice
and relay them to the well-insulated icehouse (a 1990 replica of
the original icehouse) to be packed in sawdust. Summer visitors
can peer into the cool, damp depths and see the glistening blocks
(the harvest is sold to fishermen throughout the summer to ice down
their catch), and learn about the once-common practice of ice
harvesting through photos and other exhibits in a tiny museum.
The grounds are open during daylight hours all year round; the
museum exhibits are open 1pm to 4pm Wednesday, Friday, and
Saturday in July and August. A $1 donation (50¢ for children) is
requested.

About 5 miles north of South Bristol, turn right on Pemaquid
Road, which will take you to Route 130. Along the way look for the
Harrington Meeting House (the other 1772 structure), which is
open to the public on occasional afternoons in July and August. It's
an architectural gem inside, almost painfully austere, with a small
museum of local artifacts on the second floor. Even if it's not open,
stop to wander about the lovely cemetery out back, the final resting
place of many sea captains.

Head south on Route 130 to the village of New Harbor, and look for signs to **Colonial Pemaquid** (☎ **207/677-2423**). Open daily from Memorial Day to Labor Day 9am to 5pm, this state historic site features exhibits on the original 1625 settlement here; archaeological digs take place in the summer. The $1 admission charge (free for children under 12) includes a visit to stout **Fort William Henry,** a 1907 replica of a supposedly impregnable fortress that stood over the river's entrance. (It was not impregnable, as it turned out, with tragic results for the settlement.) Nearby Pemaquid Beach allows for a bracing ocean dip and is a good spot for families.

Pemaquid Point, which is owned by the town, is the place to while away an afternoon (☎ **207/677-2494**). Bring a picnic and a book, and find a spot on the dark, fractured rocks to settle in. The ocean views are superb and the only distractions are the tenacious seagulls, which may take a profound interest in your lunch. While here, be sure to visit the **Fishermen's Museum** (☎ **207/677-2726**) in the handsome lighthouse (open daily 10am to 5pm; Sunday from 11am to 5pm). Informative exhibits depict the whys and wherefores of the local fishing trade, and should answer those questions that invariably arise while watching lobstermen at work just offshore. There's a small fee ($1 over 12, 50¢ seniors) to use the park in summer; admission to the museum is by donation.

Route 32 strikes northwest from New Harbor and it's the most scenic way to leave the peninsula if you plan to continue eastward on Route 1. Along the way look for the sign pointing to the **Rachel Carson Salt Pond Preserve,** a Nature Conservancy property. The noted naturalist Rachel Carson studied these roadside tide pools extensively while researching her 1956 bestseller *The Edge of the Sea,* and today it's still an inviting spot for budding naturalists and experts alike. Pull off your shoes and socks, and wade through the cold waters at low tide looking for starfish, green crabs, periwinkles, and other creatures.

WHERE TO STAY

Bradley Inn. Rte. 130, New Harbor, ME 04554. ☎ **207/677-2105.** Fax 207/677-3367. 14 units (including 1 cottage). TEL. Summer and fall $125–$185 double; winter and spring $95–$150. Rates include full breakfast. AE, MC, V.

The Bradley Inn is located within easy walking or biking distance to Pemaquid Point, but there's plenty of reason to lag behind at the inn. You can wander the neatly landscaped grounds, or enjoy a game of croquet or bocci in the gardens. If the fog's moved in for a spell, settle in for a game of Scrabble at the granite bar in the pub. This circa-1900 inn has been updated in a tasteful Victorian style, which borrows from the elaborate detailing of the era without embracing the whole cluttered sensibility. The rooms are tastefully appointed; the large third-floor rooms—especially #302 and #303—are the best, with high ceilings, lavish furnishings, gas fireplaces, and distant glimpses of John's Bay. Free bikes are available for guest use; two rooms have TVs, and four have gas fireplaces.

Dining: The local seafood served in the inn's restaurant includes grilled tuna, halibut, and salmon, along with more ambitious dishes like lobster cakes and duck breast served with roasted scallops. Entree prices are $18 to $25; the restaurant is open to the public nightly (closed some nights in the off-season) from 6 to 9pm.

Hotel Pemaquid. Rte. 130, Pemaquid Point (mailing address: 3098 Bristol Rd., New Harbor, ME 04554). ☎ **207/677-2312.** 23 units (4 share 2 bathrooms). Peak season $70–$125 double ($55 for shared bathroom); off season $60–$90 ($47 shared bathroom). 2-night minimum stay on weekends. No credit cards.

This 1889 coastal classic isn't directly on the water (it's about a minute's walk away from Pemaquid Point), but has the flavor of an old-time seaside boarding house. It's aggressively old-fashioned (although most guest rooms now have private bathrooms), with narrow hallways and antiques, including a great collection of old radios and phonographs. Some guests are put in the more modern annex next door, which once housed hotel staff.

WHERE TO DINE

Lovely downtown Damariscotta, just off Route 1 en route to the Pemaquid Peninsula from the south, offers a variety of informal spots for a snack or light meal. Many of these are found along the town's compact Main Street, and include the **Riverside Cafe** (☎ 207/536-6611), which specializes in tea, coffee, pastries, and imported carpets; **Breakfast Place and Bakery** (☎ 207/563-5434), which serves breakfast up to closing time at 1pm; and **Paco's Tacos** (☎ 207/563-5335), which offers burritos, tacos, and fajitas, which can be spiced up with selections from their abundant collection of hot sauces.

Shaw's Fish and Lobster Wharf. On the water, New Harbor. ☎ **207/677-2200.** Reservations not accepted. Lobster priced to market (typically $9–$13). MC, V. 11am–9pm mid-June to Labor Day; call for hours during shoulder seasons. Closed mid-Oct to late May. LOBSTER POUND.

Shaw's attracts hordes of tourists, and it's no puzzle to figure out why: It's one of the best-situated lobster pounds, with postcard-perfect views of the working harbor and the boats coming and going through the inlet that connects to the open sea. Stand in line to place your order, then wait for your name to be called. While waiting, you can stake out a seat on either the open deck or the indoor dining room (go for the deck), or order up some appetizers from the raw bar. This is one of the few lobster joints with a full liquor license.

6 Monhegan Island

Brawny, wild, and remote, Monhegan Island is Maine's premier island destination. Visited by Europeans as early as 1497 (although some historians insist that earlier Norsemen carved primitive runes on neighboring Manana Island), the island was first settled by fishermen attracted to the sea's bounty in the offshore waters. Starting in the 1870s and continuing to the present day, noted artists discovered the island and came to stay for a spell. Their roster included Rockwell Kent (the artist most closely associated with the island), George Bellows, Edward Hopper, and Robert Henri. The artists gathered in the kitchen of the lighthouse to chat and drink coffee; it's said that the wife of the lighthouse keeper accumulated a tremendously valuable collection of paintings. Today, Jamie Wyeth, scion of the Wyeth clan, claims the island as his part-time home.

It's not hard to figure why artists have been attracted to the place: There's a mystical quality to it, from the thin light to the startling contrasts of the dark cliffs and the foamy white surf. There's also a remarkable sense of tranquillity to this place, which can only help focus one's inner vision.

If you have the time, I'd strongly recommend an overnight on the island at one of the several hostelries. Day trips are popular and easily arranged, but the island's true character doesn't start to emerge until the last day boat sails away and the quiet, rustic appeal of the island starts to percolate back to the surface.

ESSENTIALS
GETTING THERE

Access to Monhegan Island is via boat from New Harbor, Boothbay Harbor, or Port Clyde. The 70-minute trip from Port Clyde is the favored route among longtime island visitors. The trip from this rugged fishing village is very picturesque as it passes the Marshall Point Lighthouse and a series of spruce-clad islands before setting out on the open sea.

Two boats now make the run to Monhegan from Port Clyde. The *Laura B.* is a doughty work boat (building supplies and boxes

Visiting Port Clyde

Port Clyde's charm lies in the fact that it's still first and foremost a fishing village. While some small-scale tourist enterprises have made their mark on the village, located at the tip of a long finger about 15 miles south of Route 1, it still caters primarily to working fishermen and the ferrymen who keep Monhegan supplied.

Here's a favorite routine for spending a couple of hours in Port Clyde, either while waiting for the ferry or just snooping around. Head to the **Port Clyde General Store** (☎ 207/372-6543) on the waterfront and soak up the cracker-barrel ambience (there's actually a decent selection of wine here, attesting to encroaching upscalism). Order a sandwich to go, then drive to the **Marshall Point Lighthouse Museum** (☎ 207/372-6450; follow the road along the harbor eastward, and bear right to the point). This small lighthouse received a few moments of fame when Forrest Gump turned around here and headed back west during his cross-country walks in the movie, but it also happens to be one of the more peaceful and scenic lighthouses in the state. Carry your lunch around to the far side of the lightkeeper's house and settle on one of the granite benches to watch the fishing boats come and go through the thoroughfare. Afterwards, tour through the small but engaging museum (free; donations encouraged) and learn a bit about the culture of lighthouses on the Maine Coast.

of food are loaded on first; passengers fill in the available niches on the deck and in the small cabin). A newer boat—the faster, passenger-oriented *Elizabeth Ann*—now also makes the run, offering a large heated cabin and more seating. You'll need to leave your car behind, so pack light and wear sturdy shoes. The fare is $25 round trip for adults; $12 for children 2 to 12 years old. Reservations are advised: **Monhegan Boat Line,** P.O. Box 238, Port Clyde, ME 04855 (☎ 207/372-8848; www.monheganboat.com). Parking is available near the dock for an additional $4 per day.

VISITOR INFORMATION

Monhegan Island has no formal visitor's center, but it's small and friendly enough that you can make inquiries of just about anyone you meet on the island pathways. The clerks at the ferry dock in Port Clyde are also quite helpful. Be sure to pick up the inexpensive map of the island's hiking trail at the boat ticket office or at the various shops around the island.

Because wildfire could destroy this breezy island in short order, smoking is prohibited outside of the village.

EXPLORING MONHEGAN

Walking is the chief activity on the island, and it's genuinely surprising how much distance you can cover on these 700 acres (about 1 1/2 miles long and a half-mile wide). The village clusters tightly around the harbor; the rest of the island is mostly wildland, laced with some 17 miles of trails. Much of the island is ringed with high, open bluffs atop fissured cliffs. Pack a picnic lunch and hike the perimeter trail, and plan to spend much of the day just sitting and reading, or enjoying the surf rolling in against the cliffs.

The inland trails are appealing in a far different way. Deep, dark **Cathedral Woods** is mossy and fragrant; sunlight only dimly filters through the evergreens to the forest floor.

Bird watching is a popular activity in the spring and fall. Monhegan Island is on the Atlantic flyway, and a wide variety of birds stop at the island along their migration routes. Swapping stories of the day's sightings is a popular activity at island inns and B&Bs.

The sole attraction on the island is the **Monhegan Museum,** located next to the 1824 lighthouse on a high point above the village. The museum, open from July through September, has a quirky collection of historic artifacts and provides some context for this rugged island's history. Also near the lighthouse is a small and select art museum that opened in 1998, featuring the works of Rockwell Kent and other island artists.

The spectacular view from the grassy slope in front of the lighthouse is the real prize. The vista sweeps across a marsh, past one of the island's most historic hotels, past melancholy Manana Island, and across the sea beyond. Get here early if you want a good seat for the sunset; it seems most visitors to the island congregate here after dinner. (Another popular place is the island's southern tip, where the wreckage of the *D.T. Sheridan,* a coal barge, washed up in 1948.)

If you time it right, you can also visit the studios of Monhegan artists, who still come here in great numbers. Artists often open their workspaces for limited hours, and are happy to have visitors stop by and look at their work, chat, and perhaps buy a canvas or sculpture. Some of the artwork runs along the lines of predictable seascapes and sunsets, but much of it rises above the banal. Look for the bulletin board along the main pathway in the village for a listing of the days and hours the studios are open.

WHERE TO STAY & DINE ON MONHEGAN

Monhegan House. Monhegan Island, ME 04852. ☎ **800/599-7983** or 207/594-7983. 33 units (all with shared bathroom). $85 double. Closed Columbus Day to Memorial Day. AE, DISC, MC, V.

The handsome Monhegan House has been accommodating guests since 1870, and it has the comfortable, worn patina of a venerable lodging house. The accommodations at this four-floor walk-up are austere but comfortable; there are no closets, and everyone uses clean dormitory-style bathrooms. The downstairs lobby with fireplace is a welcome spot to sit and take the fog-induced chill out of your bones (even in August it can be cool). The front deck is a nice place to lounge and keep a close eye on the comings and goings of the village. The restaurant offers three meals a day, with a selection of filling but simple meat and fish dishes, along with vegetarian entrees. Main courses range in price from about $9 to $16.

Trailing Yew. Monhegan Island, ME 04852. ☎ **207/596-0440.** 37 units in 4 buildings (all but 1 share bathrooms). $116 double. Rate includes breakfast, dinner, taxes, and tips. No credit cards. Closed mid-Oct to mid-May. Pets accepted.

At the end of long summer afternoons, guests congregate near the flagpole in front of the main building of this rustic hillside compound. They sit in Adirondack chairs, chat with newfound friends, and, as if at summer camp, wait for the dinner bell to ring. Inside, guests sit around long tables, introduce themselves to their neighbors, then pour an iced tea and wait for the delicious, family-style dinner. (You're given a choice, including vegetarian options, but my advice is to opt for the fresh fish whenever it's available.)

The Trailing Yew, which has been taking in guests since 1929, is a friendly, informal place, popular with hikers and bird watchers (meals are a great time to swap tales of sightings) who tend to make fast friends amid the welcome adversity of Monhegan Island. Guest rooms are eclectic and simply furnished in a pleasantly dated summer-home style; only one of the four guest buildings has electricity (most but not all bathrooms have electricity); guests in rooms without electricity are provided a kerosene lamp and instruction in its use (bring a flashlight just in case).

5

Penobscot Bay

*T*raveling eastward along the Maine Coast, those who pay attention to such things will notice that they're suddenly heading almost due north around Rockland. The culprit behind this geographic quirk is Penobscot Bay, a sizeable bite out of the Maine Coast that forces a lengthy northerly detour to cross the head of the bay where the Penobscot River flows in at Bucksport.

You'll find some of Maine's more pastoral coastal scenery in this area—spectacular offshore islands and high hills rising above the blue bay. Although the mouth of Penobscot Bay is occupied by two large islands, its waters can still churn with vigor when the tides and winds conspire.

Penobscot Bay's western shore gets a heavy stream of tourist traffic, especially along Route 1 through the scenic village of Camden. Nonetheless, this is a good destination to get a taste of the Maine coast. Services for travelers are abundant, although during the peak season a small miracle will be required to find a weekend guest room without a reservation.

1 Rockland & Environs

Few visitors refer to Rockland as "quaint." Located on the southwest edge of Penobscot Bay, Rockland has long been proud of its brick-and-blue-collar waterfront town reputation. Built around the fishing industry, Rockland historically dabbled in tourism on the side. But with the decline of the fisheries and the rise of the tourist economy in Maine, the balance is gradually shifting—Rockland is slowly being colonized by creative restaurateurs and innkeepers and other small-business folks who are painting it with an unaccustomed gloss.

There's a small park on the waterfront from which the fleet of windjammers comes and goes (see "Windjammer Tours," below), but more appealing than Rockland's waterfront is its commercial downtown—basically one long street lined with sophisticated

Penobscot Bay

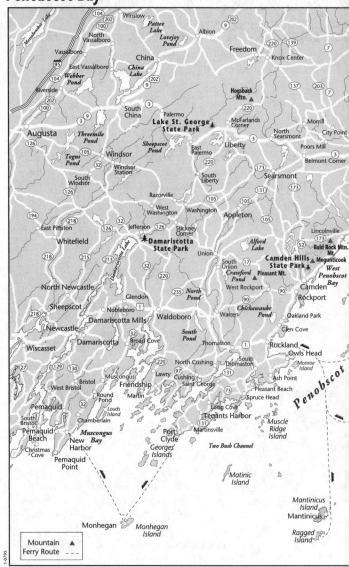

Mountain ▲
Ferry Route ---

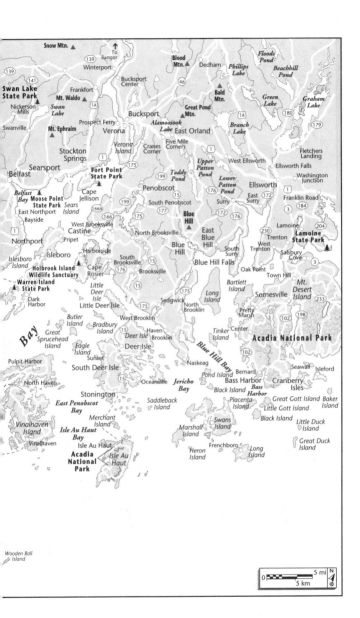

Windjammer Tours

During the long transition from sail to steam, captains of the fancy new steamships belittled the old-fashioned sailing ships as "windjammers." The term stuck, and through a curious metamorphosis the name evolved into a term of adventure and romance.

Today windjammer vacations combine adventure with limited creature comforts—sort of like lodging at a backcountry cabin on the water. Guests typically bunk in small two-person cabins, which usually offer cold running water and a porthole to let in fresh air, but not much else. (You'll conclude this isn't like a stay at a fancy inn when you see that one ship's brochure boasts "standing headroom in all 15 passenger cabins," and another crows that all cabins "are at least six feet by eight feet.")

Maine is the capital of windjammer cruising in the United States, and the two most active Maine harbors are Rockland and Camden on Penobscot Bay. Cruises last from 3 days to a week, during which these handsome, creaky vessels poke around the tidal inlets and small coves that ring the beautiful bay. It's a superb way to see Maine's coast as it's been explored historically—from the water looking in. The price runs around $100 per day per person, with modest discounts early and late in the season.

Cruises vary from ship to ship and from week to week, depending on the inclinations of the captains and the vagaries of the mercurial Maine weather. The "standard" cruise often features a stop at one or more of the myriad spruce-studded Maine islands (perhaps with a lobster bake on shore), hearty breakfasts enjoyed sitting at tables below decks (or perched cross-legged on the sunny deck), and a palpable sense of maritime history as these handsome

historic brick architecture. If it's picturesque harbor towns you're seeking, head to Camden, Rockport, Port Clyde, or Stonington. But Rockland makes a great base for exploring this beautiful coastal region, especially if you have a low tolerance for trinkets and tourist hordes.

ESSENTIALS
GETTING THERE

Route 1 passes directly through Rockland. Rockland's tiny airport is served by **Colgan Air** (☎ **800/272-5488** or 207/596-7604) with daily flights from Boston and Bar Harbor.

ships scud through frothy waters. A windjammer vacation demands you use all your senses, to smell the tang of the salt air, to hear the rhythmic creaking of the masts in the evening, and to feel the frigid ocean waters as you leap in for a bracing dip.

About a dozen windjammers offer cruises in the Penobscot Bay region during the summer season (many migrate south to the Caribbean for the winter). The ships vary widely in size and vintage, and guest accommodations range from cramped and rustic to reasonably spacious and well-appointed. Ideally, you'll have a chance to look at a couple of ships to find one that suits you before signing up. If that's not practical, call ahead to the **Maine Windjammer Association** (☎ 800/807-9463) and request a packet of brochures, which allow comparison shopping. If you're hoping for a last-minute cruise, stop by the chamber of commerce office at the Rockland waterfront (see "Essentials," above) and ask if any berths are available.

All the commercial windjammers are Coast Guard–inspected and each have unique charms. Among the ships worthy of note are the historic (1900) 40-passenger *Victory Chimes* (☎ 800/745-5651 or 207/594-0755), the largest passenger schooner in the country at 132 feet. The *Stephen Taber* (☎ 800/999-7352) is the oldest documented sailing vessel (1871) in continuous service in the nation; it carries 22 passengers. The 31-passenger *Angelique* (☎ 800/282-9989 or 207/236-8873), built in 1980 and based in Camden, may be the most handsome ship in the fleet with its dark sails and sleek lines; it features two below-deck hot-water showers.

VISITOR INFORMATION

The **Rockland/Thomaston Area Chamber of Commerce,** P.O. Box 508, Rockland, ME 04841 (☎ 800/562-2529 or 207/596-0376; e-mail rtacc@midcoast.com), staffs an information desk at Harbor Park. It's open daily 9am to 5pm Memorial Day to Labor Day, Monday to Saturday until Columbus Day, and weekdays only the rest of the year.

SPECIAL EVENTS

The **Maine Lobster Festival** (☎ 800/562-2529 or 207/596-0376) takes place at Harbor Park the first weekend in August (plus the preceding Thursday and Friday). Entertainers and vendors of all sorts of Maine products—especially the local crustacean—fill the waterfront parking lot and attract thousands of festival-goers who enjoy this pleasant event with a sort of buttery bonhomie. The event includes the Maine Sea Goddess Coronation Pageant.

TWO FINE MUSEUMS

Farnsworth Museum. 352 Main St., Rockland. ☎ **207/596-6457.** $9 adults, $8 seniors, $5 students 18 and older, free for ages 17 and under (prices discounted $1 in winter). MC, V. Summer 9am–5pm daily; winter Tues–Sat 10am–5pm, Sun 1–5pm.

Rockland, for all its rough edges, has long and historic ties to the arts. Noted sculptor Louise Nevelson grew up in Rockland, and in 1935 philanthropist Lucy Farnsworth bequeathed a fortune large enough to establish Rockland's Farnsworth Museum, which has since become one of the most respected art museums in New England. Located in the middle of downtown Rockland, the Farnsworth has a superb collection of paintings and sculptures by renowned American artists with a connection to Maine. This includes not only Nevelson and three generations of Wyeths (N.C., Andrew, and Jamie), but Rockwell Kent, Childe Hassam, and Maurice Prendergast. The exhibit halls are modern, spacious, and well-designed, and the shows professionally prepared. In June 1998, the museum expanded with the opening of the Farnsworth Center for the Wyeth Family in Maine, housed in the former Pratt Memorial Methodist Church nearby. The center houses Andrew and Betsy Wyeth's personal collection of Maine-related art.

The Farnsworth also owns two other buildings open to the public. The Farnsworth Homestead, located behind the museum, offers a glimpse into the life of prosperous coastal Victorians. And a 25-minute drive away in the village of Cushing is the Olson House, perhaps Maine's most famous home, immortalized in Andrew Wyeth's popular painting, "Christina's World." Ask at the museum for directions and information.

Owls Head Transportation Museum. Rte. 73, Owls Head. ☎ **207/594-4418.** www.ohtm.org. $6 adults, $5 seniors, $4 children 5–12, families $16. Apr–Oct daily 10am–5pm; Nov–Mar daily 10am–4pm.

You don't have to be a car or plane nut to enjoy a day at the Owls Head Transportation Museum, located 3 miles south of Rockland on Route 73. Founded in 1974, the museum has an extraordinary collection of cars, motorcycles, bicycles, and planes, nicely displayed in a tidy, hangarlike building at the edge of the Knox County

Airport. Look for the beautiful early Harley Davidson, and the sleek Rolls Royce Phantom dating from 1929. The museum is also a popular destination for hobbyists and tinkerers, who drive and fly their classic vehicles here for frequent weekend rallies in the summer. Call ahead to ask about special events.

WHERE TO STAY

Capt. Lindsey House Inn. 5 Lindsey St., Rockland, ME 04841. ☎ **800/ 523-2145** or 207/596-7950. Fax 207/596-2758. 9 units. A/C TV TEL. Peak season $95–$170 double, including continental breakfast and afternoon tea; Columbus Day to Memorial Day $65–$110. AE, DISC, MC, V.

The three-story, brick Capt. Lindsey House is located just a couple minutes' walk from the Farnsworth Museum. Guests enter through a doorway a few steps off Rockland's Main Street, and walk into an opulent first-floor common area done up in rich tones, handsome dark-wood paneling, and a well-selected mix of antique and contemporary furniture. The upstairs rooms are also tastefully decorated in a contemporary country style, generally with bold, modern colors and patterns applied to traditional design. Even the smaller rooms like #4 are well done (this in a sort of steamship nouveau style); the rooms on the third floor all feature yellow pine floors and antique oriental carpets. All rooms have nice details, like handmade bedspreads, hair dryers, down comforters, and bathrobes. Reliable pub fare is available at The Waterworks next door (see "Where to Dine," below), which is owned by the same people who own the inn.

LimeRock Inn. 96 Limerock St., Rockland, ME 04841. ☎ **800/546-3762** or 207/594-2257. 8 units. $100–$180 double. Rates include breakfast. MC, V.

This beautiful Queen Anne–style inn is located on a quiet side street just 2 blocks from Rockland's Main Street. Originally built for U.S. Rep. Charles Littlefield in 1890, it served as a doctor's residence from 1950 to 1994, after which it was renovated into a gracious inn. The innkeepers have done a fine job converting what could be a gloomy manse into one of the region's better choices for overnight accommodation. Excellent attention has been paid to detail throughout, from the choice of country Victorian furniture to the Egyptian cotton bedsheets. All the guest rooms are welcoming, but among the best choices is the Island Cottage Room, a bright and airy chamber wonderfully converted from an old shed and featuring a private deck and Jacuzzi. If it's elegance you're looking for, choose the Grand Manan Room, which has a four-poster bed the size of the Astrodome, a fireplace, and a double Jacuzzi.

Samoset Resort. 220 Warrenton St., Rockport, ME 04856. ☎ **800/ 341-1650** outside Maine, or 207/594-2511. www.samoset.com. E-mail: info@samoset.com. 150 hotel units, plus 72 town-house units. A/C TV TEL. Early July to Labor Day $215–$265 double, fall $155–$215, winter $99–$140, May to mid-June $135–$180, mid-June to early July $175–$245. Ask about packages that include meals. AE, CB, DC, DISC, MC, V.

The Samoset is a wonderful destination for those wishing for a self-contained resort that offers contemporary styling, ocean views, and lots of golf. This modern resort is located on 230 spacious acres at the mouth of Rockland Harbor. Both the hotel and town houses are surrounded by the handsome golf course, yielding wonderful views to the ocean from most every window on the property. The lobby is constructed of massive recovered timbers (from an old industrial grain silo in Portland), and the guest rooms all have balconies or terraces. Golfers love the place—it's been called Pebble Beach East— and families will always find plenty of activities for kids (there's a summer camp during high season at $40 additional per day, and baby-sitting the rest of the year). The resort also has the best sunset stroll in the state—you can ramble across the golf course to a breakwater that leads out to a picturesque lighthouse. The one downside: For the high price charged, the staff may be less polished than you would expect.

Dining/Diversions: The Samoset offers four dining areas, including the Clubhouse Grill, Breakwater Cafe, and the Poolhouse. The centerpiece restaurant is Marcel's, where specialty dinners are prepared tableside. These include lobster flambé, rack of lamb for two, and steak Diane. Prices for main courses at Marcel's range from $14 to $29.

Amenities: 18-hole golf course, indoor and outdoor pools, modern health club, hot tub, sauna, indoor video golf driving range, four tennis courts (night play), jogging and walking trails, children's program, business center, gift shops, courtesy car, valet parking, massage, free newspaper, concierge, laundry service and dry cleaning, baby-sitting, safe, and safe deposit boxes.

WHERE TO DINE

✪ **Cafe Miranda.** 15 Oak St., Rockland. ☎ **207/594-2034.** Reservations strongly encouraged. Main courses $9.50–$14.50. DISC, MC, V. Open Tues– Sat 5:30–9:30pm. WORLD CUISINE.

Hidden away on a side street, this tiny, contemporary restaurant features a huge menu with big flavors. The fare draws liberally from cuisines from around the globe ("It's comfort food for whatever planet you're from," says owner-chef Kerry Altiero), and given its wide-ranging culinary inclinations it comes as something of a surprise just how well-prepared everything is. The chargrilled pork and shrimp cakes served with a ginger-lime-coconut sauce are superb. Other creative entrees include barbecue pork ribs with a smoked jalapeño sauce, and Indian almond chicken. (The menu changes often, so don't set your heart on these dishes in particular.) Cafe Miranda provides some of the best value for the buck of any restaurant in Maine. There's also an outdoor seating area, called Karmen's Patio, that serves light fare in season from 11:30am onward.

Cod End Fish House. Next to the Town Dock, Tenants Harbor. ☎ **207/ 372-6782.** Reservations not accepted. Lunch entrees $1.25–$7.75; dinner $6.95–$13.95. DISC, MC, V. Daily July–Aug 7am–9pm; call for off-season hours; closed Nov–May. LOBSTER POUND.

Part of the great allure of Cod End is its hidden and scenic location—it's as though you've stumbled upon a great secret. Situated between the Town Landing and the East Wind Inn, Cod End is a classic lobster joint with fine views of tranquil Tenants Harbor. You walk through the cozy market (where you can buy fish or lobster to go), then place your order at the outdoor shack. While waiting to be called you can check out the dock or just sit and relax in the sun. (If it's raining, there's limited seating inside the market.) Lobsters are the draw here, naturally, but there's plenty else to choose from, including chowders, stews, linguini with seafood, rolls (like clam or haddock), and a whole menu geared to younger tastes (including a $1.50 peanut butter and jelly). As with most lobster pounds, the less complicated and less sophisticated your meal is here, the better the odds you'll be satisfied.

The Waterworks. Lindsey St., Rockland. ☎ **207/596-7950.** Reservations accepted only for parties of 6 or more. Lunch $3.25–$7.95, dinner $7.50–$14. AE, DISC, MC, V. Daily 11am–midnight (open at noon Sun). PUB FARE.

Set a half-block off Rockland's Main Street in the brick garage of the former waterworks (naturally), The Waterworks has the informal, comfortable feel of a brewpub without the brewery. The restaurant is divided into two spacious sections, both with tall windows through which the sun streams during long, lazy afternoons. Turn left when you enter for the pub side, which is open and airy, with wooden floors and long tables (eight beers are on tap). To the right is the dining room, which is also open but carpeted and quieter (no smoking). Seated on captain's chairs around wooden tables, diners can select from a selection of creative pub fare, including *gado gado* (an Indonesian dish of vegetables with a spicy peanut sauce), fish and chips, and a schooner stew ("*really* thick and decadent," promises the waitress) with lobster, sherry, and cream. The winter menu tends to favor "comfort food" (so billed) that includes roast turkey, pork loin, and meat loaf. The prices are reasonable, the atmosphere inviting.

2 Camden

For many, Camden is quintessential coastal Maine. Set at the foot of the wooded Camden Hills on a picturesque harbor that no Hollywood movie set could improve, the affluent village of Camden has attracted the gentry of the Eastern Seaboard for more than a century. The elaborate mansions of the moneyed set still dominate the shady side streets (many have been converted into bed-and-breakfasts), and Camden is possessed of a grace and sophistication that eludes many other coastal towns.

Nor have Camden's charms gone unnoticed. The village and the surrounding communities have become a haven for retired U.S. Foreign Service and CIA personnel, and it has attracted its share of summering corporate bigwigs, including former Apple Computer C.E.O. John Sculley. (The area seems to be the destination of choice for retired computer executives: the family of Thomas Watson, the former C.E.O. of IBM, has a summer compound just offshore at North Haven.) More recently, the town received an economic injection from the rapid growth of MBNA, a national credit card company that has restored historic buildings and contributed significantly to Camden's current prosperity. It also explains the high number of clean-cut young men in white shirts and ties you may see in and around town.

The best way to enjoy Camden is to park your car as soon as you can—which may mean driving a block or two off Route 1. The village is of a perfect scale to reconnoiter on foot, which allows a leisurely browse of boutiques and galleries. Don't miss the hidden town park (look behind the library), which was designed by the landscape firm of Frederick Law Olmsted, the nation's most lauded landscape architect.

On the downside: All this attention and Camden's growing appeal to bus tours is having a deleterious impact, say some longtime visitors. The merchandise at the shops seems to be trending downward to appeal to a lower denominator, and the constant summer congestion distracts somewhat from the village's inherent charm. If you don't come expecting a pristine and undiscovered village, you're likely to enjoy the place all the more.

ESSENTIALS
GETTING THERE

Camden is on Route 1. Coming from the south, travelers can shave a few minutes off their trip by turning left on Route 90 six miles past Waldoboro, bypassing Rockland. The most traffic-free route from southern Maine is to Augusta via the Maine Turnpike, then via Route 17 to Route 90 to Route 1.

VISITOR INFORMATION

The **Rockport-Camden-Lincolnville Chamber of Commerce,** P.O. Box 919, Camden, ME 04843 (☎ **800/223-5459** or 207/236-4404), dispenses helpful information from its center at the Public Landing in Camden. The chamber is open year-round weekdays from 9am to 5pm and Saturdays 10am to 5pm. In summer, it's also open Sundays 10am to 4pm.

EXPLORING CAMDEN

Camden Hills State Park (☎ **207/236-3109**) is about a mile north of the village center on Route 1. This 6,500-acre park features an oceanside picnic area, camping at 112 sites, a winding toll road up 800-foot Mt. Battie with spectacular views from the summit, and a variety of well-marked hiking trails. The day use fee is $2 adults, 50¢ for children 5 to 11.

One fairly easy **hike** I'd recommend strongly is an ascent to the ledges of **Mount Megunticook,** preferably early in the morning before the crowds have amassed and when the mist still lingers in the valleys. Leave from near the campground and follow the well-maintained trail to these open ledges, which requires only about 30 to 45 minutes' exertion. Spectacular, almost improbable, views of the harbor await, as well as glimpses inland to the gentle vales. Depending on your stamina and desires, you can continue on the park's trail network to Mount Battie, or into the less-trammeled woodlands on the east side of the Camden Hills.

For a view from the water back to the hills, **Maine Sports Outfitters** (☎ **800/722-0826** or 207/236-8797) offers **sea-kayaking** tours of Camden's scenic harbor. The standard tour lasts 2 hours and costs $30, and takes paddlers out to Curtis Island at the outer edge of the harbor. This beginners' tour is offered three or four times daily, and is an easy, delightful way to get a taste of the area's maritime culture. Longer trips and instruction are also available. The outfitter's main shop, on Route 1 in Rockport, has a good selection of outdoor gear and is worth a stop for outdoor enthusiasts gearing up for local adventures or heading on to Acadia.

The Camden area also lends itself well to exploring by **bike.** A pleasant loop of several miles takes you from Camden into the village of Rockport, which has an equally scenic harbor and less tourist traffic. Bike rentals ($15 per day, $9 half-day), maps, and local riding advice is available at **Brown Dog Bikes** (☎ **207/236-6664**) at 53 Chestnut St. in Camden.

Try this bike route: Take Bayview Street from the center of town out along the bay, passing by opulent seaside estates. The road soon narrows and becomes quiet and pastoral, overarched with leafy trees. At the stop sign just past the cemetery, turn left and follow this route into Rockport. Along the way, you'll pass the local version of "landscape with cows": in this case, a small herd of belted Galloways. In Rockport, snoop around the historic harbor, then stop by **Maine Coast Artists** (Russell Avenue; ☎ **207/236-2875**), a stately gallery that offers rotating exhibits of local painters, sculptors, and craftsmen. Admission is free.

Come winter, there's **skiing** at the **Camden Snow Bowl** (☎ **207/236-3438**) just outside of town on Hosmer's Pond Road. This small, family-oriented ski area has a handful of trails and a modest vertical drop of 950 feet, but it has good views of the open ocean and an exhilarating toboggan run. Toboggans are available for rent, or you can bring your own.

What to do in the evening? Besides quaffing a lager or ale at the Sea Dog Brewing Co. (see "Where to Dine," below), you might take in a foreign or art film at the **Bayview Street Cinema** (10 Bayview St.; ☎ **207/236-8722**), on the second floor a short stroll from Camden's main intersection. The theater boasts a superb sound system, and there's an excellent lineup of frequently changing films throughout the year.

WHERE TO STAY

Camden vies with Kennebunkport and Manchester, Vt., for the title of bed-and-breakfast capital of New England. They're everywhere. Route 1 north of the village center—locally called High Street—is a virtual bed-and-breakfast alley, with many handsome homes converted to lodging. Others are tucked on side streets. One note of caution: High Street is thick with cars and RVs during the summer months, and you may find the steady hum of traffic diminishes the small-town charm of the establishments that flank this otherwise stately, shady road. Restless sleepers should request rooms at the rear of the property.

Despite the preponderance of B&Bs, the total number of guest rooms is fairly limited, and during peak season lodging is tight. It's best to reserve well in advance. You might also try **Camden Accommodations and Reservations** (☎ **800/236-1920**), which offers assistance with everything from booking rooms at local B&Bs to finding cottages for seasonal rental.

If the inns and B&Bs listed below are booked up or too pricey, a handful of area motels and hotels may be able to accommodate you. South of the village center are the **Cedar Crest Motel** (115 Elm St.; ☎ **800/422-4964** or 207/236-4839), a handsome compound with coffee shop and a trolley connection downtown; and longtime mainstay **Towne Motel** (68 Elm St.; ☎ **207/236-3377**), which is within walking distance of the village. Also right in town, just across the footbridge, is the modern if generic **Best Western Camden Riverhouse Hotel** (11 Tannery Lane; ☎ **800/755-7483** or 207/236-0500), which has an indoor pool and fitness center.

Finally, there's camping at **Camden Hills State Park** (see "Exploring Camden," above).

The Belmont. 6 Belmont St., Camden, ME 04843. ☎ **800/238-8053** or 207/236-8053. E-mail: foodeez@midcoast.com. 6 units. 2-night minimum stay: $260–$360 double includes 2 nights' accommodation, 1 dinner, 2 breakfasts. MC, V. Closed Oct–Apr. From south on Rte. 1: Turn right at first stop sign in Camden; continue straight for 1 block; inn is on the left. From north: after passing through town on Rte. 1, turn left at blinking yellow light; continue straight for 1 block; inn is on the left.

The Belmont is in a handsome, shingle-style 1890s home set in a quiet residential neighborhood of unassuming homes. Step inside, though, and you're instantly transported to a world of elegance and repose. The Belmont has a strong sense of understated style throughout—think of it as the mid-19th century as interpreted by the 1940s. All the guest rooms are nicely furnished with eclectic antiques and have polished wood floors; the simple style lets this house of clean, uncluttered lines speak for itself. Downstairs there's an elegant common room with a fireplace alcove and two built-in benches; adjacent is a cozy bar.

Dining: The dining room seats about 50 (open to the public), with diners choosing from a plum-carpeted main room, or a sun porch with wood floors and contemporary sculpture. The meals are among Camden's finest, with the menu changing weekly. A typical meal around foliage time might include lobster risotto, or veal loin with wild mushrooms. The dining room is open daily except

Wednesday from 6 to 9pm; entrees are $16 to $28; reservations are encouraged.

Cedarholm Cottages. Rte. 1, Lincolnville Beach, ME 04849. ☎ **207/ 236-3886.** 6 units (includes 3 two-bedroom cottages). TV. Oceanfront cottages $225–$300 double (up to 4 guests); oceanview cottages $80–$135 double. Rates include breakfast. 2-night minimum stay in some cottages. MC, V.

Cedarholm began as a small cottage court with just four cottages north of Camden along Route 1 that was operated more or less as a hobby. Then Joyce and Barry Jobson—the daughter of the former owners and her husband—took over in 1995, built a road down to the 460 feet of dramatic shoreline along a cobblestone beach, and constructed two modern, steeply gabled cedar cottages, each with two bedrooms. These are uniquely wonderful places, with great detailing like pocket doors, cobblestone fireplaces, handsome kitchenettes, and Jacuzzis. They're easily among the region's most quiet and peaceful retreats. Guests staying up the hill in the smaller, older (but recently updated) cottages can still wander down to the shore and lounge on the common deck overlooking the upper reaches of Penobscot Bay. It's noisier up above, where it's closer to Route 1, and the prices reflect that.

Inn at Sunrise Point. Rte. 1 (P.O. Box 1344), Camden, ME 04843. ☎ **800/ 435-6278** or 207/236-7716. Fax 207/236-0820. 7 units (4 in cottages). TV TEL. $175–$225 rooms; $250–$350 cottages. Rates include a full breakfast. AE, MC, V. Closed Nov to late May. Children not accepted.

This peaceful, private sanctuary 4 miles north of Camden Harbor seems a world apart from the bustling town. The service is crisp and helpful, and the setting can't be beat. Situated on the edge of Penobscot Bay down a long, tree-lined gravel road, the Inn at Sunrise Point consists of a cluster of contemporary but classic shingled buildings set amid a nicely landscaped yard full of birches. The predominant sounds here are of birds and waves lapping at the cobblestone shore. A granite bench and Adirondack chairs are arrayed on the front lawn to allow guests to enjoy the bay view; breakfasts are served in a sunny conservatory. The guest rooms are spacious and comfortable and full of amenities, including VCRs (for those rainy days) and individual heat controls. The cottages are at the deluxe end of the scale, and all feature double Jacuzzis, fireplaces, wet bars, and private decks.

✪ **Maine Stay.** 22 High St., Camden, ME 04843. ☎ **207/236-9636.** www.mainestay.com. E-mail: mainstay@midcoast.com. 8 units. $100–$140 double. Rates include breakfast. Discounts available during the off-season. AE, MC, V. Children over 10 accepted.

This is Camden's premier bed-and-breakfast. Located in a home dating to 1802 but expanded in Greek Revival style in 1840, the Maine Stay is a classic slate-roofed New England homestead set in a shady yard within walking distance of both downtown and Camden Hills State Park. The eight guest rooms on three floors all have ceiling fans and are distinctively furnished with antiques and special decorative touches. My favorite: the downstairs Carriage House Room, which is away from the buzz of traffic on Route 1 and boasts its own stone patio.

The downstairs common rooms are perfect for unwinding, and the country kitchen is open to guests at all times. Hikers can set out on trails right from the yard into the Camden Hills. Perhaps the most memorable part of a stay here, however, will be the hospitality of the three hosts—Peter Smith, his wife Donny, and her twin sister, Diana Robson. The trio is genuinely interested in their guests' well-being, and they offer dozens of day trip suggestions, which are conveniently printed out from the inn's computer for guests to take with them.

✪ **Norumbega.** 61 High St., Camden, ME 04843. ☎ **207/236-4646.** Fax 207/236-0824. www.norumbegainn.com. 13 units. TV TEL. July to mid-Oct $155–$450 double; mid-May to June and late Oct, $125–375; Nov to mid-May $99–$295. All rates include full breakfast and evening refreshments. 2-night minimum stay on weekends and holidays. AE, DISC, MC, V. Children over 7 accepted.

You'll have no problem finding Norumbega. Just head north of the village and look for travelers pulled over taking photos of this Victorian-era stone castle overlooking the bay. The 1886 structure is both wonderfully eccentric and finely built, full of wondrous curves and angles throughout. There's extravagant carved-oak woodwork in the lobby, and a stunning oak and mahogany inlaid floor. The downstairs billiards room is the place to pretend you're a 19th-century railroad baron.

The guest rooms have been meticulously restored and furnished with antiques. Five of the rooms have fireplaces, and the three "garden-level rooms" (they're off the downstairs billiards room) have private decks. Two rooms rank among the finest and most unique in this country—the Library Suite, housed in the original two-story library with interior balcony, and the sprawling Penthouse with its superlative views. The inn is big enough to ensure privacy, but also intimate enough to get to know the other guests—mingling often occurs at breakfast, at the optional evening social hour, and in the afternoon, when the inn puts out its famous fresh-baked cookies.

The Spouter Inn. Rte. 1 (P.O. Box 270), Linconville Beach, ME 04849. ☎ **207/789-5171.** E-mail: terrapin@tidewater.net. 7 units. A/C. Summer and early fall $75–$165; off season $65–$135. Rates include full breakfast. 2-night minimum stay on all reservations Memorial Day through Labor Day. AE, DISC, MC, V. Children 8 and over accepted.

The Spouter Inn is located about 5 miles north of Camden in Lincolnville Beach, just far enough from of the congestion to imbue your stay with a slower pace. This elegantly restored 1832 farmhouse with seven guest rooms is also within walking distance of everything there is to do in Lincolnville, which is blessedly little. You can loll around on the beach across the road, enjoy a lobster at a nearby restaurant, take a kayak trip (ask the innkeepers), or rent a bike from the inn ($15 per day) and catch the ferry to the gracious island of Isleboro for an afternoon adventure.

The inn itself is in a handsome pale-yellow farmhouse, and the rooms are furnished in a light country style. All the rooms have at least glimpses of the water; some have full-blown views and decks. Note that the inn is on Route 1, which can be noisy at times. Among the best rooms are the two suites, both of which feature Jacuzzi, decks, and plenty of space. The guest rooms in a 1995 addition blend well inside and out with the rest of the inn, and all have great bay views and wood-burning fireplaces. Televisions are available by request.

Sunrise Motor Court. Rte. 1 (R.R.3, Box 545), Lincolnville Beach, ME 04849. ☎ **207/236-3191.** 13 cottages (all shower only). TV. Peak season $49–$69 double; off season $41–$61. Rates include continental breakfast. Located 4.5 miles north of Camden. DISC, MC, V. Closed Columbus Day to Memorial Day weekend.

The Sunrise Motor Court, about 10 minutes north of Camden on Route 1, is a vintage 1950s-era establishment with excellent views of Penobscot Bay—though these views are regrettably across noisy Route 1 and through a latticework of utility lines. Yet, the place boasts a time-worn comfort, like a favorite old sweatshirt. The 13 cozy cottages are arrayed along a grassy hillside at the edge of a wood, and each is simply furnished with a bed and maybe a few chairs. All boast small decks and outdoor chairs, allowing guests to relax and enjoy the serene view. (Note that two cabins behind the manager's house lack a view.) This is a good bet for budget-conscious travelers who want to explore the Camden area, yet not spend a small fortune doing so.

Whitehall Inn. 52 High St., Camden, ME 04843. ☎ **800/789-6565** or 207/
236-3391. www.whitehall-inn.com. E-mail: stay@whitehall-inn.com. 50 units
(8 units share 4 baths). July to late Oct $140–$180 double, including breakfast and dinner ($110–$150 with breakfast only). Call for off-season rates.
AE, MC, V. Closed late Oct to late May.

The Whitehall is a venerable Camden establishment. Set at the edge
of town on Route 1 in a structure that dates to 1834, this three-story
inn has a striking architectural integrity with its columns, gables, and
long roofline. This is the place you think of when you think of the
classic New England summer inn. The only downside is its location
on Route 1—the traffic noise tends to persist through the evening,
then start up early in the morning. (Ask for a room away from the
road.)

Inside, the antique furnishings—including the handsome Seth
Thomas clock, Oriental carpets, and cane-seated rockers on the front
porch—are impeccably well cared for. Guest rooms are simple but
appealing; only some rooms have phones. The Whitehall also occupies a minor footnote in the annals of American literature—a young
local poet recited her poems here for guests in 1912, stunning the
audience with her eloquence. Her name? Edna St. Vincent Millay.

Dining: The Whitehall's dining room boasts a slightly faded
glory and service that occasionally limps along, but remains a good
destination for reliable fare like veal with sweet vermouth, sage, and
prosciutto; or baked haddock stuffed with Maine shrimp. (Entrees
$15 to $18.) And, of course, there's always lobster.

Amenities: Tennis court, tour desk, nature trails, conference
rooms, baby-sitting, guest safe, afternoon tea.

WHERE TO DINE

For sandwiches and snacks to go, head to the atmospheric **Boynton-
McKay** grocery shop, located smack in the middle of Camden at
30 Main St. (☎ **207/236-2465**). A landmark pharmacy and soda
fountain since 1893, the shop today offers upscale snacks, basic gro-
ceries, and a to-go menu that includes bagels, spicy Thai noodles,
and a variety of wraps. This is the spot to stock up on the goods for
a picnic at Camden Hills State Park. Note the original tin ceiling
and tile floors.

Cork Bistro. 37 Bayview St. ☎ **207/230-0533.** Reservations recommended.
Main courses $14–$23. AE, DISC, MC, V. Summer daily 5:30–9pm; off-season
closed Sun–Tues. WINE BAR.

This unassuming second-floor eatery attracts those hoping to decompress by means of sipping good wines and nibbling cheeses a notch above the ordinary. (A cheese board with four cheeses is $15.) The place also manages to serve some very fine meals along the way. The menu changes with availability of ingredients, but might include crab cakes served on spinach, or pork chops with a cognac-peppercorn sauce.

Marriner's Restaurant. 35 Main St., Camden. ☎ **207/236-2647.** Breakfast $2.75–$5.95; sandwiches $4.25–$6.95. MC, V. Open Mon–Sat 6am–3pm; Sun 6am–2pm. Hours limited during the off-season. LUNCHEONETTE.

"The last local luncheonette" is how Marriner's sums itself up, along with the legend "Down Home, Down East, No Ferns, No Quiche." As you might guess, this is a fairly small and simple affair, done up in a not-very-subtle nautical theme with pine booths and vinyl seats, some of which are held together with duct tape. This is the place for early risers to get a quick start on the day—those getting here later in summer will likely find themselves facing a wait. As you might expect, there's nothing on the menu to wow gourmands, but it's decent, reliable fare served up with plenty of local color.

Peter Ott's. 16 Bayview St., Camden. ☎ **207/236-4032.** Reservations not accepted. Main courses $13.95–$22.95. MC, V. Peak season daily 5:30–9:30pm; call for off-season hours. AMERICAN.

Peter Ott's has attracted a steady stream of satisfied local customers and repeat-visitor yachtsmen since it opened smack in the middle of Camden in 1974. While it poses as a steak house with its simple wooden tables and chairs and its manly meat dishes (like charbroiled Black Angus with mushrooms and onions, and sirloin steak dijonaise), it's grown beyond that to satisfy more diverse tastes. In fact, the restaurant offers some of the better prepared seafood in town, including a pan-blackened seafood sampler and grilled salmon served with a lemon-caper sauce. Be sure to leave room for the specialty coffees and famous deserts, like the lemon-almond crumb tart.

Sea Dog Brewing Co. 43 Mechanic St., Camden. ☎ **207/236-6863.** Reservations not accepted. Main courses $6.95–$12.95. AE, DISC, MC, V. Daily 11:30am–9pm (kitchen closed 2–5pm in off-season). Located at Knox Mill 1 block west of Elm St. PUB FARE.

The Sea Dog Brewing Co. is one of a handful of brewpubs that have found quick acceptance in Maine, and it makes a reasonable destination for quick and reliable fare such as nachos or hamburgers. It won't set your taste buds to dancing, but it will satisfy basic cravings. Located in the ground floor of an old woolen mill that's been renovated by MBNA, a national credit card company, the restaurant has a pleasing, comfortable brewpub atmosphere with its booths, handsome bar, and views through tall windows of the old millrace. And the beers are consistently excellent, although some suffer from a regrettable cuteness in naming (for example, Old Gollywobbler Brown Ale).

The Waterfront. Bayview St. on Camden Harbor. ☎ **207/236-3747.** Reservations not accepted. Main courses, lunch $6.95–$13.95; dinner $12.95–$22.95. AE, MC, V. Daily 11:30am–2:30pm and 5–9pm. SEAFOOD.

The Waterfont disproves the restaurant rule of thumb that "the better the view, the worse the food." Here you can watch multimillion-dollar yachts and handsome windjammers come and go as you eat (angle for a harborside seat on the deck), yet still be impressed by the food. The house specialty is fresh seafood of all kinds, and the proprietors sell a lot of it. Both lunch and dinner menus offer an enterprising mix of old favorites and creative originals. On the old-favorites side are fried clams, crab cakes, boiled lobster, and a fisherman's platter piled with fried seafood. On the more adventurous side, you'll find black sesame shrimp salad (served on noodles with a Thai vinaigrette), or a seafood linguini with shrimp, mussels, squid, and carmelized balsamic onions. More earthbound fare for non-seafood eaters includes burgers, pitas, and strip steaks.

3   Belfast to Bucksport

The northerly stretch of Penobscot Bay is rich in history, especially maritime history. In the mid-19th century, Belfast and Searsport produced more than their share of ships, along with the captains to pilot them on trading ventures around the globe. In 1856 alone, 24 ships of more than 1,000 tons were launched from Belfast. The now-sleepy village of Searsport once had 17 active shipyards, which turned out some 200 ships over the years.

When shipbuilding died out, the Belfast area was sustained by a thriving poultry industry. Alas, that too declined as the industry moved south. In recent decades, the area has attracted artisans of various stripes, who sell their wares at various shops. Tourists tend to pass through the region quickly, en route from the tourist enclave of Camden to the tourist enclave of Bar Harbor. It's worth slowing down for.

ESSENTIALS
GETTING THERE
Route 1 connects Belfast, Searsport, and Bucksport.

VISITOR IMFORMATION
The **Belfast Area Chamber of Commerce,** P.O. Box 58, Belfast,
ME 04915 (☎ **207/338-5900**), staffs an information booth near
the waterfront that's open 10am to 6pm daily in summer. For
information on accommodations and activities further up the
bay, try the **Bucksport Bay Area Chamber of Commerce,**
P.O. Box 1880, Bucksport, ME 04416 (☎ **207/469-6818**).

EXPLORING THE REGION
Splendid historic homes may be viewed by veering off Route 1 and
approaching downtown Belfast via High Street (look for the first
"Downtown Belfast" sign). The **Primrose Hill District** along High
Street was the most fashionable place for prosperous merchants to
settle during the early and mid-19th century, and their stately homes
reflect an era when stature was equal to both the size of one's home
and the care one took in designing and embellishing it. Downtown
Belfast also has some superb examples of historic brick commercial
architecture, including the elaborate High Victorian Gothic–style
building on Main Street that formerly housed the Belfast National
Bank.

Near Belfast's small waterfront park you can take a diverting
excursion on the scenic **Belfast and Moosehead Lake Railroad**
(☎ **800/392-5500** or 207/948-5500). The railroad was chartered
in 1867 and financed primarily by the town; in fact, until 1991, the
B&ML railroad was the only railroad in the nation owned by a
municipality. The rail line was purchased by entrepreneurs, who
have spruced it up considerably. In 1995, the company acquired 11
vintage railcars from Sweden, including a 1913 steam locomotive,
and opened a new station in Unity, near the end of the 33-mile-long
line. (The steam train departs from Unity; a diesel train runs from
Belfast.)

The 2-hour tour offers a wonderful glimpse of inland Maine and
its thick forests and rich farmland. (The train also edges along
Passagassawakeag River, a name which provokes considerable amusement in all but the most melancholy of children.) The train features
a dining car, and entertainment in the form of a hold-up by some
unsavory desperados known as the Waldo Station Gang. An

optional tour of northern Penobscot Bay on a handsome riverboat can also be packaged with the train excursions.

The train runs daily from mid-May to the end of October. The fare is $14 for adults, $10 for teens, $7 for children 2 to 12.

If you'd like to explore the Passagassawakeag by water, call Harvey Schiller at **Belfast Water Tours** (☎ 207/382-6204), or just show up at the Belfast City Pier boat ramp. With a great deal of charm and even more enthusiasm, Harvey will take provide paddle instruction and take you out for a guided tour. Trips last 1½ hours and cost $16 per adult, $14 for kids aged 10 to 15, and are available from 9am to 6pm daily (except in inclement weather) from July to Labor Day. Call for off-season hours and group rates.

At the northern tip of Penobscot Bay, the Penobscot River squeezes through a dramatic gorge near Verona Island, which Route 1 spans on an attractive suspension bridge. This easily defended pinch in the river was perceived to be of strategic importance in the 1840s, when solid and imposing **Fort Knox** was constructed. While it was never attacked, the fort was manned during the Civil and Spanish-American wars, and today is run as a state park (☎ 207/469-7719). It's an impressive edifice to explore, with graceful granite staircases and subterranean chambers that produce wonderful echoes. Admission is $2 for adults, 50¢ for children under 12.

Across the river in the paper mill town of Bucksport is **Northeast Historic Film** (☎ 800/639-1636 or 207/469-0924), an organization founded in 1986 dedicated to preserving and showing early films related to New England. In 1992 the group bought Bucksport's Alamo Theatre, which was built in 1916 and closed (after a showing of "Godzilla") in 1956. Renovations are coming along gradually, but films are regularly shown at the bare-bones theater. Call to ask about ongoing film series. Visitors can also stop by the store at the front of the Alamo to browse through available videos and other items.

THE SEAFARING LIFE

✪ **Penobscot Marine Museum.** Church St. at Rte. 1, Searsport. ☎ 207/548-2529. Adults $6, seniors $5, children 7–15 $2, family $14. Open daily Memorial Day through mid-Oct 10am–5pm (open noon on Sun).

The Penobscot Marine Museum is one of the best small museums in New England. Housed in a cluster of eight historic buildings atop a gentle rise in tiny downtown Searsport, the museum does a deft job in educating visitors about the vitality of the local shipbuilding industry, the essential role of international trade to daily life in the 19th century, and the hazards of life at sea. The exhibits are uncommonly well organized, and wandering from building to building induces a keen sense of wonderment at the vast enterprise that was Maine's maritime trade.

Among the more intriguing exhibits are a wide selection of dramatic marine paintings (including one stunning rendition of whaling in the Arctic), black and white photographs of many of the 286 weathered sea captains who once called Searsport home, exceptional photographs of a 1902 voyage to Argentina, and an early home decorated in the style of sea captain, complete with lacquered furniture and accessories hauled back from trade missions to the Orient. Throughout, the curators have done a fine job both educating and entertaining visitors. It's well worth the price if you're at all interested in Maine's rich culture of the sea.

WHERE TO STAY

✪ **The White House.** 1 Church St., Belfast. ☎ **888/290-1901** or 207/338-1901. Fax 207/338-5161. www.mainebb.com. E-mail: whitehouse@mainebb.com. 6 units (1 with private hall bathroom). TEL. Peak season $75–$125 double including full breakfast. Call for off-season rates. MC, V, DISC.

This lovely B&B in a stately Greek Revival home is just a 10-minute walk from downtown. Originally built as a sea captain's home in the 1840s and topped with a striking eight-sided cupola, the James P. White House has recently been refurnished, painted, wallpapered, and redecorated—and the results are spectacular. Downstairs, guests have the run of a library, an elegant parlor area, and a dining room where the hearty breakfasts are served. Against a backdrop of ornate ceiling medallions, marble fireplaces, and intricate moldings, glass cases display glass and china collections and elegant furniture poses gracefully. Bedrooms are as fine, but feel cozier. Each features a private bathroom with hair dryer and gorgeously soft Egyptian cotton towels and robes. One of the nicest (and also the priciest) is the Belfast Bay with fireplace, whirlpool, and water views. Two of the less expensive rooms are suites with room for three.

WHERE TO DINE

Darby's. 155 High St., Belfast. ☎ **207/338-2339.** Reservations suggested after 7pm. Main courses, lunch $3.95–$8.95; dinner $5.75–$13.95. DISC, MC. V. Daily 11am–10pm. AMERICAN/ECLECTIC.

This dark, often smoky restaurant centers around a handsome bar and offers filling fare that goes the extra culinary mile. Located in a

Civil War–era pub with attractive stamped tin ceilings and a beautiful back bar with Corinthian columns, Darby's is a popular local hangout that boasts a comfortable, neighborhoody feel. Order up a Maine beer or single-malt whisky while you peruse the menu, which is surprisingly creative. Darby's offers most pub favorites, like burgers and Cajun chicken on a bulkie, but also features imports like pad Thai, enchilada verde, and Thai chicken salad. Try the Bombay chicken curry or the pecan haddock with Cuban mojita sauce. And if you like the artwork on the wall, ask about it. It's probably done by a local artist, and it's probably for sale.

The Rhumb Line. 200 East Maine St. (Rte. 1), Searsport. ☎ **207/548-2600.** Reservations suggested. Main courses $16–$21. MC, V. Peak season 6–9pm daily, call for off-season hours. NEW AMERICAN.

At press time, The Rhumb Line had just completed its first season, and judging from the quality of the food, this is a place that's around to stay. Most of the ingredients are locally grown—the tomatoes and basil in a mozzarella salad had just been picked from the garden in back of the inn, and the tender horseradish-crusted salmon was farmed in nearby Ellsworth. If you're not in the mood to start with one of the fresh salads, try the wonderful smoky-flavored lentil and chicken soup. As far as entrees go, avoid the cream-laden pasta dishes, which can be on the heavy side, and stick with the sirloin served with garlic mashed potatoes or one of the fish dishes.

Young's Lobster Pound. Mitchell Ave., East Belfast. ☎ **207/338-1160.** Reservations not accepted. Main courses $5.95–$16.95. MC, V. Daily 7am–8pm (until 7pm in shoulder seasons). Closed Dec through Mar. From Belfast, take Rte. 1 eastward across the river; look for signs. LOBSTER POUND.

When you first pull down to the dirt parking lot and come upon the unlovely red corrugated industrial building on the waterfront, you'll think: "There must be some mistake." This doesn't look much like a restaurant at all. But head inside the hangar-sized door, and you'll find a counter where folks will take your order amid the long, green lobster tanks loudly gushing water. After placing your order, scope out the operation and then stake out a seat. You can eat upstairs, where picnic tables are arrayed in an open, barnlike area, or out on the deck, with views across the river to Belfast. This is a place to get good and messy without embarrassment. While you can order from a variety of dishes, the smart money sticks to the shore dinners and steers away from the stews, which are a bit bland and thin.

6

Blue Hill Peninsula

*T*he Blue Hill Peninsula is a backroads paradise. If you're of a mind to get lost on country lanes that suddenly dead-end at the sea or inexplicably start to loop back on themselves, this is the place. In contrast to the western shores of Penobscot Bay, the Blue Hill Peninsula attracts few tourists, and has more of a lost-in-time character. The roads are hilly, winding, and narrow, passing through leafy forests, along venerable saltwater farms, and touching on the edge of an azure inlet here or there. By and large it's overlooked by the majority of Maine's tourists, especially those who like their itineraries well-structured and their destinations clear and simple.

1 Castine & Environs

Castine gets my vote for the most gracious village in Maine. It's not so much the stunningly handsome, meticulously maintained mid-19th-century homes that fill the side streets. Nor is it the location on a quiet peninsula, 16 miles south of tourist-clotted Route 1. No, what lends Castine most of its charm are the splendid, towering elm trees, which still overarch many of the village streets. Before Dutch elm disease ravaged the nation's tree-lined streets, much of America once looked like this, and it's easy to slip into a debilitating nostalgia for this most graceful tree, even if you're too young to remember the America of the elms. Through perseverance and a measure of luck, Castine has managed to keep several hundred elms alive, and it's worth the drive here for this alone.

For American history buffs, Castine offers more than trees. This outpost served as a strategic town in various battles among British, Dutch, French, and feisty colonials in the centuries following its settlement in 1613. It was occupied by each of those groups at some point, and historical personages like Miles Standish and Paul Revere passed through during one epoch or another. (Paul Revere, in one of his less heroic feats, was involved in the horrendous British routing of 44 American ships during the Revolution, a setback that followed a failed colonial attack on British-held Castine.) The town has a dignified, aristocratic bearing, and it somehow seems appropriate that Tory-dominated Castine welcomed the British with open arms during the Revolution.

An excellent brief history of Castine by Elizabeth J. Duff is published in brochure form by the Castine Merchant's Association. The brochure, which also includes a walking tour of Castine, is entitled "Welcome to Castine" and is available at several shops in town, at the town hall, and at most state information centers.

Castine is also home to the **Maine Maritime Academy** (☎ **207/ 326-8545**), which trains sailors for the rigors of life at sea with the merchant marine. The campus is on the western edge of the village, and the *S.S. Maine,* the hulking gray training ship, is often docked in Castine, threatening to overwhelm the village with its sheer size. Free half-hour tours of the ship are offered in summer (assuming the ship is in port) from 10am to noon, and 1 to 4pm.

One final note: Castine is most likely to appeal to those who can entertain themselves. It's a peaceful place to sit and read, or take an afternoon walk. If it's outlet shopping or cute boutiques you're looking for, you're better off moving on. "This is not Bar Harbor," one local innkeeper noted dryly.

ESSENTIALS
GETTING THERE

Castine is located 16 miles south of Route 1. Turn south on Route 175 in Orland (east of Bucksport) and follow this to Route 166, which winds its way to Castine. Route 166A offers an alternate route along Penobscot Bay.

VISITOR INFORMATION

Castine lacks a formal information center, but the clerk at the **Town Office** (☎ **207/326-4502**) is often helpful with local questions.

EXPLORING CASTINE

One of the town's more intriguing attractions is the **Wilson Museum** (☎ **207/326-8753** during the day, or between 5 and 9pm call the curator at ☎ 207/326-8545) on Perkins Street, an attractive and quirky anthropological museum constructed in 1921. This small museum contains the collections of John Howard Wilson, an archaeologist and collector of prehistoric artifacts from around the globe. His gleanings are neatly arranged in a staid, classical arrangement of the sort that proliferated in the late-19th and early-20th centuries. The museum is open 2 to 5pm from the end of May to the end of September daily except Monday; admission is free.

Next door is the **John Perkins House,** Castine's oldest home. It was occupied by the British during the Revolution and the War of 1812, and a tour features demonstrations of old-fashioned cooking techniques. The Perkins House is open 2 to 5pm July and August on Wednesday and Sunday only. Admission is $2.

Also worth exploring is **Dyce's Head Light** at the extreme western end of Battle Avenue. While the 1828 light itself is not open to the public, it's well worth scrambling down the trail to the rocky shoreline along the Penobscot River just beneath the lighthouse. A small sign indicates the start of the public trail.

A TOUR OF CAPE ROSIER

Across the Bagaduce River from Castine is **Cape Rosier,** one of Maine's better-kept secrets. The bad news is, to reach the cape you need to backtrack to Route 175, head south toward Deer Isle, then follow Route 176 to the turnoff to Cape Rosier—about 18 miles of driving to cross 1 mile of water. As a dead-end peninsula, there's no through traffic and roads suddenly turn to dirt in sections. The cape still has a wild, unkempt flavor with salty views of Penobscot Bay; it's not hard to imagine that you're back in the Maine of the 1940s.

A loop of 15 miles or so around the cape starting on Goose Falls Road is suitable by mountain bike or as a leisurely car trip. The views are uncommonly beautiful, with a mix of blueberry barrens, boreal forest, farmsteads, summer estate houses, and coves dotted with yachts and lobster boats. There's virtually no commercial development of any sort. It's no accident that Helen and Scott Nearing, the late back-to-the-land gurus and authors of *Living the Good Life,* chose to settle here when Vermont became too developed for their tastes. A number of Nearing acolytes continue to live on Cape Rosier.

If the weather's agreeable, stop for a walk on the state-owned **Holbrook Island Sanctuary,** a 1,200-acre preserve laced with trails and abandoned roads. The sanctuary is located at the northern end of the cape (look for signs). Among the choices: The Backshore Trail passes along open meadows to the shoreline; the Summit Trail is all mossy, mushroomy, and medieval, with teasing glimpses of the water from the top.

WHERE TO STAY

Castine Harbor Lodge. Perkins St. (P.O. Box 215), Castine, ME 04421. ☎ **207/326-4861.** 9 units (2 share 1 bathroom; 1 with private hall bathroom). $75–$115 double. Rates include continental breakfast. DC, DISC, MC, V. Closed Nov–May. Pets accepted.

This is a wonderful spot for families. Housed in a grand 1893 mansion (the only inn on the water in Castine), it's run with an informal good cheer that kids simply eat up. The main parlor is dominated by a Ping-Pong table, and there's also Scrabble and Nintendo. The front porch has views that extend across the bay to the Camden Hills, and is one of the best places to unwind in all of Maine. The spacious rooms are eclectically furnished, with some antiques and some modern furnishings. Though this is a great family choice, anyone who prefers well-worn comfort to high-end elegance will enjoy staying here. Last word: The bathrooms have the best views of any in the state.

Castine Inn. Main St. (P.O. Box 41), Castine, ME 04421. ☎ **207/326-4365.** Fax 207/326-4570. www.castineinn.com. E-mail: relax@castineinn.com. 20 units. $85–$135 double. Rates include full breakfast. 2-night minimum stay in July and Aug. MC, V. Closed mid-Dec to May. Children over 7 accepted.

The Castine Inn is a Maine Coast rarity—a hotel that was originally built as a hotel (not as a residence), in this case in 1898. This handsome cream-colored village inn, designed in an eclectic Georgian-Federal revival style, has a fine front porch and attractive gardens. Inside, the lobby takes its cue from the 1940s, with wingback chairs and love seats, and a fireplace in the parlor. There's also an intimate, dark lounge decked out in rich green hues, reminiscent of an Irish pub. The guest rooms on the two upper floors are attractively if unevenly furnished in Early American style—the innkeepers are revamping the rooms one by one to an even gloss, even adding luxe touches. Until they're all renovated, it may be wise to view the available rooms before you sign in.

Dining: The elegant dining room serves up some of the best fare in town. Chef/owner Tom Gutow served a stint at Bouley in New York, and isn't timid in experimenting with local meats and produce. The menu changes nightly with ingredients varying by the season, but you might expect to find dishes such as lobster with wild mushrooms, leeks, corn, and a tarragon sauce; or veal sweetbreads spiced with cloves and served with a soy-honey glaze. Entrees range from $17 to $24.

Pentagöet Inn. Main St. (P.O. Box 4), Castine, ME 04421. ☎ **800/845-1701** or 207/326-8616. Fax 207/326-9382. E-mail: pentagoet@hypernet.com. 16 units (2 with private hallway baths). $99–$129 double, including buffet breakfast. 2-night minimum stay in peak season. MC, V. Closed 3rd week of Oct through early May. Pets accepted by reservation. Children 12 and over accepted.

Here's the big activity at the Pentagöet: Sit on the wraparound front porch on cane-seated rockers and watch the slow-paced activity on

Main Street. That's not likely to be overly appealing to those looking for a fast-paced vacation, but it's the perfect salve for someone seeking respite from urban life. This quirky yellow and green 1894 structure with its prominent turret is tastefully furnished downstairs with hardwood floors, oval braided rugs, and a woodstove. It's comfortable without being overly elegant, professional without being chilly, personal without being overly intimate. High tea is served to guests every afternoon, as are cocktails and canapés in the evening.

The rooms on the upper two floors of the main house are furnished eclectically, with a mix of antiques and old collectibles. The five guest rooms in the adjacent Perkins Street building—a more austere Federal-era house—are furnished simply and feature painted floors. There's no air-conditioning, but all rooms have ceiling or window fans.

WHERE TO DINE

The best dinner in town is indisputably at the Castine Inn (see above). For lunch or more informal dinner fare, try the following.

Dennett's Wharf. Sea St. (next to the Town Dock). ☎ **207/326-9045.** Reservations recommended in summer and for parties of 6 or more. Lunch $5.50–$17.95, dinner $8.95–$17.95. Daily 11am–midnight. Closed mid-Oct to Apr 30. PUB FARE.

Located in a soaring waterfront sail loft with dollar bills tacked all over the high ceiling, Dennett's Wharf offers upscale bar food amid a lively setting leavened with a good selection of microbrews. If the weather's decent, there's outside dining under a bright yellow awning with great harbor views. Look for grilled sandwiches, roll-ups, and salads at lunch; dinner includes lobster, stir-fry, and steak teriyaki. And how did all those bills get on the ceiling? Ask your server. It will cost you exactly $1 to find out.

2 Deer Isle

Deer Isle is well off the beaten path, but worth the long detour off Route 1 if your tastes run to pastoral countryside with a nautical edge. Loopy, winding roads cross through forest and farmland, and travelers are rewarded with sudden glimpses of the sun-dappled ocean and mint-green coves. An occasional settlement crops up now and again.

Deer Isle doesn't cater exclusively to tourists, as many coastal regions do. It's still occupied by fifth-generation fishermen, farmers, longtime rusticators, and artists who prize their seclusion.

The village of Deer Isle has a handful of inns and galleries, but its primary focus is to serve locals and summer residents, not transients. The village of Stonington, on the southern tip, is a rough-hewn sea town. Despite serious incursions the past 5 years by galleries and enterprises dependent on seasonal tourism, it remains dominated in spirit by fishermen and the occasional quarry worker.

ESSENTIALS
GETTING THERE

Deer Isle is accessible via several winding country roads from Route 1. Coming from the west, head south on Route 175 off Route 1 in Orland, then connect to Route 15 to Deer Isle. From the east, head south on Route 172 to Blue Hill, where you can pick up Route 15. Deer Isle is connected to the mainland via a high, narrow, and graceful suspension bridge, built in 1938, which can be somewhat harrowing to cross in high winds.

VISITOR INFORMATION

The **Deer Isle-Stonington Chamber of Commerce** (☎ **207/ 348-6124**) staffs a seasonal information booth just beyond the bridge on Little Deer Isle. The booth is open daily in summer from 10am to 4pm, depending on volunteer availability.

EXPLORING DEER ISLE

Deer Isle, with its network of narrow roads to nowhere, is ideal for perfunctory rambling. It's a pleasure to explore by car, and is also inviting to travel by bike, although hasty and careening fishermen in pickups can make this unnerving at times. Especially tranquil is the narrow road between Deer Isle and Sunshine to the east. Plan to stop and explore the rocky coves and inlets along the way. To get here, head toward Stonington on Route 15. Just south of the village of Deer Isle, turn east toward Stinson Neck and continue along this scenic byway for about 10 miles over bridges and causeways.

Along this road, watch for the **Haystack Mountain School of Crafts** (☎ **207/348-2306**). The campus of this respected summer crafts school is stunning. Designed in the early 1960s by Edward Larrabee Barnes, the campus is set on a steep hillside overlooking the cerulean waters of Jericho Bay. Barnes cleverly managed to play up the views while respecting the delicate landscape by building a series of small buildings on pilings that seem to float above the earth. The classrooms and studios are linked by boardwalks, many of which are connected to a wide central staircase, ending at the "Flag Deck," a sort of open-air commons just above the shoreline.

The buildings and classrooms are closed to the public, but summer visitors are welcome to walk to the Flag Deck and stroll the nature trail adjacent to the campus. There's also one public tour weekly on Wednesday at 1pm, during which you can catch glimpses of the studios. Donations are appreciated. Call for further information.

Stonington, at the very southern tip of Deer Isle, consists of one commercial street that wraps along the harbor's edge. While bed-and-breakfasts and boutiques have made some inroads here, it's still mostly a rough-and-tumble waterfront town with strong links to the sea, and you're likely to observe lots of activity in the harbor as lobstermen come and go. If you hear industrial sounds emanating from just offshore, that's probably the stone quarry on Crotch Island, which has been supplying architectural granite to builders nationwide for more than a century.

You can learn more about the stone industry at the **Deer Isle Granite Museum** on Main Street (☎ **207/367-6331**). The museum features some historical artifacts from the quarry's golden years, but the real draw is a working diorama (8 by 15 feet) of Crotch Island as it would have appeared around 1900. It features a little railroad, little boats, and little cranes moving little stones around. Kids under 10 years old find it endlessly fascinating. The museum is open from late May through August daily 10am to 5pm. (Sunday it opens at 1pm.) Donations are requested.

While wandering the town, be sure to note the doll house–sized model of the town next to Eagull Antiques on East Main Street in Stonington. This quirky collection of 15 miniature buildings—the tallest is the church at about 5 feet—was originally displayed outside the home of the creator, Everett Knowlton. It's now owned by the city and on public display.

A DAY TRIP TO ISLE AU HAUT

Rocky and remote Isle au Haut offers the most unique hiking and camping experience in northern New England. This 6 × 3–mile island, 6 miles south of Stonington, was originally named Ille Haut—or High Island—in 1604 by French explorer Samuel de Champlain. The name and its pronunciation evolved—today, it's generally pronounced "aisle-a-ho"—but the island itself has remained steadfastly unchanged over the centuries.

About half of the island is owned by the National Park Service and maintained as an outpost of Acadia National Park (see chapter 7). A 60-passenger mail boat makes a stop in the morning and late afternoon at Duck Harbor, allowing for a solid day of hiking while still returning to Stonington by nightfall. At Duck Harbor, the National Park Service also maintains a cluster of five Adirondack-style lean-tos, which are available for overnight camping. (Advance reservations are essential. Contact **Acadia National Park,** Bar Harbor, ME 04609, or call ☎ **207/288-3338.**)

A network of superb hiking trails radiates from Duck Harbor. Be sure to ascend the island's highest point, 543-foot Duck Harbor Mountain, for exceptional views of the Camden Hills to the west and Mount Desert Island to the east. Nor should you miss the Cliff or Western Head trails, which track along high, rocky bluffs and coastal outcroppings capped with damp, tangled fog forests of spruce. The trails periodically descend to cobblestone coves, which issue forth a deep rumble with every incoming wave. A hand pump near Duck Harbor provides drinking water, but be sure to bring food and other refreshments for hiking.

The other half of the island is privately owned, some of it by fishermen who can trace their island ancestry back 3 centuries, and some by summer rusticators, whose forebears discovered the bucolic splendor of Isle au Haut in the 1880s. The summer population of the island is about 300, with some 50 die-hards remaining year-round. The mail boat also stops at the small harborside village, which has a few old homes, a handsome church, and a tiny schoolhouse, post office, and store. Day-trippers will be better served ferrying straight to Duck Harbor.

The mail boat (☎ **207/367-5193** or 207/367-6516) to Isle au Haut leaves from the pier at the end of Sea Breeze Avenue in Stonington. From mid-June to mid-September, the *Miss Lizzie* departs for the village of Isle au Haut daily at 7 and 11:30am, and 4:30pm; the *Mink* departs for Duck Harbor daily at 10am and 4:30pm. (It makes limited trips to Isle au Haut the remainder of the year.) The round-trip boat fare is $24 for adults to either the village or Duck Harbor. Children under 12 are $10. Reservations are not accepted; it's best to arrive about a half hour before departure.

WHERE TO STAY

✪ **Goose Cove Lodge.** Goose Cove Rd. (P.O. Box 40), Sunset, ME 04683. ☎ **207/348-2508.** Fax 207/348-2624. 25 units. Open mid-May to mid-Oct; July and August 2-night minimum stay (1 week minimum in cottages). Low-season rates $98–$185 double including full breakfast; high season $160–$286 double including breakfast and dinner. MC, V.

Goose Cove Lodge, a rustic compound adjacent to a nature preserve on a remote coastal point, is a superb destination for families and lovers of the outdoors. Exploring the grounds offers an adventure

Sea Kayaking & Camping Along "Merchant's Row"

Peer southward from Stonington and you'll see dozens of spruce-studded islands between here and the dark, foreboding ridges of Isle au Haut. These islands, ringed with salmon-pink granite, are collectively called Merchant's Row, and they're invariably ranked by experienced coastal boaters as among the most beautiful in the state. Because of these exceptional islands, Stonington is among Maine's most popular destinations for sea kayaking. Many of the islands are open to day visitors and overnight camping, and one of the Nature Conservancy islands even hosts a flock of sheep. Experienced kayakers should contact the **Maine Island Trail Association** (☎ **207/761-8225**) for more information about paddling here; several of the islands are open only to association members. Aspiring kayakers who lack seafaring experience should sign up for a guided trip. No outfitter is currently based in Stonington (they've come and gone in the past, so it can't hurt to ask around), but several Maine-based outfitters lead multiday camping trips to Merchant's Row and Isle au Haut. Contact **Maine Island Kayak Co.** (☎ 207/766-2373), **Maine Sports Outfitters** (☎ 207/236-8797), or **The Phoenix Centre** (☎ 207/374-2113).

every day. You can hike out at low tide to salty Barred Island, or take a guided nature hike on any of five trails. You can mess around in boats in the cove (the inn has kayaks and canoes), or borrow one of the inn's bikes for an excursion. And after dinner there's astronomy. When fog or rain puts a damper on things, curl up with a book in front of a fireplace. (Twenty of the rooms offer fireplaces or Franklin stoves.) Two new (1997) architecturally designed modern cottages sleep six, and are available through the winter. My favorites? Elm and Linnea, cozy cabins tucked privately in the woods on a rise overlooking the beach.

Dining: Meals here are excellent—far above what anyone would sensibly expect to find at the end of remote dirt road. Each evening begins with a cocktail hour at 5:30 in the lodge, followed by dinner. The maple-floored dining room wraps in a semicircle around the living room, and guests dine while enjoying views of the cove and distant islands, swapping information on the day's adventures (guests are typically seated family style with other guests). There's always a vegetarian option at dinner, along with one or two other entrees, like beef tenderloin with a pepper crust with horseradish spaetzle, or salmon with wild mushroom couscous and white truffle essence. The dining room is open to the public; come by for lunch on the deck, or for dinner if space permits (reservations are essential; fixed price $33, Sunday $25).

Oakland House/Shore Oaks. Herrick Rd., Brooksville, ME 04617. ☎ **800/ 359-7352** or 207/359-8521. www.acadia.net/oaklandhouse. 10 inn rooms, 15 cottages. (3 inn units share 1 bathroom.) Inn: summer $146–$190 double including breakfast and dinner; off-season $75–$115 double including breakfast. Cottages: $1,195–$1,573 double per week including breakfast and dinner. MC, V. 2-night minimum stay for inn on weekends. Closed mid-Oct to early May. No children in inn. Pets accepted in some cottages; $9 additional per day.

On the mainland just north of the bridge to Deer Isle, Oakland House is a classic summer resort that's been in the same family since the American Revolution. For the past half-century, the main draw has been the cluster of shoreside cottages, tucked among 50 acres and a half mile of shorefront with superlative water views. These are usually set aside for weeklong stays (Saturday to Saturday). The cottages are of varying vintages but most have fireplaces with wood delivered daily. For shorter visits, a grand 1907 shorefront home has been converted to a 10-room inn called Shore Oaks; innkeepers Jim and Sally Littlefield have been making it over in recent years in an Arts and Crafts–inspired style. In peak season, guests take their meals at the old 1889 hotel, with tasty options such as broiled swordfish, roast pork loin, or chicken and lobster verdicchio.

Activities on the grounds include hiking trails (be sure to ask about the Blue Dot Trail to Lookout Rock), dubbing around in rowboats, swimming in the frigid salt water, hiking to a (warmer) lake for swimming (shared with a kids' summer camp), and watching videos in the barn after dinner. Boat charters and a weekly lobster bake are summer options.

Pilgrim's Inn. Main St., Deer Isle, ME 04627. ☎ **207/348-6615.** www.pilgrimsinn.com. 13 units, 2 cottages (3 rms with shared bathroom). $160–$225 double, including breakfast and dinner. MC, V. Closed mid-Oct to mid-May (cottages open year-round). Children 10 and over accepted.

Set just off a town road and between an open bay and a millpond, the Pilgrim's Inn is a historic, handsomely renovated inn in a lovely setting. This four-story, gambrel-roofed structure will especially appeal to those intrigued by early American history. (Two nearby cottages are also available.) The interior of this 1793 inn is tastefully decorated in a style that's informed by early Americana, but not beholden to historic authenticity. The guest rooms are well-appointed with antiques and painted in muted colonial colors; especially intriguing are the rooms on the top floor with impressive diagonal beams. Activities here include strolling around the village, using the inn's bikes to explore (free), and setting off on scenic drives. Ask about bird-watching weekends in May.

Dining: Dinners start with cocktails and hors d'oeuvres in the common room at 6pm, followed by one seating at 7pm in the adjacent barn dining room. Only one entree is served, but the creative American cuisine is not likely to disappoint. Dinner is open to the public by reservation at a fixed price of $29.50.

WHERE TO DINE

For fine dining, check out Goose Cove Lodge or the Pilgrim's Inn (see "Where to Stay," above).

Fisherman's Friend. School St., Stonington. ☎ **207/367-2442.** Reservations recommended in peak season and on weekends. Sandwiches $2–$6; dinner entrees $7–$15. No credit cards. Daily 11am–9pm. Closed Nov–Mar. Up the hill from the harbor past the Opera House. SEAFOOD.

This lively, boisterous restaurant is usually as crowded as it is unpretentious. Simple tables fill a large room, and long-experienced waitresses hustle about to keep up with demand. The menu typically includes a wide range of fresh fish, prepared in a variety of styles. (The locals seem to like it fried.) If you find yourself beset with a fierce craving for lobster, do yourself a favor and bypass the same-old-same-old boiled lobster with bib. Instead, head straight for the lobster stew, which is brimming with meaty lobster chunks and is flavored perfectly. It's not a light meal, but travelers often find themselves making excuses to linger in Stonington the next day to indulge in yet another hearty bowl. Bring your own wine, beer, or cocktails.

3 Blue Hill

Blue Hill, pop. 1,900, is fairly easy to find—just look for gently domed, eponymous Blue Hill Mountain, which lords it over the northern end of Blue Hill Bay. Set between the mountain and the bay is the quiet and historic town of Blue Hill, clustering along the bay shore and a burbling stream. There's never much going on, and that seems to be exactly what attracts summer visitors back time and again—and may explain why two excellent bookstores are located here. Many old-money families maintain retreats set along the water or in the rolling inland hills, but Blue Hill offers several excellent choices for lodging if you're not well endowed with local relatives. It's a good destination for an escape, and will especially appeal to those deft at crafting their own entertainment.

When in the area, be sure to tune into the **local community radio station,** WERU, at 89.9 FM. It started some years back in the chicken coop. The idea was to spread around good music and provocative ideas. It's become slicker and more professional in recent years, but still maintains a pleasantly homespun flavor.

ESSENTIALS
GETTING THERE

Blue Hill is southeast of Ellsworth on Route 172. Coming from the west, head south on Route 15 five miles east of Bucksport (it's well marked with road signs).

VISITOR INFORMATION

Blue Hill does not maintain a visitor information booth. Look for the "Blue Hill, Maine" brochure and map at state information centers, or write the **Blue Hill Chamber of Commerce,** P.O. Box 520, Blue Hill, ME 04614. The staffs at area inns and restaurants are usually able to answer any questions you might have.

SPECIAL EVENTS

The **Blue Hill Fair** (☎ **207/374-9976** for information) is a traditional country fair with livestock competitions, displays of vegetables, and carnival rides. The fair takes place at the fairgrounds northwest of the village on Route 172 on Labor Day weekend.

EXPLORING BLUE HILL

A good way to start your exploration is to ascend the open summit of **Blue Hill Mountain,** from which you'll have superb views of the azure bay and the rocky balds on nearby Mount Desert Island. To reach the trailhead from the village, drive north on Route 172, then turn west (left) on Mountain Road at the Blue Hill Fairgrounds. Drive 0.8 mile and look for the well-marked trail. An ascent of the "mountain" (elevation 940 feet) is about a mile, and requires about 45 minutes. Bring a picnic lunch and enjoy the vistas.

Blue Hill has traditionally attracted more than its fair share of artists, especially, it seems, potters. On Union Street, stop by **Rowantrees Pottery** (☎ **207/374-5535**), which has been a Blue Hill institution for more than half a century. The shop was founded by Adelaide Pearson, who was inspired to pursue pottery as a career after a conversation with Mahatma Gandhi in India. Rowantrees' pottery is richly hued, and the potters who've succeeded Pearson continue to use glazes made from local resources.

Another inventive shop, the family-run **Rackliffe Pottery** on Ellsworth Road (☎ **207/374-2297**), uses native clay and lead-free glazes, and the bowls, vases, and plates produced here have a lustrous, silky feel. Visitors are welcome to watch the potters at work. Both shops are open year-round.

Even if you've never been given to swooning over historic homes, you owe yourself a visit to the intriguing **Parson Fisher House** (contact Blue Hill Tea & Tobacco, ☎ **207/374-2161**, for information), located on routes 176 and 15 a half mile west of the village. Parson Fisher, Blue Hill's first permanent minister, was a rustic version of a Renaissance man when he settled here in 1796. Educated at Harvard, Fisher not only delivered sermons in six different languages, including Aramaic, but was a writer, painter, and minor inventor whose energy was evidently boundless. On a tour of his home, which he built in 1814, you can see a clock with wooden works he made, and samples of the books he not only wrote but published and bound himself.

Parson Fisher House is open from July to mid-September daily except Sunday from 2 to 5pm. Admission is $2 for adults; children under 12 are admitted free.

If you're an ardent antique hunter or bibliophile, it's worth your while to detour to the **Big Chicken Barn** (☎ **207/667-7308**) on Route 1 between Ellsworth and Bucksport (it's 9 miles west of Ellsworth and 11 miles east of Bucksport). This sprawling antique mall and bookstore is of nearly shopping mall proportions—more than 21,000 square feet of stuff in an old poultry barn. The first floor has a mix of very old and recent-old antiques in dozens of stalls maintained by local dealers. Most things for sale are of a size you'll tote away in a bag, although there's some furniture as well. Upstairs are some 90,000 books, which are unusually well organized by category. There's a huge selection of old magazines in plastic sleeves that are great for browsing through on rainy afternoons. It's open daily in summer 9am to 7pm.

WHERE TO STAY

Blue Hill Farm Country Inn. Rte. 15 (P.O. Box 437), Blue Hill, ME 04614. ☎ **207/374-5126.** www.bluehillfarminn.com. 14 units (7 share 4 bathrooms). June–Oct $80–$95 double; off-season $65–$75. All rates include continental breakfast. AE, MC, V.

Comfortably situated on 48 acres 2 miles north of the village of Blue Hill, the Blue Hill Country Farm Inn offers some of the most relaxing and comfortable common areas you'll find anywhere. The first floor of a vast barn has been converted to a spacious living room for guests, with a handful of sitting areas arrayed such that you can opt for privacy or the company of others. Or you can relax in the cozy common room in the adjoining old farmhouse, amply stocked with a good selection of books. There's also the old kitchen, no longer used for cooking, but a fine place to linger, as well as walking trails on the property.

It's fortunate that the common areas are so exceptionally well done, because you're not likely to spend much time in the guest rooms, which tend to be small and sparely furnished. The more modern rooms are upstairs in the barn loft and are nicely decorated in a country farmhouse style. But these are a bit motel-like, with rooms set off a central hallway. The older rooms with shared bath in the farmhouse have more character.

Blue Hill Inn. Union St. (P.O. Box 403), Blue Hill, ME 04614. ☎ **207/ 374-2844.** Fax 207/374-2829. www.bluehillinn.com. E-mail: bluhilin@ downeast.net. 12 units. $140–$190 double; suite $200–$260. Rates include breakfast and dinner. 2-night minimum stay on summer weekends. DISC, MC, V. Closed Dec to mid-May. Children 13 and over accepted.

The Blue Hill Inn has been hosting travelers since 1840, so it should come as no surprise that the place has figured out how to deliver hospitality. Situated on one of Blue Hill's busy streets and within walking distance of most everything, this Federal-style inn features a convincing colonial American motif throughout, with the authenticity enhanced by creaky floors and doorjambs slightly out of true. Innkeepers Mary and Don Hartley have furnished all the rooms pleasantly with antiques and down comforters; four rooms feature wood-burning fireplaces. A more contemporary suite is located in an adjacent building, which features cathedral ceiling, fireplace, kitchen, and deck.

Dining: The one part of the inn that doesn't feel old is the dining room, which was built in a boxy, shedlike addition to the old house. But the superb country French–style cooking of chef Andre Strong makes up for the less interesting atmosphere. The meals are made chiefly with local, organic ingredients. Among the creative dishes are lobster with a vanilla beurre blanc and roast duck with green peppercorn sauce. The wine selection is excellent.

The fixed-price dinner ($30) is served Wednesday through Sunday and is open to the public; reservations are required.

۞ John Peters Inn. Rte. 176 E. (P.O. Box 916), Blue Hill, ME 04614. ☎ **207/374-2116.** www.johnpetersinn.com. E-mail: jpi@downeast.net. 14 units. $105–$165 double. Rates include full breakfast. MC, V. Closed Nov–Apr.

The long and narrow dirt driveway of the John Peters Inn sends a signal that you're entering into another world. You ascend a gentle hill between a row of stately maples; to the right are glimpses of the bay, to the left is the handsome 1810 home that, with its later architectural embellishments, could be a modest antebellum plantation home.

Inside, it's strictly New England and decorated in antiques with an uncommon elegance and an eye to detail by the innkeepers. There's nothing grand—it's all simple Early American style done with exceptionally good taste. The guest rooms, nine of which boast fireplaces and four of which have private phones, all feature love seats or sofas, and are hard to tear oneself out of. But do try. The inn sits on 25 lovely shorefront acres, and has been lightly landscaped—to do more would be to gild the lily. There's also an unheated outdoor pool that will appeal mostly to those of stout constitution, and a rowboat, sailboat, and canoe for low-key exploring. Breakfast in the simply decorated dining room is a sublime treat, with offerings like freshly squeezed orange juice, poached eggs with asparagus, lobster omelets, and a variety of waffles.

WHERE TO DINE

۞ Firepond. Main St., Blue Hill. ☎ **207/374-9970.** Reservations recommended. Lunch $4–$12, dinner entrees $16–$30 (mostly $18–$20). DISC, MC, V. Daily lunch 11:30–2:30; happy hour (light fare) 3–5pm; dinner 5:30–9:30pm. Closed Nov to mid-May. ECLECTIC.

Firepond, located right in the village of Blue Hill, is a drop-dead-gorgeous restaurant that happens to serve exceptionally fine food. Ideally sited along a small stream in a former blacksmith's shop, Firepond has old-pine floors and is lavishly decorated with dry and live flowers. The decor flirts with a Martha-Stewart-Run-Amok look, but it pulls back in the nick of time and carries its elegance unusually well. The best seats are downstairs in the covered porch overhanging the stream, but it's hard to go wrong anywhere here for setting a romantic mood. If you're not sure this is the place for you, try this: Stop by the handsome bar with its wrought-iron stools for a drink and an appetizer. The odds are you'll decide that staying for dinner is a good idea.

The meals are adventurous. Traditional regional fare updated for the 1990s dominates, and the restaurant is noted for its fresh fish specials, which change daily. You might also find wild boar, ostrich, or rack of New Zealand lamb. They also serve plain boiled lobster in response to customer demand, but what's the point? Be adventurous, and expect your meal to be prepared with a deft touch.

Jean-Paul's Bistro. Main St., Blue Hill. ☎ **207/374-5852.** Lunch $6.95–$8.95. MC, V. Daily 11am–5pm. Closed mid-Sept to June 30. Located at the intersection of routes 172 and 15. UPSCALE SANDWICHES.

You get a lot of elegance for a moderate price at Jean-Paul's, which serves up lunch and tea during its brief summer season (it's open in July, August, and early September only). This is the place to head when the sun's shining overhead and summer blazes in its full glory. Behind this old farmhouse in the village center are stone terraces and a lawn that slopes down to the head of Blue Hill Bay. Choose a table on the terraces, or plop yourself into one of the wide-armed Adirondack chairs on the lawn overlooking the water. (The lawn is a popular spot for solo diners who prefer to eat in the company of a good book.) Lunches tend toward quiche, croissant sandwiches, and salads. The walnut tarragon chicken salad is tasty; the delicious desserts make liberal use of local blueberries.

Jonathan's. Main St., Blue Hill. ☎ **207/374-5226.** Reservations recommended. Main courses $15.95–$21.95. MC, V. Daily 5–9:30pm; Closed Mon–Tues Nov–May. ECLECTIC.

Right in the middle of Blue Hill, Jonathan's appeals to most everyone—from the younger local crowd to the old-money summer denizens. The background music is jazz or light rock, the service brisk and professional, and the wine list extensive and creative. Guests choose between the barnlike back room with a comfortable knotty-pine feel, or the less elegantly decorated front room facing Main Street, done up in green tablecloths, captain's chairs, and booths of white pine. The menu changes frequently, but among the dishes typically served here are *churrasco* (a Cuban-style marinated flank steak with Caribbean condiments), mixed grill of quail, rabbit, and venison sausage, and a simple poached salmon with dill sauce. Appetizers run along the lines of warm salad of smoked mussels and chevre, or Indonesian shrimp satay.

7

Mount Desert Island & Acadia National Park

*M*ount Desert Island is home to spectacular Acadia National Park, and for many visitors the two places are one and the same. Yes, Acadia drives the economy and defines the spirit of Maine's largest island. And the park does contain the most dramatic coastal real estate on the Eastern Seaboard.

Yet the park holdings are only part of the appeal of this immensely popular island, which is connected to the mainland via a short, two-lane causeway. Beyond the parklands are scenic harborside villages and remote backcountry roads, quaint B&Bs and unusually fine restaurants, oversized 19th-century summer "cottages" and the unrepentant tourist trap of Bar Harbor. Those who arrive on the island expecting untamed wilderness invariably leave disappointed. Those who understand that Acadia National Park is but one chapter (albeit a very large one) in the intriguing story of Mount Desert Island will enjoy their visit more thoroughly.

Mount Desert (pronounced "de-*sert*") is divided into two lobes separated by Somes Sound, the only legitimate fjord in the continental U.S. (A fjord is a valley carved by a glacier that is subsequently filled with rising ocean water.) Those with a poetic imagination see Mount Desert shaped as lobster, with one large claw and one small. Most of the parkland is on the meatier east claw, although large swaths of national park exist on the leaner west claw as well. The eastern side is more developed, with Bar Harbor the center of commerce and entertainment. The western side has a more quiet, settled air, and teems with more wildlife than tourists. The island isn't huge—it's only about 15 miles from the causeway to the island's southernmost tip at Bass Harbor Head—and visitors can do a lot of adventuring in such a compact space. The best plan is to take it slow, exploring whenever possible by foot, bicycle, canoe, or kayak.

1   Acadia National Park

It's not hard to fathom why Acadia is consistently one of the biggest draws in the U.S. national park system. The park's landscape is a rich tapestry of rugged cliffs, restless ocean, and deep, silent woods. Acadia's landscape, like so much of the rest of northern New England, was carved by glaciers some 18,000 years ago. A mile-high ice sheet shaped the land by scouring valleys into their distinctive U shapes, rounding many of the once-jagged peaks and depositing huge boulders about the landscape, such as the famous 10-foot-high "Bubble Rock," which appears to be perched precariously on the side of South Bubble Mountain.

The park's more recent roots can be traced back to the 1840s, when noted Hudson River School painter Thomas Cole packed his sketchbooks and easels for a trip to this remote island, then home to a small number of fishermen and boat builders. His stunning renditions of the surging surf pounding against coastal granite were later displayed in New York and triggered an early tourism boom as urbanites flocked to the island to "rusticate." By 1872, national magazines were touting Eden (Bar Harbor's name until 1919) as a desirable summer resort. It attracted the attention of wealthy industrialists, and soon became summer home to Carnegies, Rockefellers, Astors, and Vanderbilts, who built massive summer cottages with literally dozens of rooms (one "cottage" even boasted 28 bathrooms). More recently, lifestyle doyenne Martha Stewart bought a multimillion-dollar hilltop compound originally built by Edsel Ford.

By early in this century, the huge popularity and growing development of the island began to concern its most ardent supporters. Boston textile heir and conservationist George Dorr and Harvard president Charles Eliot, aided by the largesse of John D. Rockefeller Jr., started acquiring large tracts for the public's enjoyment. These parcels were eventually donated to the federal government, and in 1919 the public land was designated Lafayette National Park, the first national park east of the Mississippi. Renamed Acadia in 1929, the park has grown to encompass nearly half the island, with holdings scattered piecemeal here and there.

Rockefeller purchased and donated about 11,000 acres—about one third of the park. He's also responsible for one of the park's most extraordinary features. Around 1905 a dispute erupted over whether to allow noisy new motorcars onto the island. Resident islanders wanted these new conveniences to boost their mobility; John D. Rockefeller Jr., whose fortune was from the oil industry (students of irony take note), strenuously objected, preferring the tranquillity of the car-free island. Rockefeller went down to defeat on this issue, and the island was opened to cars in 1913. In response, the multimillionaire set about building an elaborate 57-mile system of private carriage roads, featuring a dozen gracefully handcrafted stone bridges. These roads, which are today open only to equestrians, bicyclists, and pedestrians, are concentrated most densely around Jordan Pond, but also ascend to some of the most scenic open peaks and wind through sylvan valleys.

JUST THE FACTS

GETTING THERE

Acadia National Park is reached from the town of Ellsworth via Route 3. If you're coming from southern Maine, you can avoid the coastal congestion along Route 1 by taking the Maine Turnpike to Bangor, picking up I-395 to Route 1A, then continuing south on Route 1A to Ellsworth. While this looks longer on the map, it's by far the quickest route in summer.

Daily flights from Boston to the airport in Trenton, just across the causeway from Mt. Desert Island, are offered year-round by Continental affiliate **Colgan Air** (☎ **800/523-3273** or 207/ 667-7171).

ENTRY POINTS & FEES

A 1-week park pass, which includes unlimited trips on Park Loop Road, costs $10 per car (no extra charge per passenger). A daily pass is no longer available. The main point of entry to Park Loop Road, the park's most scenic byway, is at the visitor center at **Hulls Cove.** Mount Desert Island consists of an interwoven network of park and town roads, allowing visitors to enter the park at numerous points. A glance at a park map (available at the visitor center) will make these access points self-evident. The entry fee is collected at a toll- booth on Park Loop Road, one-half mile north of Sand Beach.

VISITOR CENTERS

Acadia staffs two visitor centers. The **Thompson Island Informa- tion Center** (☎ **207/288-3411**) on Route 3 is the first you'll pass as you enter Mount Desert Island. This center is maintained by the local chambers of commerce, but park personnel are often on hand to answer inquiries. It's open May through mid-October, and is a

Mount Desert Island/Acadia National Park

good stop for general lodging and restaurant information; if you're primarily interested in information about the park itself, continue on Route 3 to the National Park Service's **Hulls Cove Visitor Center** about 7.5 miles beyond Thompson Island. This attractive stone-walled center includes professionally prepared park service displays, such as a large relief map of the island, natural history exhibits, and a short introductory film. You can also request free brochures about hiking trails and the carriage roads, or purchase postcards and more detailed guidebooks. The center is open mid-April through October. Information is also available year-round, by phone or in person, from the park's **headquarters** (☎ **207/288-3338**) on Route 233 between Bar Harbor and Somesville.

Your questions might also be answered in advance on the park's Web page at **www.nps.gov/acad/anp.html**.

PARK ACCOMMODATIONS

The national park itself offers no overnight accommodations other than two campgrounds (see below). But visitors don't have to go far to find a room. That's especially true for Bar Harbor, which is teeming with motels and inns. The rest of the island also has a good if scattered selection of places to spend the night. See "Where to Stay," below.

SEASONS

Visit Acadia in September if you can. Between Labor Day and the foliage season of early October, the days are often warm and clear, the nights have a crisp northerly tang, and you can avoid the hassles of congestion, crowds, and pesky insects. Not that the park is empty in September. Bus tours seem to proliferate this month, which results in great knots of tourists at the most popular sites. Not to worry: If you walk just a minute or two off the road you can find solitude and an agreeable peacefulness. Hikers and bikers have the trails and carriage roads to themselves.

Summer, of course, is peak season at Acadia. The weather is perfect for just about any outdoor activity in July and August. Most days are warm (in the 70s or 80s), with afternoons frequently cooler than mornings owing to ocean breezes. While sun seems to be the norm, come prepared for rain and fog, which are both frequent visitors to the Maine Coast. And once or twice each summer a heat wave will settle into the area, producing temperatures in the 90s, dense haze, and stifling humidity, but this rarely lasts more than 2 or 3 days. Soon enough, a brisk north wind will blow in from the Canadian Arctic, churning up the waters and forcing visitors into sweaters at night. Sometime during the last 2 weeks of August, a cold wind will blow through at night and you'll smell the approach of autumn, with winter not far behind it.

Avoiding Crowds at Acadia

Early fall is the best time to miss out on the mobs yet still enjoy the weather. If you do come midsummer, try to venture out early mornings and early evenings to see the most popular spots, like the Thunder Hole or the summit of Cadillac Mountain. Setting off into the woods at every opportunity is also a good strategy. About four out of five visitors restrict their tours to the loop road and a handful of other major attractions, leaving the Acadia backcountry open for more adventurous spirits.

The best guarantee of solitude is to head to the more remote outposts managed by Acadia, especially Isle au Haut and Schoodic Peninsula. See chapters 6 and 8, respectively.

REGULATIONS

The usual national park rules apply. Guns may not be used in the park; if you have a gun, it must be "cased, broken down, or otherwise packaged against use." Fires and camping are allowed only at designated areas. Pets must be on a leash at all times. Seat belts must be worn in the national park (this is a federal law). Don't remove anything from the park, either man-made or natural; this includes cobblestones from the shore.

RANGER PROGRAMS

Frequent ranger programs are offered throughout the year. These include talks at campground amphitheaters and tours of various locations around the island. Examples are the Otter Point nature hike, Mr. Rockefeller's bridges walk, a Frenchman Bay cruise (rangers provide commentary on commercial trips; make reservations with commercial tour boat owners), and a discussion of changes in Acadia's landscape. Ask for a schedule of events or more information at either of the two visitor centers or campgrounds.

ENJOYING THE PARK
DRIVING THE PARK LOOP ROAD

This almost goes without saying, since it's the park's premier attraction. This 20-mile road runs along the island's eastern shore, then loops inland along Jordan Pond and Eagle Lake. The road runs alternately high along the shoulders of dramatic coastal mountains, then dips down along the boulder-strewn coastlines. The dark granite is broken by the spires of spruce and fir, and the earthy tones contrast sharply with the frothy white surf and the steely, azure sea. The two-lane road is one-way along the coastal stretches; the right lane is set aside for parking, so it's easy to make frequent stops to admire the vistas.

Ideally, visitors will make at least two trips on the loop road. The first is for the sheer exhilaration and to suss out the lay of the land. On the second trip, plan to stop frequently, leaving your car behind while you explore trails and coastline.

Attractions along the coastal loop include scenic **Sand Beach,** which is the only sand beach on the island; **Thunder Hole** is a shallow oceanside cavern into which the surf surges, compresses, and bursts out with explosive force and a concussive sound, and **Cadillac Mountain,** at 1,530 feet the highest point on the island and the place first touched by the sun in the U.S. during much of the year.

The mountaintop is accessible by car along an old carriage road, but the lot at the summit is often crowded and drivers testy. You're better off hiking to the top, or scaling a more remote peak.

✪ BIKING CARRIAGE ROAD

The 57 miles of carriage road built by John D. Rockefeller, Jr. are among the park's most extraordinary hidden treasures. After Rockefeller's death in 1960, the roads became somewhat shaggy and overgrown until a major restoration effort beginning in 1990 brought them back. Today these roads are superbly restored and maintained, and though built for horse and carriage, they are ideal for cruising by mountain bike and offer some of the most scenic, relaxing biking found anywhere in the United States. Park near Jordan Pond and plumb the tree-shrouded lanes that lace the area, taking time to admire the stonework on the uncommonly fine bridges. Afterwards, stop for tea and popovers at the **Jordan Pond House,** which has been a popular island destination for over a century, although it's unlikely as much Lycra was in evidence 100 years ago.

A decent map of the carriage roads is available free at the park's visitor center. (Where the carriage roads cross private land—generally between Seal Harbor and Northeast Harbor—the roads are closed to mountain bikes.) More detailed guidebooks are sold at area bookstores.

Mountain bikes may be rented along Cottage Street in Bar Harbor, with rates around $15 to $17 for a full day, $10 to $12 for a half day. Most bike shops include locks and helmets as basic equipment, but ask what's included before you rent. Also ask about closing times, since you'll be able to get a couple extra hours in with a later-closing shop. **Bar Harbor Bicycle Shop** (☎ 207/288-3886) at 141 Cottage St. gets my vote for the most convenient and friendliest; you might also try **Acadia Outfitters** (☎ 207/288-8118) at 106 Cottage St., or **Acadia Bike & Coastal Kayak** (☎ 207/288-9605) at 48 Cottage St.

CANOEING

Mount Desert's several ponds offer scenic if limited canoeing, and most have public boat access. Canoe rentals are available at the north end of Long Pond in Somesville from **National Park Canoe Rentals** (☎ 207/244-5854). The cost is $22 for 4 hours. Long Pond is the largest of the island ponds, and offers good exploring. Pack a picnic and spend a few hours reconnoitering the pond's 3-mile length. Much of the west shore and the southern tip lie within

Acadia National Park. Jet Skis, incidentally, are banned in the national park.

HIKING A MOUNTIAN

This quintessential Acadia experience shouldn't be missed. The park is studded with low "mountains" (they'd be called hills elsewhere) that offer superb views over the island and the open ocean. The trails weren't simply hacked out of the hillside; many were crafted by experienced stonemasons and others with high aesthetic intent. The routes aren't the most direct, or the easiest to build. But they're often the most scenic, taking advantage of fractures in the rocks, picturesque ledges, and sudden vistas. Acadia National Park has 120 miles of hiking trails in addition to the carriage roads. The Hulls Cove Visitor Center offers a one-page chart of area hikes; combined with the park map, this is all you'll need since the trails are well maintained and well marked. It's not hard to cobble together loop hikes to make your trips more varied. Coordinate your hiking with the weather; if it's damp or foggy, you'll stay drier and warmer strolling the carriage roads. If it's clear and dry, head for the highest peaks with the best views.

Among my favorite trails is the **Dorr Ladder Trail,** which departs from Route 3 near The Tarn just south of the Sieur de Monts entrance to the Loop Road. This trail begins with a series of massive stone steps ascending along the base of a vast slab of granite, then passes through crevasses (not for the wide of girth) and up ladders affixed to the granite. The views east and south are superb.

An easy lowland hike is around **Jordan Pond,** with the northward leg along the pond's east shore on a hiking trail, and the return via carriage road. It's mostly level, with the total loop measuring just over 3 miles. At the north end of Jordan Pond, consider heading up the prominent, oddly symmetrical mounds called **The Bubbles.** These detours shouldn't take much more than 20 minutes each; look for signs off the Jordan Pond Shore Trail.

On the western side of the island, an ascent of **Acadia Mountain** and return takes about an hour and a half, but hikers should schedule in some time for lingering while they enjoy the view of Somes Sound and the smaller islands off Mount Desert's southern shores. This 2.5-mile loop hike begins off Route 102 at a trailhead 3 miles south of Somesville. Head eastward through rolling mixed forest, then begin an ascent over ledgy terrain. Be sure to visit both the east and west peaks (the east peak has the better views), and look for hidden balds in the summit forest that open up to unexpected vistas.

TAKING A CARRIAGE RIDE

Carriage rides are offered by **Wildwood Stables** (☎ 207/276-3622), a national park concessioner located a half-mile south of Jordan Pond House. The 1-hour Day Mountain trip departs three times daily, yields wonderful views, and costs $13 for adults, $7 for children 6 to 12, and $4 for children 2 to 5. Longer tours and charters are also available, as is a special carriage designed to accommodate handicapped passengers; reservations are encouraged.

ROCK CLIMBING

Many of the oceanside rock faces attract experienced rock climbers, as much for the beauty of the climbing areas as the challenge of the climbs. For curious novices, **Acadia Mountain Guides** (☎ 207/288-8186) offers rock climbing lessons and guide services, ranging from a half-day introduction to rock climbing to intensive workshops on self-rescue and instruction on how to lead climbs. The Bar Harbor shop is located at the corner of Main Street and Mt. Desert Street.

SEA KAYAKING

Experienced sea kayakers flock to Acadia to test their paddling skills along the surf at the base of rocky cliffs, to venture out to the offshore islands, and to probe the still, silent waters of Somes Sound. Novice sea kayakers also come to Acadia to try their hand with guided tours, which are offered by several outfitters. Many new paddlers have found their inaugural experiences gratifying; others have complained that the quantity of paddlers taken out on quick tours during peak season makes the experience a little too much like a cattle drive to truly enjoy. Ask how many paddlers have already signed up if crowding is an issue for you. (Insider tip: rainy days can be magical on the water and surprisingly dry once you're sealed inside a kayak; you're also likely to have a much less crowded experience.) You can turn up a variety of tours, ranging from a $2^1/_2$-hour harbor tour to a 7-hour full-day tour by contacting the following guide services: **Acadia Outfitters** (☎ 207/288-8118) at 106 Cottage St.; **Coastal Kayaking Tours** (☎ 207/288-9605) at 48 Cottage St., and **National Park Sea Kayak Tours** (☎ 207/288-0342) at 137 Cottage St. Rates range from $34 per person for a 2-hour harbor tour to $65 for a full-day excursion.

CAMPING

The National Park Service maintains two campgrounds within Acadia National Park. Both are extremely popular; during July and August expect both to fill by early to mid-morning.

The more popular of the two is **Blackwoods** (☎ 207/ 288-3274), located on the island's eastern side. Access is from Route 3 five miles south of Bar Harbor. Bikers and pedestrians can easily reach the loop road from the campground via a short trail. The campground has no public showers, but an enterprising business offers showers for a modest fee just outside the campground entrance. Camping fees are $14 and limited reservations are accepted; call ☎ **800/365-2267.** (This number is for a national reservation service, whose contract is revisited from time to time by the park service; if it's non-working, call the campground directly to ask for the current toll-free reservation number.)

Seawall (☎ 207/244-3600) is on the quieter, western half of the island near the fishing village of Bass Harbor. This is a good base for road biking, and several short coastal hikes are within easy striking distance. Many of the sites are walk-ins, which require carrying your gear a hundred yards or so to the site. The campground is open late May through September on a first-come, first-served basis. In general, if you get here by 9 or 10am, you'll be pretty much assured of a campsite, especially if you're a tent camper. No showers, but they're available nearby. The fee is $14 for those arriving by car, $10 for those coming by foot or bike.

Private campgrounds handle the overflow. The region from Ellsworth south boasts some 14 private campgrounds, which offer varying amenities. The **Thompson Island Information Center** (☎ 207/288-3411) posts up-to-the-minute information on which campgrounds still have vacancies; it's a good first stop for those arriving without camping reservations.

To my mind, two private campgrounds stand above the rest. **Bar Harbor Campground** (Route 3, Salisbury Cove; ☎ 207/ 288-5185) on the main route between the causeway and Bar Harbor doesn't take reservations, and you can often find a good selection of sites if you arrive before noon, even during the peak season. Some of its 300 sites are set in piney woods; others are on an open hillside edged with blueberry barrens. The wooded sites are quite private. There's a pool for campers, uncommonly clean bathhouses, and campers always get to pick their own sites rather than be arbitrarily assigned to one. Rates range from $18 for a basic, no-services site, to $25 for all hookups.

At the head of Somes Sound is **Mount Desert Campground** (Route 198; ☎ **207/244-3710**), which is especially well suited for campers (RVs to a maximum of 20 feet only). This heavily wooded campground has very few undesirable sites, and a great many desirable ones, including some walk-in sites right at the water's edge. The rate is $22 per night. (*Note:* This campground should not be confused with the Mount Desert Narrows Campground, which is more RV-oriented and located closer to the causeway.)

Another option is **Lamoine State Park** (☎ **207/667-4778**), which faces Mount Desert from the mainland across the cold waters of northernmost Frenchman Bay. This is an exceptionally pleasant, quiet park with private sites and a small beach about a half-hour's drive from the action at Bar Harbor. The campground finally has been discovered by travelers in recent years, but still rarely fills to capacity.

2 Bar Harbor

Bar Harbor has historical roots in the grand resort era of the late 19th century. The region was discovered by wealthy rusticators, drawn by the mid-19th-century landscape paintings that were exhibited in Boston and New York. Later, sprawling hotels and boarding houses cluttered the shores and hillsides as the newly affluent middle class flocked here in summer by steamboat and rail from Eastern Seaboard cities. When the resort was at its zenith near the turn of the last century, Bar Harbor had rooms enough to accommodate some 5,000 visitors. Along with the hotels and guest houses, hundreds of cottages were built by the wealthiest rusticators who came here season after season.

The tourist business continued to grow through the early part of the 1900s, then all but collapsed as the Great Depression and the growing popularity of automobile travel doomed the era of the extended vacation. Bar Harbor was dealt a further blow in 1947 when a fire fueled by an unusually dry summer and fierce northwest winds leveled many of the most opulent cottages and much of the rest of the town. (To this day, no one knows with any certainty how the fire started.) The fire destroyed five hotels, 67 grand cottages, and 170 homes. In all, some 17,000 acres of the island were burned. Downtown Bar Harbor was spared, and many of the in-town mansions along the oceanfront were missed by the conflagration.

After a period of quiet slumber (some storefronts were still boarded up as late as the 1970s), Bar Harbor has been rejuvenated

Bar Harbor

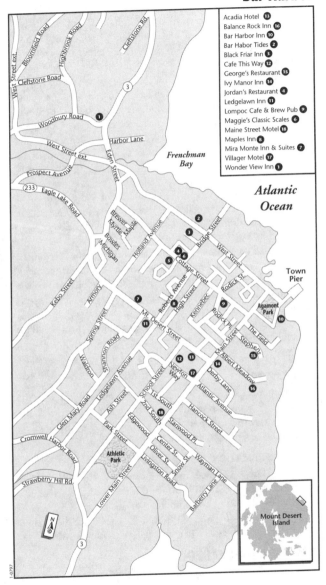

Acadia Hotel **13**
Balance Rock Inn **16**
Bar Harbor Inn **10**
Bar Habor Tides **2**
Black Friar Inn **3**
Cafe This Way **12**
George's Restaurant **15**
Ivy Manor Inn **14**
Jordan's Restaurant **4**
Ledgelawn Inn **11**
Lompoc Cafe & Brew Pub **9**
Maggie's Classic Scales **6**
Maine Street Motel **18**
Maples Inn **8**
Mira Monte Inn & Suites **7**
Villager Motel **17**
Wonder View Inn **1**

Frenchman Bay

Atlantic Ocean

Town Pier

Mount Desert Island

and rediscovered in recent years as tourists have poured in, followed by entrepreneurs who have opened dozens of restaurants, shops, and boutiques. The less charitable regard Bar Harbor as just another tacky tourist mecca—Pigeon Forge, Tennessee, with moose horns and spruce. And it does share some of those traits—the downtown hosts a proliferation of T-shirt vendors, ice-cream cone shops, and souvenir palaces. Crowds spill off the sidewalk and into the street in midsummer, and the traffic and congestion can be truly appalling.

Yet Bar Harbor's vibrant history, distinguished architecture, and beautiful location along Frenchman Bay allow it to rise above its station as mild diversion for tourists. Most of the island's inns, motels, and B&Bs are located here, as are dozens of fine restaurants, making it a desirable base of operations. Bar Harbor is also the best destination for the usual supplies and services; there's a decent grocery story and Laundromat, and you can stock up on other necessities of life.

As for the congestion, it's fortunate that Bar Harbor is compact enough that once you find a parking space or a room for the night, the whole town can be navigated conveniently on foot. Arriving here early in the morning also considerably improves your odds of securing parking within easy striking distance of the town center. *Suggestion:* Explore Bar Harbor before and after breakfast, then set off for the hills, woods, and coast the rest of the day.

ESSENTIALS
GETTING THERE

Bar Harbor is located on Route 3 about 10 miles southeast of the causeway. Seasonal bus service is available in summer; for schedules contact **Vermont Transit Lines** (☎ **800/451-3292** or 800/642-3133) or **Concord Trailways** (☎ **800/639-3317**).

VISITOR INFORMATION

The **Bar Harbor Chamber of Commerce,** P.O. Box 158, Bar Harbor, ME 04609 (☎ **207/288-5103;** www.acadia.net/bhcc), stockpiles a huge amount of information about local attractions at its offices at 93 Cottage St. Write, call, or e-mail (bhcc@acadia.net) in advance for a full guide to area lodging and attractions.

EXPLORING BAR HARBOR

Wandering the compact downtown on foot is a good way to get a taste of the town. Among the best views in town are those from the foot of Main Street at grassy **Agamont Park,** which overlooks the town pier and Frenchman Bay. From here, set off past the Bar Harbor Inn on the **Shore Path,** a winding, wide trail that follows the shoreline for a short distance along a public right-of-way. The pathway passes in front of many of the elegant summer homes (some converted to inns), offering a superb vantage point to view the area's architecture.

From the path, you'll also have an open view of **The Porcupines,** a cluster of spruce-studded islands just offshore. This is a good spot to witness the powerful force of glacial action. The south-moving glacier ground away at the islands, creating a gentle slope facing north. On the south shore, away from the glacial push (glaciers simply melted when they retreated north), is a more abrupt, clifflike shore. The resulting islands look like a small group of porcupines migrating southward—or so early visitors imagined.

One of the most elaborate of Bar Harbor's magnificent summer cottages—called The Turrets—is now part of the campus of the **College of the Atlantic** (☎ 207/288-5015), a school founded in 1969 with a strong emphasis on environmental education. The Turrets is an impressively turreted castle built in 1895, and features a broad porch and drop-dead spectacular views of the bay. Part of the ground floor has been converted to a fine, small natural history museum, which is open to the public. The exhibits are well prepared and informative; museum guides often have hands-on activities for kids. Allow an hour to explore the museum and wander the exceptional campus.

The college is on Route 3 northwest of the village center; it's about a 15-minute walk from downtown, or you can drive (parking is no problem on campus). The museum is open daily 9am to 5pm June 15 to Columbus Day (10am to 4pm from Labor Day on); admission is $2.50 adults, $1.50 seniors and teens, and $1 children 12 and under.

For an eye-opening adventure, consider taking in the sunrise from atop Cadillac Mountain, followed by a zippy bike descent back to Bar Harbor. **Acadia Downhill** (part of Acadia Bike and Coastal Kayaking, 48 Cottage St; ☎ 207/288-9605) will haul you and a rental bike to the top of the island's highest peak via van, serve you coffee and a light breakfast while you watch the sun creep up over the eastern horizon, then lead you on a brisk coasting and pedaling trip 6 miles back down the mountain and into Bar Harbor. Beware that this is a really early morning adventure: Tours meet at about 3:30am in June (about 5am by August), and last about 3 hours.

Trips are offered Monday through Friday during the peak summer season, and reservations are recommended; the price is $34 per person.

One of downtown's less obvious attractions is the **Criterion Theater** (☎ 207/288-3441), a movie house built in 1932 in a classic art deco style that so far has avoided the degradation of multiplexification. The 900-seat theater, located on Cottage Street, shows first-run movies in summer and is worth the price of admission for the fantastic if somewhat faded interiors; the movie is secondary. As once was the case at most movie palaces, it still costs extra to sit in the more exclusive loges upstairs.

SHOPPING

Bar Harbor is clotted with boutiques and souvenir shops along the two intersecting commercial streets—Main Street and Cottage Street. Many are the usual T-shirt and coffee-mug emporia; a number, however, offer more original items.

Bar Harbor Hemporium. 116 Main St. ☎ **207/288-3014.** www.barharborhemp.com.

It's not what you think it is. The Hemporium is dedicated to promoting products made from hemp, an environmentally friendly (and nonpsychoactive) fibrous plant that can be used in making paper, clothing, and more.

Bowl and Board. 160 Main St. ☎ **207/288-4519.**

Wood products from Maine are the focus here, with items including—in addition to bowls and cutting boards—children's games and puzzles, peg coat racks, and spice racks. Upstairs is the North Woods Center, where you can learn about efforts to create a North Woods National Park in northern Maine.

Island Artisans. 99 Main St. ☎ **207/288-4214.**

This is the place to browse for locally made products. Most are a size you can bring home in a knapsack, and include tiles, sweet-grass baskets, pottery, jewelry, and soaps.

RainWise. 25 Federal St. ☎ **800/762-5723** or 207/288-5169. www.rainwise.com.

Bar Harbor–based RainWise manufactures high-end weather stations for the serious hobbyist. The factory store, located off Cottage Street, sells the firm's products, along with a variety of third-party thermometers and barometers.

Window Panes. 166 Main St. ☎ **800/519-4889** or 207/288-9550.

Unique and creative housewares and garden accessories are nicely displayed at this attractive shop.

ON THE WATER

Bar Harbor makes a memorable base for several ocean endeavors, including **whale watching.** Several tour operators offer excursions in search of humpbacks, finbacks, minkes, and the rarely seen endangered right whale. Reservations are encouraged during July and August.

The largest of the fleet is the **Friendship V** (☎ **800/942-5374** or 207/288-2386), which operates from the Holiday Inn wharf 1 mile north of Bar Harbor. Tours are on a fast, twin-hulled, three-level excursion boat that can hold 200 passengers in two heated cabins. The tours run 3 hours plus; the cost is $31 per adult (which is refunded if you fail to see a whale).

Sea Bird Watcher Company (☎ **800/247-3794** or 207/288-2025) runs whale-and-puffin tours on a 72-foot boat from the Golden Anchor Pier in Bar Harbor; the 4-hour tour is $33 per adult; a 2-hour puffin trip is also offered for $18.

Whale Watcher (☎ **800/508-1499** or 207/288-3322) takes passengers in search of whales aboard the 116-foot, two-deck **Atlantis.** The 3-hour trip is $30. The same folks offer somewhat more rustic bay tours aboard the 42-foot **Katherine** (☎ **207/288-3322**), which is especially popular among younger children. You'll stop to haul lobster traps and inspect the contents, and look at and handle urchins, starfish, and other inhabitants of the briny deep. Spotting harbor seals sunning on the rocks is often the most memorable part of the trip for kids. The 1¹/₂-hour tour costs $16.75 for adults, $12.75 for children. Trips depart from next to Bar Harbor's municipal pier.

For a rather more romantic view of the coast, sign up for a sailing tour. **Downeast Windjamming and Lighthouse Cruises** (☎ **207/288-4585** or 207/288-2373) offers three trips daily aboard a recently built 151-foot, four-masted schooner, the only four-masted schooner regularly plying New England's waters. It lacks some of the creaky romanticism of older sailing vessels (the ship is mostly made of steel), but the sunset sail is appealing. If the weather and wind cooperate, you can watch the day come to a peaceful close while enjoying sweeping views of the impressive hills. Tours leave from the Bar Harbor Inn Pier near Agamont Park, last about

2 hours, and cost $25 for adults, $15 for children under 12. The ticket office is at 27 Main St.

WHERE TO STAY
EXPENSIVE

✪ **Balance Rock Inn.** 21 Albert Meadow, Bar Harbor, ME 04609. ☎ **800/ 753-0494** or 207/288-2610. 21 units. A/C MINIBAR TV TEL. Peak season $195–$410 double, including breakfast; early summer and late fall $125–$255; spring $95–$195. Closed Nov to late Apr. Albert Meadow is off Main St. at Butterfield's grocery store. AE, DISC, MC, V.

It's quite simple: If you can afford it, stay here. Built in 1903, the mansion is an architecturally elaborate affair of gray shingles with cream, maroon, and forest-green trim. The common rooms are expansive yet comfortable, with pilasters and coffered ceilings, arched doorways, and leaded windows. The favored spot among serious loungers is the front covered patio with its green wicker furniture and a recessed bar off to the side. The sound of the sea drifts up gently. And then there's the view, which is among the best in Maine: You look across a wonderful pool and down a verdant lawn framed by hardwoods to the rich, blue waters of Frenchman Bay.

The rooms are wonderfully appointed with a contemporary styling; most may be reached by elevator, and many feature whirlpool baths or fireplaces. About half of the rooms are done up in softer, floral decor, and half in darker, more masculine tones. The top-floor rooms (in the former attic) tend to be a bit tighter with odd angles, but are still bright and comfortable. Among the most outstanding rooms: #304 with a private roof deck and sauna ($275), and the deluxe suite (#408) with full kitchen, outside deck, and upstairs Jacuzzi with spectacular ocean view ($525). The inn also features a fitness center in an air-conditioned carriage house on the property.

The Bar Harbor Inn. Newport Dr. (P.O. Box 7), Bar Harbor, ME 04609. ☎ **800/248-3351** or 207/288-3351. www.barharborinn.com. 153 units. A/C TV TEL. Peak season $155–$395 double; spring and late fall $75–$199. All rates include continental breakfast. AE, DISC, MC, V. Closed Dec to late Mar.

The Bar Harbor Inn, just off Agamont Park, manages to mix traditional and contemporary nicely. Situated on shady waterfront grounds just a minute's stroll from downtown boutiques (it's also at the start of the Shore Path), the inn offers both convenience and gracious charm. The main shingled inn, which dates back to the turn of the century, has a settled, old-money feel, with its semicircular dining room with ocean views, and the button-down elegance of the lobby. The guest rooms, located in the main inn and two additional structures, are decidedly more contemporary. Guest rooms in the Oceanfront and Main Inn both offer spectacular views of the bay, and many have private balconies; the less expensive Newport building lacks views but is comfortable and up-to-date. The inn offers attractive packages in the shoulder seasons.

Dining: The inn's semiformal dining room serves up well-regarded meals along with one of the best ocean views in town. Entrees include charred tuna with a pineapple kiwi salsa, and boneless lamb loin with wild mushrooms. Prices are $16.95 to $22.95. An outdoor grill, serving simpler fare like chowders, salads, and boiled lobster, overlooks the bay and is open daily for lunch and dinner.

Amenities: Heated outdoor pool, hot tub, morning newspaper, conference space, limited room service, afternoon coffee and cookies.

The Bar Harbor Tides. 119 West St., Bar Harbor, ME 04609. ☎ **207/ 288-4968.** www.barharbortides.com. E-mail: info@barharbortides.com. 4 units. TV. Peak season $150–$275 double; off-season $95–$175. Rates include full breakfast. DISC, MC, V.

The Tides features just four guest rooms, and they're wonderfully situated—in a sprawling, 1887 cream-colored mansion at the head of a long, lush lawn that descends to the water's edge. The inn is on $1^1/_2$ in-town acres in a neighborhood of imposing homes and within easy strolling distance of the village center.

When you first enter, it seems as though you're visiting someone else's great aunt—someone's *very rich* great aunt. But soon enough it feels like home, as you unwind in the two spacious living rooms (one upstairs and one down) or, more likely, on the veranda, which has its own fireplace. Breakfast is served on the porch in good weather; otherwise it's enjoyed in the regal dining room with polished wood floors and views out to Bar Island. Plan to be back by sunset to wander down to the foot of the lawn for the spectacular show.

Inn at Canoe Point. Rte. 3, Bar Harbor, ME 04609. ☎ **207/288-9511.** www.innatcanoepoint.com. E-mail: canoe.point@juno.com. 5 units. Peak season $140–$245 double; off season $80–$150. Rates include breakfast. DISC, MC, V. Children 16 and over accepted.

The Inn at Canoe Point boasts the best deck on the island—it virtually hangs over the ocean tucked away in a rocky cove, with great views across the northern bay. There's even a cluster of Adirondack chairs arrayed for sprawling. The inn itself is equally magical, built in 1889 in a style that might best be described as "storybook Tudor." Guests arrive down a short, winding road through an attractive stand of pines. Although the inn is just 75 yards or so off bustling Route 3, you might as well be on an island far away. The interior is sleekly contemporary and comfortable. The guests' living room has a stunning modern stone fireplace, superb views, and a great selection of reading material. Rooms vary, but all are attractively appointed. The Garret Suite occupies the whole third floor and is quite spacious; the tiny Garden Room makes up for its relatively diminutive size with wonderful windows on three sides. The main trick here is actually getting a room; they tend to be booked up weeks in advance, so reserve well ahead (or come in the off-season).

Ivy Manor Inn. 194 Main St., Bar Harbor, ME 04609. ☎ **207/288-2138.** E-mail: ivymanor@acadia.net. 7 units. A/C TV TEL. Mid-May to mid-Oct $150–$275; mid-Oct to mid-Mar $85–$135; mid-Mar to mid-May $85–$185. Rates include full breakfast. 2-night minimum stay on holiday weekends. AE, DISC, MC, V. Children over 12 accepted.

The Ivy Manor opened in 1997 and is one of Bar Harbor's newest additions to the upscale lodging pool. Located in a 1940s-era Tudor-style house that was once the home and office of a doctor, the Ivy Manor was thoroughly done over in an understated French Victorian style, mostly in lush, rich colors like burgundy. The rooms are nicely sized; most are carpeted and furnished with attractive, tasteful antiques from the innkeeper's collection. Some rooms have antique claw-foot tubs; others have small outdoor sitting decks (none with views to speak of). Among the best rooms are #6, a small suite with a private sitting room and small fireplace, and #1, the honeymoon room with an imposing walnut headboard and matching armoire. All rooms have small TVs. Leave time for a cocktail in the cozy first-floor lounge after you return from your day's outing.

Dining: See the entry for Michelle's under "Where to Dine," below.

MODERATE

Black Friar Inn. 10 Summer St., Bar Harbor, ME 04609. ☎ **207/288-5091.** Fax 207/288-4197. E-mail: blackfriar@acadia.net. 7 units (3 with private hall bathrooms). A/C. $90–$140 double. Rates include full breakfast. 2-night minimum stay mid-June to mid-Oct. DISC, MC, V. Closed Dec–Apr. Children 12 and overaccepted.

The Black Friar Inn, tucked on a side street overlooking the municipal building parking lot, is easily overlooked. But this yellow-shingled structure with quirky pediments and a somewhat eccentric air offers surprises inside. A former owner "collected" interiors and installed them throughout the house. Among them is a replica of the namesake Black Friar Pub in London, complete with elaborate carved wood paneling (it's now a common room), stamped tin walls in the breakfast room, and a doctor's office (now a guest room). The Black Friar's rooms are carpeted and furnished with a mix of antiques, and most are rather small and cozy. The least expensive are the two garret rooms on the third floor, which have private bathrooms down a hall. The inn's friendly Brittany, named Falke, has the run of the place.

Ledgelawn Inn. 66 Mt. Desert St., Bar Harbor, ME 04609. ☎ **800/274-5334** or 207/288-4596. Fax 207/288-9968. 33 units. A/C TV TEL. July–Aug $125–$225 double. Rates include full breakfast. Discounts in the off-season. AE, DISC, MC, V. Closed late Oct to early May.

If you want a great location and far more flair than a motel, this is a good bet. This hulking cream and maroon 1904 "cottage" sits on a village lot amid towering oaks and maples. The place has a mid-century elegance updated with such modern amenities as a small, no-frills pool. The Ledgelawn first gets your attention with a handsome sun-porch lounge with a full bar, and when you first set foot here you half expect to find Bogart flirting with Bacall in a corner. It has that kind of pleasantly lost-in-time aura. The guest rooms all vary somewhat as to size and mood, but all are comfortably if not stylishly furnished with antiques and reproductions. Some rooms feature fireplaces that burn Duraflame-style logs; others have bathrooms wedged into small spaces.

Maples Inn. 16 Roberts Ave., Bar Harbor, ME 04609. ☎ **207/288-3443.** E-mail: maplesinn@acadia.net. 6 units (1 with private hall bathroom). Mid-June to mid-Oct $90–$150 double, off-season $60–$95. Rates include full breakfast. DISC, MC, V. 2-night minimum stay on holiday weekends. No small children.

The Maples is a popular destination among those attracted to outdoor activities. You'll often find guests swapping stories of the day's adventure on the handsome front porch, or lingering over breakfast to compare notes about the best hiking trails. The rather modest (by Bar Harbor standards) yellow farmhouse-style home is tucked away on a leafy side street among other B&Bs; it's an easy walk downtown to a movie or dinner. The innkeepers have a good way of making guests comfortable, with board games and paperbacks scattered about, and down comforters in all rooms. The rooms aren't huge, but you're not likely to feel cramped either. (The suite with fireplace is the largest.) Breakfasts—including dishes like Bananas Holland America—are appropriately filling for a full day outdoors.

Mira Monte Inn. 69 Mt. Desert St., Bar Harbor, ME 04609. ☎ **800/ 553-5109** or 207/288-4263. Fax 207/288-3115. E-mail: mburns@acadia.net. 12 units, 3 suites. A/C TV TEL. $125–$155 double; suites $180. Rates include breakfast. 2-night minimum stay in midsummer. AE, DC, DISC, MC, V. Closed Nov–May (suites available by week in winter).

A stay at this impressive grayish-green Italianate mansion, built in 1864, feels a bit like a trip to grandmother's house—a grandmother who inherited most of her furniture from *her* grandmother. The antiques are more intriguing than elegant, and the common rooms are furnished in a pleasant country Victorian style. The 2-acre grounds, located within a few minutes' walk of Bar Harbor's restaurants and attractions, are attractively landscaped and include a cutting garden to keep the house in flowers. There's a nice brick terrace away from the street, which makes a fine place to enjoy breakfast on warm summer mornings. The guest rooms are blessed with a profusion of balconies and fireplaces—most rooms have one or the other or both. The room styles vary widely; some are heavy on the Victorian, others have the feel of a country farmhouse. If you're a light sleeper, avoid the rooms facing Mt. Desert Street; those facing the gardens in the rear are far more peaceful. Families should inquire about the suites in the adjacent outbuilding.

INEXPENSIVE

Acadia Hotel. 20 Mt. Desert St., Bar Harbor, ME 04609. ☎ **207/288-5721.** 10 units. A/C TV. Peak season $65–$115 double; off-season $45–$95 double. AE, DISC, MC, V.

The Acadia Hotel is perfectly situated overlooking the Village Green, and easily accessible to all in-town activities. This handsome, simple home dating from the late 19th century has a wraparound porch (where you can enjoy the continental breakfast in the summer) and attractive guest rooms decorated in a pleasant floral motif. The rooms vary widely in size and amenities: two have whirlpools, two have phones, and one has a kitchenette. Ask for the specifics when you book.

The Colony. Rte. 3 (P.O. Box 56), Hulls Cove, ME 04644. ☎ **800/524-1159** or 207/288-3383. 55 units. $60–$90 double. AE, DC, DISC, MC, V. Closed mid-Oct to early June.

The Colony is a classic motor court consisting of a handful of motel rooms and a battery of 55 cottages arrayed around a long green. It will be most appreciated by those with a taste for retro chic; others might decide to look for something with more modern amenities. The rooms are furnished in a simple '70s style that won't win any awards for decor, but all are comfortable; many have kitchenettes. It's situated just across Route 3 from a cobblestone beach, and a 10-minute drive from Bar Harbor. The Colony offers one of the better values on the island.

St. Saviour's Parish Hall Youth Hostel. 27 Kennebec St. (P.O. Box 32), Bar Harbor, ME 04609. ☎ **207/288-5587.** 20 beds (all with shared bathroom). $15 single ($12 Hostelling International members). No credit cards. Closed Sept 1 to mid-June.

Tucked down a leafy side street behind the impressive St. Saviour's church, this youth hostel offers inexpensive dorm-style accommodations for both men and women. It's housed in a handsomely shingled building, and is handy to everything in Bar Harbor. This is a good bet if low cost is a high priority for you and privacy is a low one. There's parking and a group kitchen as well. Be aware that it's filled every night it's open, and reservations are accepted by mail only with check or cash enclosed—and then only if your payment arrives a week or more before you do. Alternatively, you can stop by to see if beds are available. (When the office is closed, the number of available beds that night is posted on the door.) The hostel office is open daily from 7 to 9am and 5 to 10pm.

WHERE TO DINE
EXPENSIVE

✪ **George's.** 7 Stephens Lane. ☎ **207/288-4505.** Reservations recommended. Entrees $24; appetizer, entree, and dessert packages $33–$36. AE, DISC, MC, V. Daily 5:30–10pm; shorter hours after Labor Day. Closed Nov to early May. CONTEMPORARY MEDITERRANEAN.

George's takes some sleuthing to find, but it's worth the effort to visit this Bar Harbor classic, which has offered fine dining in informal surroundings for nearly 2 decades. (It's in the small clapboard cottage behind Main Street's First National Bank.) George's captures the joyous feel of summer nicely with four smallish dining rooms (and plenty of open windows) and additional seating on the terrace outside, which is the best place to watch the gentle dusk settle over town. The service is upbeat, and the meals wonderfully prepared. All entrees sell for one price ($24), and

Pillow Talk

Bar Harbor is the bedroom community for Mount Desert Island, with hundreds of hotel, motel, and inn rooms. While varied in size, shape, cost, and decor, all share one thing in common: They're filled during the busy days of midsummer. It's essential to book your room as early as possible.

A number of modern hotels and motels cluster along Route 3 just northwest of the village center; this is your best bet if you arrive without reservations. Be aware that even the most basic of rooms can be expensive in July and August. It will require a small miracle to find a motel for less than $60 during the summer; bed-and-breakfasts start at about $85.

In the full reviews on the adjacent pages there's space enough to review just a handful of the better choices. These represent only a fraction of the accommodations available. Don't despair if you can't book a room in any of these fine establishments. There are still dozens of other good options, including those listed below.

The **Acadia Inn** (98 Eden St.; ☎ **800/638-3636** or 207/288-3500) is a modern if unintriguing three-story hotel on busy Route 3, with amenities including a playground, outdoor pool, and Jacuzzi. The village is 5 minutes away by foot. Peak season rates are $139 to $159 and include continental breakfast.

The **Golden Anchor** (55 West St.; ☎ **800/328-5033** or 207/288-5033) is smack on the waterfront, with some rooms looking across the harbor toward the town pier and others out to Bar Island. (The less expensive rooms have no view at all.) There's a pool and hot tub right at the harbor's edge, and an oceanfront dining room that serves basic fare. Peak season rates range from $110 to $165.

The **Town Motel and Guest House** (12 Atlantic Ave.; ☎ **800/458-8644** or 207/288-5548) has both comfortable motel rooms and inn rooms in a Victorian manor; it's located within walking distance of downtown attractions. Peak-season rates are $92 to $140.

include salad, vegetable, and potato or rice. You won't go wrong with the basic choices, like steamed lobster or roast chicken, but you're even better off opting for the more adventurous fare like

The Park Entrance Oceanfront Motel (Route 3; ☎ **800/ 288-9703** or 207/288-9703) is nicely situated on 10 handsome waterfront acres close to the park visitor's center. The inn has an attractive private pier and cobblestone beach, and an outdoor swimming pool and Jacuzzi. Summer rates are $129 to $159; suites are $169 to $299.

Great views greet guests at the **Atlantic Eyrie Lodge** (Highbrook Road; ☎ **207/288-9786**), perched on a hillside above Route 3. Peak rates are $99 to $153. Some units have kitchenettes and balconies; all share access to the oceanview pool.

The Aurora Motel (51 Holland Ave.; ☎ **800/841-8925** or 207/288-3771) is nicely situated downtown, has 10 basic rooms decorated in a modern country style, and offers easy access to the village for rates of $80 to $96.

Convenient to the Nova Scotia ferry on nicely landscaped grounds is the family-friendly **Bar Harbor Motel** (100 Eden St.; ☎ **800/388-3453** or 207/288-3453), which has a heated outdoor pool and a small playground. Two-bedroom units for families are $135 in midsummer; standard rooms run $102 to $112.

Those looking for a bit more quiet and who don't feel the need to be right downtown have a good option in the **Edgewater Motel and Cottages** (off Route 3, Salisbury Cove; ☎ **207/288-3491**). The 11 cottages are just up from the water's edge (the name doesn't lie), where you can enjoy the early morning sun with your morning coffee, and prowl around watery crevices at low tide. Rates are $78 to $105 during peak season, which are a good value.

Reputable motels and hotels offering at least some rooms under $100 include the conveniently located, budget-priced **Villager Motel** (207 Main St.; ☎ **207/288-3211**), a family-run motel with 63 rooms; the 79-room **Wonder View Inn** (50 Eden St.; ☎ **800/ 341-1553** or 207/288-3358), with sweeping bay views (pets accepted); and the downtown **Maine Street Motel** (315 Main St.; ☎ **800/333-3188** or 207/288-3188).

lobster strudel or the house-specialty lamb in its many incarnations, including charcoal-grilled lamb tenderloin and rolled lamb stuffed with wild mushrooms.

Michelle's. 194 Main St. ☎ **207/288-0038.** Reservations recommended during peak season. Main courses $19–$42 (mostly $24–$28). Daily 6:30–9:30pm. Closed late Oct to early May. FRENCH.

Michelle's is located in the graceful Ivy Manor Inn (see "Where to Stay," above), and soon caught the attention of the state's gourmands when it opened in 1997. The three dining rooms are elegant and set with fresh roses and candles (there's outside seating when the weather's good). The extensive menu elaborates on traditional French cuisine with New England twists. The appetizers ($7 to $16) include smoked salmon layered with a chervil mousse, and foie gras with black truffles. Main courses are elaborate affairs, with dishes like chateâubriand for two carved at the table, and oven-roasted duckling with a ragout of cranberries and apricot. Appropriately for Bar Harbor, the seafood selection is extensive. The "chilled seafood bounty" for two ($80) should sate any craving for local fare from the sea; it includes lobster, mussels, clams, oysters, scallops, and crab.

MODERATE

Café This Way. 14¹/₂ Mt. Desert St. ☎ **207/288-4483.** Reservations recommended for dinner. Main courses, breakfast $3.25–$5.95; dinner $11–$18. MC, V. Summer daily 7–11am (8am–1pm Sunday) and 6–9pm. Closed for dinner and open for lunch in winter. CONTEMPORARY CAFE.

Café This Way has the feel of a casually hip coffee house, and is much more airy than one might guess upon first looking at this cottage tucked on a side street across from the village green. Bookshelves line one wall, and there's a small bar tucked in a nook. The breakfasts are excellent and mildly sinful, with offerings like eggs Benedict with spinach, artichoke, and tomato. The red-skinned potatoes are crispy and delicious; the robust coffee requires two creamers to lighten it. Dinners are equally appetizing, with tasty dishes like butternut squash ravioli, crab cakes with a tequila-lime sauce, and filet mignon grilled with fresh basil. This is the kind of place I love, where they know how to do great things with relatively simple ingredients.

Elaine's. 76 West St. ☎ **207/288-3287.** Reservations not accepted. Main courses $6.95–$12.95. Wed–Mon 5pm–9:30pm (closes earlier in off-season). Closed Nov–May 1. VEGETARIAN.

Bar Harbor's only fully vegetarian restaurant, Elaine's, opened in 1998 and has been happily embraced by herbivorous visitors. Located near the waterfront on West Street in a cozy, contemporary space, the menu includes house specialties "beef" burgundy (made

Lobster by the Pound

The ingredients for a proper feed at a local lobster pound are a pot of boiling water, a tank of lobsters, some well-worn picnic tables, a good view, and a six-pack of Maine beer—no pretensions, no frills.

One of the best destinations for lobster is **Beal's Lobster Pier** (☎ 207/244-7178) in Southwest Harbor, one of the oldest pounds in the area. **Thurston's Lobster Pound** (☎ 207/244-7600) in tiny Bernard (across the water from Bass Harbor) was atmospheric enough to be used as a backdrop for the Stephen King miniseries "Storm of the Century"; it's a fine place to linger toward dusk. **Abel's Lobster Pound** (☎ 207/276-5827), on Route 198 five miles north of Northeast Harbor, overlooks the deep blue waters of Somes Sound; eat at picnic tables under the pines or indoors at the restaurant. It's quite a bit pricier than other lobster restaurants at first glance, but they don't charge for the extras like many other lobster joints, and some visitors claim that lobsters here are more succulent.

On the mainland just north of the causeway is the wonderful **Oak Point Lobster Pound** (☎ 207/667-6998). This is off the beaten path (although still popular and often crowded), where you can enjoy your lobster with a sensational view of the island's rocky hills. To get here, turn west off Route 3 onto Route 230 before crossing to Mt. Desert, then continue 4 miles to the restaurant.

---

with seitan), and a Tijuana tofu bake. Other offerings on the menu are veggie burgers, tempeh, penne with steamed cabbage, and a broccoli and shiitake stir-fry. Deserts are rich and tasty, especially the homemade cheesecake.

Lompoc Cafe and Brewpub. 36 Rodick St. ☎ **207/288-9392.** Reservations not accepted. Sandwiches $4.50–$6.50; dinner $8.95–$15.95. MC, V. May–Nov daily 11:30am–1am. Closed Dec–Apr. AMERICAN/ECLECTIC.

The Lompoc Cafe has a well-worn, neighborhood bar feel to it, and it's little wonder that waiters and waitresses from around Bar Harbor congregate here after hours. The cafe consists of three sections— there's the original bar in the pine-floored dining room, a trim and tidy garden just outside (try your hand at bocce), and a small, open barnlike structure at the garden's edge to handle the overflow. The on-site brewery produces several unique beers, including a blueberry ale (intriguing concept, but ask for a sample before you order a full glass), and the smooth Coal Porter, available in sizes up to the 20-ounce "fatty." Whisky drinkers will be busy here: The Lompoc claims the largest selection of single-malts north of Boston. Bar menus are usually predictable and tiresome, but this one has some pleasant surprises, like the Persian plate (hummus and grape leaves), Szechuan eggplant wrap, and crab and shrimp cakes. A number of vegetarian entrees are offered. Live music is offered some evenings, when there's a small cover charge.

Maggie's Classic Scales. 6 Summer St. ☎ **207/288-9007.** Reservations recommended in July and Aug. Main courses $12.95–$20.95. DISC, MC, V. Daily 5–10pm; closed mid-Oct to mid-June. SEAFOOD.

The slogan for Maggie's is "notably fresh seafood," and the place invariably delivers on that understated promise. (Only fish caught on the island are used.) It's a causally elegant spot tucked off Cottage Street, good for a romantic evening with soothing music and good service. Appetizers include the smoked salmon (recommended) and charbroiled shrimp brochettes. Main courses range from basic boiled lobster and crabmeat–stuffed sole, to more adventurous offerings like Maine seafood provençal and sautéed scallops with fresh corn, bacon, and peppers. The servings are usually quite sizeable. Deserts are homemade and well worth leaving room for.

INEXPENSIVE

Jordan's Restaurant. 80 Cottage St. ☎ **207/288-3586.** Reservations not accepted. Breakfast $2–$6.95; lunch $2.75–$7.95. No credit cards. Daily 5am–2pm. Closed Jan through Mar. DINER.

Jordan's is the place for an early and filling breakfast, and is a good destination for those looking to get fed and into the park before the crowds. It's a popular haunt of local working folks; diners can settle into one of the pine booths or at a laminated table and order off the place-mat menu, choosing fare like omelets, blueberry pancakes (recommended!), and Belgian waffles. Lunch offerings include homemade soups and chowders, but the big breakfasts are the real draw.

Village Green Bakery Café. 195 Main St. ☎ **207/288-9450.** Reservations not accepted. Main courses $4.25–$16.95 (mostly $6–$8). DISC, MC, V. Daily 6am–8pm. Closed January. BASIC FARE.

The Village Green is where busy locals head to lunch, and it's the best place for basic, quick fare like burgers, wraps, and salads. Housed in an attractive old storefront just south of the green, the place is unpretentious and (when not harried) quite friendly. Be sure to check the specials menu, which might include such light-on-the-wallet options as fried scallops with french fries and coleslaw for $4.95.

3 Elsewhere on Mount Desert Island

Acadia National Park is the main island attraction, of course, and Bar Harbor has a boisterous charm and plenty of character. But there's plenty else to explore outside of these areas. Quiet fishing villages, deep woodlands, and unexpected ocean views are among the jewels that turn up when one peers beyond the usual places.

ESSENTIALS
GETTING AROUND

The east half of the island is best navigated on Route 3, which forms the better part of a loop from Bar Harbor through Seal Harbor and past Northeast Harbor before returning up the eastern shore of Somes Sound. Routes 102 and 102A provide access to the island's western half.

VISITOR INFORMATION

The best source of information on the island is at the **Thompson Island Information Center** (☎ **207/288-3411**) on Route 3 just south of the causeway connecting Mount Desert Island with the mainland. Another reliable source of local information is **Mount Desert Chamber of Commerce,** P.O. Box 675, Northeast Harbor, ME 04662 (☎ **207/276-5040**).

EXPLORING THE REST OF THE ISLAND

On the tip of the eastern lobe of Mount Desert Island is the staid, prosperous community of **Northeast Harbor,** long one of the favored retreats among the Eastern Seaboard's upper crust. Those without personal invitations to come as houseguests will need be satisfied with glimpses of the shingled palaces set in the fragrant spruce forests and along the rocky shore. But the village itself is worth investigating. Situated on a scenic, narrow harbor, with the once-grand Asticou Inn at its head, Northeast Harbor is possessed of a refined sense of elegance that's best appreciated by finding a vantage point, then sitting and admiring.

One of the best, least publicized places for enjoying views of the harbor is from the understatedly spectacular ✪ **Asticou Terraces** (☎ **207/276-5130**). Finding the parking lot can be tricky: Head one-half mile east (toward Seal Harbor) on Route 3 from the junction with Route 198, and look for the small gravel lot on the water side of the road with a sign reading ASTICOU TERRACES. Park here, cross the road on foot, and set off up a magnificent path made of local rock that ascends the sheer hillside with expanding views of the harbor and the town. This pathway, with its precise stonework and the occasional bench and gazebo, is one of the nation's hidden marvels of landscape architecture. Created by Boston landscape architect Joseph Curtis, who summered here for many years prior to his death in 1928, the pathway seems to blend in almost preternaturally with its spruce-and-fir surroundings, as if it were created by an act of god rather than of man. Curtis donated the property to the public for quiet enjoyment.

Continue on the trail at the top of the hillside and you'll soon arrive at Curtis's cabin (open to the public daily in summer), behind which lie the formal **Thuya Gardens,** which are as manicured as the terraces are natural. These wonderfully maintained gardens, designed by noted landscape architect Charles K. Savage, attract flower enthusiasts, students of landscape architecture, and local folks looking for a quiet place to rest. It's well worth the trip. A donation of $2 is requested of visitors to the garden; the terraces are free.

From the harbor, visitors can depart on a seaward trip to the beguilingly remote **Cranberry Islands.** You have a couple of options: Either travel with a national park guide to Baker Island, the most distant of this small cluster of low islands, and explore the natural terrain; or hop one of the ferries to either Great or Little Cranberry Island and explore on your own. From Northeast Harbor, **Beal & Bunker** (☎ 207/244-3575) offers year-round ferry service to the island starting at 7:30am (10am Sundays) and running to late afternoon or early evening. The round-trip fare is around $10. On Little Cranberry there's a small historical museum run by the National Park Service that's worth seeing, along with a wharf restaurant that serves pricey but decent meals. Both islands feature a sense of being well away from it all, but neither offers much in the way of shelter or tourist amenities, so travelers should head out prepared for the possibility of shifting weather.

When leaving Northeast Harbor, plan to drive out via **Sargent Drive.** This one-way route runs through Acadia National Park along the shore of Somes Sound, affording superb views of this glacially carved inlet.

On the far side of Somes Sound, there's good **hiking** (see above), and the towns of **Southwest Harbor** and **Bass Harbor.** These are both home to fishermen and boatbuilders, and are rather more humble than the settlements of the landed gentry at Northeast and Seal harbors across the way. Those with confidence in their navigational skills can rent powerboats and sailboats (ranging from 16 to 30 feet) to cruise the Sound and around the Cranberry Islands from **Manset Yacht Service** (☎ 207/244-4040), near Southwest Harbor.

In Southwest Harbor, look for the intriguing **Wendell Gilley Museum of Bird Carving** (☎ 207/244-7555) on Route 102 just north of town. Housed in a modern building constructed specifically to display fine woodcarving, the museum contains the masterwork of Wendell Gilley, a plumber who took up carving birds as a hobby in 1930. His creations, ranging from regal bald eagles to delicate chickadees, are startlingly lifelike and beautiful. The museum offers woodcarving classes for those inspired by the displays, and a gift shop offers fine woodcarving for sale. It's open daily 10am to 4pm except Monday June through October; open Friday through Sunday in May, November, and December. The museum is closed January through April. Admission is $3 adults, $1 children 5 to 12.

WHERE TO STAY

✪ **Claremont.** P.O. Box 137, Claremont Road, Southwest Harbor, ME 04679. ☎ **800/244-5036** or 207/244-5036. 42 units. TEL. July to Labor Day $135–$145 double, including breakfast, $160–$200 including breakfast and dinner; off-season from $95 double. Cottages: July–Labor Day $158–$198, off-season $100–$140. 3-day minimum stay in cottages. No credit cards. Closed mid-Oct to early June.

The early prints of the Claremont, built in 1884, show an austere four-story wooden building with a single severe gable overlooking Somes Sound from a low, grassy rise. And the place hasn't changed all that much since then. The Claremont offers nothing fancy or elaborate, just simple, classic New England grace. It's wildly appropriate that the state's most high-profile and combative croquet tournament takes place here annually in early August; all those folks in their whites seem right at home. The common areas and dining rooms are pleasantly appointed in an affable country style. There's a library with rockers, a fireplace, and jigsaw puzzles waiting to be assembled. Two other fireplaces in the lobby take the chill out of the morning air.

Most of the guest rooms are bright and airy, furnished with antiques and some old furniture that doesn't quite qualify as antique. The bathrooms are modern. Guests opting for the full meal plan at the inn are given preference in reserving rooms overlooking the water; it's almost worth it, although dinners can be lackluster. There's also a series of cottages, available for a 3-day minimum. Some are set rustically in the piney woods; others offer pleasing views of the sound.

Dining: The dining room is open nightly. Meals are mainly reprises of American classics like salmon, grilled lamb, and steamed lobster. The dining room is open to the public; entrees are $17 to $22.

Facilities: One clay tennis court, rowboats, bicycles (free to guests), croquet court.

Inn at Southwest. 371 Main St. (P.O. Box 593), Southwest Harbor, ME 04679. ☎ **207/244-3835.** www.acadia.net/iaswh. E-mail: innatsw@acadia.net. 9 units (2 with private hall bathrooms). Summer and early fall $95–$145 double; off-season $65–$105 double. Rates include full breakfast. May–Oct. DISC, MC, V.

Innkeeper Jill Lewis acquired the architecturally quirky Inn at Southwest in 1995, and she's done a fine job making this mansard-roofed Victorian a hospitable place. There's a decidedly turn-of-the-century air to this elegant home, but it's restrained on the frills. The guest rooms are named after Maine lighthouses, and are furnished with both contemporary and antique furniture. All rooms have ceiling fans and down comforters. Among the most pleasant rooms is Blue Hill Bay on the third floor, with its large bathroom, sturdy oak bed and bureau, and glimpses of the scenic harbor. Breakfasts offer ample reason to rise and shine, featuring specialties like vanilla Belgian waffles with raspberry sauce, and crab potato bake.

✪ **Lindenwood Inn.** 118 Clark Point Rd. (P.O. Box 1328), Southwest Harbor, ME 04679. ☎ **207/244-5335.** 22 units (some with shower only), 1 suite. July and Aug $95–$185 double; Sept to mid-Oct $85–$165; mid-Oct to June $75–$145 (suite $30 additional). Rates include full breakfast. AE, MC, V.

The Lindenwood offers a refreshing change from the fusty, overly draperied inns that tend to proliferate along Maine's coast. Housed in a handsome 1902 Queen Anne–style home at the harbor's edge, the inn features rooms that are modern and uncluttered, the colors simple and bold. The adornments are relatively few (those that do exist are mostly from the innkeeper's collection of African and Pacific art and artifacts), but clean lines and bright natural light more than create a relaxing mood—you'll even begin to view the cobblestone doorstops as works of art. Especially appealing is the spacious suite, which features great harbor views. If you're on a tighter budget, ask for a room in the annex, housed in an 1883 home just a minute's walk down the block. The rooms are somewhat less expansive and more simply decorated, but still offer nice touches (like bright halogen reading lamps) and make a superb base from which to explore the area. Eight of the rooms feature fireplaces; most also have telephones, but ask when you book if this is important to you.

Dining: The Lindenwood's dining room attracted serious attention from around the island when it started offering dinner in 1996, but it was closed in the summer of 1998 following some unexpected turnover in kitchen staff. Innkeeper Jim King was anticipating reopening the dining room in 1999 as of press time, but it's safest to call first.

Facilities: Jacuzzi, heated outdoor pool, boat dock.

WHERE TO DINE

For a quick bite or a picnic to go, try the informal **Little Notch Cafe** (340 Main St., Southwest Harbor; ☎ 207/244-3357) in the village of Southwest Harbor. It's part upscale pizzeria and part wonderful bakery. The sandwiches ($3.95 to $5.95) include prosciutto with asiago cheese and roasted peppers, and grilled flank steak. All are served on homemade bread, rolls, or focaccia. The pizzas ($6 and up, depending on toppings) go beyond mushroom and pepperoni, and feature options like roasted onions, turkey sausage, and sun-dried tomato. It's open 11am to 8pm Monday to Saturday. There's limited inside dining.

The Burning Tree. Rte. 3, Otter Creek. ☎ **207/288-9331.** Reservations recommended. Main courses $14–$20. Wed–Mon 5–9pm, daily in Aug. Closed Columbus Day to mid-June. REGIONAL/ORGANIC.

Located on busy Route 3 between Bar Harbor and Northeast Harbor, The Burning Tree is an easy restaurant to speed right by. But that's a mistake. This low-key place, with its bright, open and sometimes noisy dining room, serves up the freshest food in the area. Much of the produce and herbs come from its own gardens, with the rest of the ingredients supplied locally wherever possible. Seafood is the specialty here, and it's consistently prepared with equal parts imagination and skill. The menu changes often to reflect local availability. Typical appetizers might include chili-orange noodle and scallop salad, and smoked salmon served with a corn and caper relish. Entrees could feature Cajun crab and lobster au gratin, grilled swordfish with a watercress-lime sauce, or monkfish baked with clams, artichokes, and olives and served with a saffron orzo.

Jordan Pond House. Park Loop Rd., Acadia National Park (near Seal Harbor). ☎ **207/276-3316.** Reservations recommended for lunch, tea, and dinner. Lunch $6.25–$12.75, afternoon tea $5.75–$6.75, dinner $7.25–$17.50. AE, DISC, MC, V. Mid-May to late Oct daily 11:30am–8pm (until 9pm July–Aug). AMERICAN.

The secret to the Jordan Pond House? Location, location, location. The restaurant traces its roots back to 1847, when an early farm was established on this picturesque property at the southern tip of a pond looking toward The Bubbles, a pair of towering, glacially sculpted mounds. If the weather's agreeable, ask for a seat on the lawn with its unrivaled views. Afternoon tea is a hallowed Jordan Pond House tradition. Ladies Who Lunch sit next to Mountain Bikers Who Wear Lycra, and everyone feasts on the huge, tasty popovers and strawberry jam served with a choice of teas or fresh lemonade. Dinners are reasonably priced, and include classic resort entrees like prime rib, steamed lobster, and baked haddock.

Keenan's. Rte. 102A, Bass Harbor. ☎ **207/244-3403.** Reservations suggested for parties of 5 or more. Sandwiches and main courses $5–$17. No credit cards. Summers Tues–Sun 4:30–10pm; weekends only in off-season. SEAFOOD.

This classic, informal seafood shack at a fork in the road is one of those local secrets that most travelers zip right by without a second thought. But do yourself a favor and make an effort to stop here and order up some of the best seafood value for your money. The fried clams are well prepared, and the spicy gumbo packs a kick. If you're of a mind to gorge, go with the seafood sampler, which includes lobster, crab, mussels, clams, and corn, all for around $17, which is what you'd pay for a lobster alone at some of the snootier coastal joints.

Redfield's. Main St., Northeast Harbor. ☎ **207/276-5283.** Reservations strongly recommended in summer. Main courses $17.95–$20.95. AE, MC, V. June–Oct Mon–Sat 6–9pm; Nov–May Fri–Sat only. CONTEMPORARY.

Located in a storefront in Northeast Harbor's tiny downtown, this elegant restaurant is decorated with a subtle and restrained touch. A couple of large sprays of flowers set the tone. Patrons can enjoy a libation at the wonderful marble bar (it was taken from an old soda fountain), then settle in and peruse the short but tempting menu, which draws its inspiration from cuisines around the world. Choices change with some frequency, but might include appetizers of Stilton cheese fondue over artichoke hearts, or smoked lobster with a sauce of corn, tomato, and serrano chili. The entrees are usually prepared with style and care, and include a sesame-dipped salmon fillet with ginger-tamari sauce, and venison with dried cranberry and port compote.

Restaurant XYZ. Shore Rd., Manset. ☎ **207/244-5221.** Reservations recommended. Main courses $13–$15. MC, V. Daily in summer 5:30–9pm; limited hours (usually weekends only) during the shoulder seasons. Closed Columbus Day to Memorial Day. MEXICAN.

Restaurant XYZ doesn't promise much at first: It's on the ground floor beneath a run-of-the-mill motel overlooking the harbor, and the interior is adorned with kitschy imports from Mexico that might best be described as "stuff." But the food! Drawing on the traditions of central Mexico and the Yucatán, the fare here is spicy, earthy, and tangy. Expect a remarkably savory mole (especially good with chicken), and a chipotle salsa that sings. Start with one of the stand-out margaritas (made with fresh lime juice), and then head straight to the main courses. (The appetizers don't offer especially good value.) Among the more notable entrees are the pork dishes, including *tatemado* (a pork loin baked with guajillo and ancho chiles), and Yucatecan-style pork rubbed with achiote paste and marinated with citrus before baking. Aficionados of authentic Mexican cooking will be delightfully surprised to find such excellent dining deep in the home turf of boiled lobster and fried clams.

8

The Downeast Coast

*T*he term "Downeast" comes from the old sailing ship days. Ships heading east had the prevailing winds at their backs, making it an easy "downhill" run to the eastern ports. Heading the other way took a bit more skill and determination.

Today, it's a rare traveler who gets far Downeast to explore the rugged coastline of Washington County—few tourists venture beyond Acadia National Park. But Downeast Maine has substantial appeal. There's an authenticity and remoteness that's been lost in much of coastal Maine. After the turnoff to Mt. Desert Island, Route 1 becomes rather lonesome, and the 2-hour drive to the Canadian border from Ellsworth offers a glimpse of Maine as it was a half-century ago. Those hoping to see a rugged, hardscrabble way of life where independence is revered above all else aren't likely to go away disappointed.

Many residents of the region survive as their forebears did—by scratching a living from the land. Lobstering and fishing remain major sources of income, as do logging and other forest work. Picking wild blueberries in the barrens in late summer and tipping fir trees and making wreaths in late fall round out the income. In recent years, aquaculture has become an important part of the economy around Passamaquoddy Bay; travelers are likely to see vast floating pens where salmon are raised for markets worldwide. More than likely, locals you'll come across stitch together their livelihood with some of each, changing occupations as the seasons roll through.

I've cobbled together a driving tour that could be done in a leisurely 2 or 3 days, or in an abbreviated fashion in one hellishly long day from Mount Desert Island (not recommended).

1 Essentials

GETTING THERE

Downeast Maine is most commonly reached via Route 1 from Ellsworth. Those heading directly to Washington County in summer can take a more direct, less congested route via Route 9 from Bangor, connecting south to Route 1 via Route 193 or Route 192.

Downeast Coast

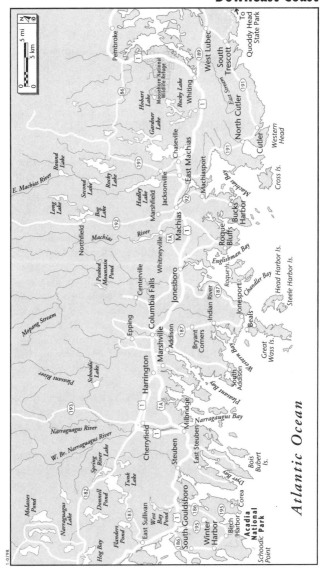

VISITOR INFORMATION

The **Machias Bay Area Chamber of Commerce,** P.O. Box 606, Machias, ME 04654 (☎ **207/255-4402**), provides tourist information from its offices at 23 E. Main St. (Route 1). The offices are open 9am to 5pm Tuesday through Saturday (also open Monday in summer).

A COASTAL DRIVING TOUR

To begin, head east from Ellsworth on Route 1 for 17 miles to West Gouldsboro, then turn south on Route 186 to Winter Harbor. Outside of Winter Harbor, look for the familiar brown-and-white National Park signs indicating:

1. **Schoodic Point.** A pleasing loop drive hooks around the tip of Schoodic Point, which is part of Acadia National Park. The one-way road (no charge) winds along the water and through forests of spruce and fir. Good views of the mountains of Acadia open up across Frenchman Bay; you'll also see buildings of an historic naval station housed on the point. Park near the tip of this isolated promontory and explore the salmon-colored rocks that plunge into the ocean. It's especially dramatic when the seas are agitated and the surf crashes loudly.

   From here, continue back to Route 186, then continue on through Prospect Harbor to rejoin Route 1 at Gouldsboro. Head eastward, detour off the highway at Columbia Falls, and look for signs to the historic:

2. **Ruggles House** (☎ **207/483-4637**). This fine Federal home dates from 1818, and was built for Thomas Ruggles, an early timber merchant and civic leader. The home is very grand and opulent, but in an oddly miniature sort of way. There's a flying staircase in the central hallway, pine doors hand-painted to resemble mahogany, and extraordinary wood carvings in the main parlor, done over the course of 3 years by an English craftsman equipped, legend says, with only a penknife. Locals once said his hand was guided by an angel. The Ruggles House is open June through mid-October daily from 9:30am to 4:30pm (Sundays open at 11 am). Tours last 20 minutes to a half-hour, and a donation is requested.

   East of Columbia Falls, head south on Route 187 to the rough-hewn fishing village of Jonesport. Look for signs to Beals Island. Cross the bridge; bear right at the fork after crossing the causeway to Great Wass Island. The pavement soon ends; continue slowly past the lobster pound to a small parking lot on the left, providing access to:

3. **Great Wass Preserve.** This exceptional 1,524-acre parcel was acquired by the Nature Conservancy in 1978, and contains an excellent 5-mile loop hike covering a wide cross-section of native terrain, including bogs, heath, rocky coastline, and forests of twisted jack pines. Maps and a birding checklist are found in a stand at the parking lot. Follow one fork of the trail to the shoreline; work your way along the storm-tossed boulders to the other fork, then make your way back to your car. If a heavy fog has settled into the area, as often happens, don't let that deter your hike. The dense mist creates a medieval tableau that makes for magical hiking.

Continue along Route 187 back to Route 1, then head eastward to Machias. After crossing the bridge over the Machias River falls, take your second left to:

4. **Burnham Tavern** (☎ **207/255-4432**). In June 1775, a month after the Battle of Lexington in Massachusetts, a group of patriots hatched a plan at the gambrel-roofed Burnham Tavern that led to the first naval battle of the Revolutionary War. The armed schooner *Margaretta* was in Machias harbor to obtain wood for British barracks. The patriots didn't think much of this idea, and attacked the ship using much smaller boats they had commandeered, along with muskets, swords, axes, and pitchforks. The patriots prevailed, killing the captain of the *Margaretta* in the process.

Visitors can learn all about this episode during a tour of the tavern, which was built on a rise overlooking the river in 1770. On display is booty taken from the British ship, along with the original tap table and other historic furniture and ephemera. The 1-hour tours cost $2 for adults and 25¢ for children, and are held June through September Monday through Friday from 9am to 5pm.

From Machias, continue east on Route 1. At the riverside town of East Machias, turn south on Route 191. The road twists and winds past unremarkable homes and through an undistinguished landscape until you pass a huge radar installation used by the U.S. military as a communications outpost. (You'll know it by the towering antennae.) Afterwards, you'll come upon classic ocean views, framed with islands studded with spruce and fir, and an open boreal landscape of barrens and heaths. The Route 191 detour doesn't fit into any mold of classic New England beauty (you're never far from a mobile home), but there's a certain spare beauty to the entire area.

The town of **Cutler** has, to my mind, one of the most beautiful small harbors in the state, flanked by a cluster of homes—some old, some new—on the hillside above. The town has a village store and not much else, other than a certain stalwart grace in the face of a difficult economy and an unforgiving sea.

A couple of miles outside of Cutler, keep an eye on the right for:

5. ✪ **Cutler Coastal Trail.** Marked by a sign at a small parking lot, this dramatic loop trail passes through diverse ecosystems, including bogs, barrens, and dark and tangled spruce forests. But the highlight of this trail, which traverses state-owned land, is the mile-long segment along the rocky headlands high above the restless ocean. Some of the most dramatic coastal views in the state are along this isolated stretch, which overlooks dark-gray-to-black rocks and an often tumultuous sea. Visible on the horizon across the Bay of Fundy is the low, flat Canadian island of Grand Manan. Plan on at least 2 or 3 hours for the whole loop, although more time spent whiling away the afternoon hours on the rocks is well worthwhile. If it's damp or foggy, rain pants are advised to fend off the moisture from the low brush along the trail.

Back at your car, continue eastward, and after the harborside hamlet of South Trescott look for a right turn at a white farmhouse with green trim. This is a backroad shortcut to West Quoddy Head, over a narrow road that is partly paved, partly gravel, and which affords some glimpses of the ocean.

At the next stop sign, turn right and head to:

6. **West Quoddy Head Light.** This famed red-and-white light (it's been likened to a barbershop pole and a candy cane) marks the easternmost point of the United States, and ushers boats into the Lubec Channel between the U.S. and Canada. The light is operated by the Coast Guard and isn't open to the public, but visitors can walk along the high headlands at the adjacent state park, which has several miles of hiking trails. The park overlooks rocky shoals that are ceaselessly battered by high winds, pounding waves, and some of the most powerful tides in the world. Watch for fishing boats straining against the currents, or seals playing in the waves and sunning on the offshore rocks. The big landmass in the distance is Canada's Grand Manan Island.

From the lighthouse, head to Route 1, backtracking partway on South Lubec Road, then turn right into Lubec. Follow the signs to the international bridge leading to:

7. **Campobello Island,** and take a brief excursion out of the country and across the time zone. The U.S. and Canada maintain a joint national park here, called the **Roosevelt Campobello International Park** (☎ **506/752-2922**). Head to the visitor's center to collect information on hiking at the 2,721-acre park (some relaxing oceanside hikes await you along the 8 miles of trails), but at the very least take a self-guided tour through the wondrous Roosevelt "cottage," an 18-bedroom shingled summer home purchased by James Roosevelt in 1910. James was the father of President Franklin Delano Roosevelt, who summered here most every year between 1883 and 1921, when he was stricken with polio. A brief and informative film at the visitor's center helps set the stage; docents at the home can answer any questions you might have. The park is open daily Memorial Day weekend through mid-October from 10am to 6pm Eastern time. Admission is free.

2 Where to Stay & Dine

✪ **Le Domaine.** Rte. 1 (P.O. Box 496), Hancock, ME 04640. www.ledomain\e. com. E-mail: ledomaine@acadia.net. ☎ **800/554-8498** or 207/422-3395. Fax 207/422-2316. 7 units. $200 double including breakfast and dinner. AE, DISC, MC, V.

A gourmand's delight, Le Domaine has firmly established its reputation as one of the most elegant and delightful destinations in Maine. Set on Route 1 about 10 minutes east of Ellsworth, this inn has the continental flair of an impeccable auberge. While the highway in front can be a bit noisy, the garden and woodland walks out back offer plenty of serenity. The rooms are comfortable and tastefully appointed without being pretentious, but the real draw here is the exquisite dining room.

Dining: Chef Nicole Purslow carries on the tradition begun by her mother in 1946 by offering superb French country cooking in the handsome candlelit dining room with its pinewood floors and sizeable fireplace. The ever-changing sauces make the entrees sing here, and might feature the Atlantic salmon with a sorrel and shallot sauce, or rabbit served with a robust prune sauce. Plan to check in by 5:30pm; dinner is served between 6pm and 9pm.

Index

Page numbers in italic refer to maps.